Modern Satanism

Anatomy of a Radical Subculture

CHRIS MATHEWS

Westport, Connecticut
London

Library of Congress Cataloging-in-Publication Data

Mathews, Chris.
   Modern Satanism : anatomy of a radical subculture / Chris Mathews.
      p. cm.
   Includes bibliographical references and index.
   ISBN 978–0–313–36639–0 (alk. paper)
 1. Satanism.   I. Title.
   BF1548.M38   2009
   299—dc22   2008045522

British Library Cataloguing in Publication Data is available.

Library of Congress Catalog Card Number: 2008045522
ISBN: 978–0–313–36639–0

First published in 2009

Praeger Publishers, 88 Post Road West, Westport, CT 06881
An imprint of Greenwood Publishing Group, Inc.
www.praeger.com

Printed in the United States of America

The paper used in this book complies with the
Permanent Paper Standard issued by the National
Information Standards Organization (Z39.48–1984).

10 9 8 7 6 5 4 3 2 1

To my parents

With thanks to the help, criticism and support of:
Andrew Jones
Geoffrey Roche
Yoko Arai

Contents

Introduction

COUNTER THE COUNTERCULTURE

The Birth of Modern Satanism

> Death to the weakling, wealth to the strong!
> —Anton Szandor LaVey, *The Satanic Bible*, p. 30

Walpurgisnacht (Walpurgis Night) is an annual pagan festival, falling on April 30 or May 1, marking the final triumph of spring over winter. It is considered the most potent magical date of the year, and legends tell of witches meeting on the night, celebrating the change of season with wild revels and Black Masses as huge bonfires burn away the last vestiges of winter. The festival is named after Saint Walburga, a English nun who traveled to Germany to convert German pagans to Christianity in the eighth century. Following her death in Heidenheim in 778, her memorial—May 1—was confused with the pagan festival. The festival was, like so many pagan observances, adapted for the Christian era. The so-called Easter fires came to signify the driving out of evil spirits. Its original heritage, however, became widely known after its role in Goethe's *Faust*, where Mephistopheles takes Faust to witness the proceedings on Walpurgisnacht and "mix with the devils." In keeping with tradition, the revels are taking place on the Blocksberg, an atmospheric 1,142-meter peak in Germany's Harz Mountains:

> We creep as slowly as a snail;
> Far, far ahead the witches sail.
> When to the Devil's home they speed,
> Women by a thousand paces lead.[1]

In San Francisco in 1966, Walpurgisnacht marked more than just another sabbat, as a group of modern-day devils met to celebrate their own rites. The auspices of April 30–May 1, 1966 witnessed the inauguration of the Church of Satan, the world's first openly Satanic church. With due ceremony, Anton LaVey—a 36-year-old explorer of the dark arts—shaved his head, donned a black priest's collar, and proclaimed the Age of Satan to his small private assembly. No stranger to theatrics, LaVey was already a mild celebrity in the Bay Area, an ex-circus and carnival worker known for taking his 500-pound pet lion Togare to local schools and holding Friday night seminars on occult topics in his foreboding 13-room home. Cannibalism, voodoo, lycanthropy, phrenology, hexes, Ouija boards, fortune telling, tea-leaf reading—there was no topic too bizarre to be included. Bizarreness, in fact, was the main criteria. Quickly generating publicity with a Satanic wedding and other sensational antics, the Church of Satan steadily attracted members and worked to bring the demonic and the occult out of the shadows.

LaVey and his fledgling court were strangely out of place. San Francisco in the 1960s was synonymous with peace, love, and happiness. The spiritual home to the flower power movement—physical home to tens of thousands of bohemians with no direction home—it was an unexpected place to find a diabolical order. Taking up the standard of the Beatniks, the hippie movement had renounced the conservative social values of the 1950s and begun an exploration of political, individual, religious, and sexual freedom. San Francisco's Haight-Ashbury district became the magnetic hub of a global movement, with an estimated 100,000 starry-eyed idealists gravitating there for 1967's Summer of Love. Once there, they were greeted in Golden Gate Park by Timothy Leary's evocation to "turn on, tune in, drop out." Anton LaVey was not impressed. "I found the hippie movement distasteful on a personal level. Suddenly the ingestion of lysergic acid made every man a king."[2] The loosening of conventional mores was, however, a boon to the young Church of Satan, which its newly ordained magus later noted:

> Concurrent with the increasingly liberal social climate of the 60s, many former taboos became relaxed. The Dark Side displayed itself in polite society, where beatnik poets and bongo drummers had flourished, where witches and tarot readers held court. To most theologians only a single entity was responsible for everything from prophesy to meditation. No matter how innocuous an esoteric act or voluble its practitioner's disclaimer, the Devil was to blame.[3]

He had reason to be grateful, however. It was the "increasingly liberal social climate" that provided the space instinctive fringe-dwellers like LaVey needed to maneuver in. The heralds of the counterculture were slowly bringing exploration of the esoteric and arcane into the mainstream by dabbling in paganism, witchcraft, and Eastern mysticism—activities the conservative establishment generally identified as the work of the archfiend.

And maneuver LaVey did. His evocation was of a thoroughly different type than what was happening a few kilometers away in Haight-Ashbury or Golden Gate Park. LaVey took the Black Mass, an inversion of the Christian Mass, and made it the ritual centerpiece of his new order. The Mass was the time-honored method of witches and black arts practitioners to parody the Christian service while paying homage to their own deity or spirits. The Mass's subversive, clandestine history and diametric opposition to conventional religious practices made it a powerful vehicle for the Satanists, both symbolically and magically. LaVey incorporated a sinister carnivalesque element, draping a long black cloak over his shoulders and wearing a traditional priest's uniform and horned skull cap over his shaven head. The ceremony was conducted with a naked acolyte reclining on an altar and a large Baphomet framing the background. The infernal names—titles of gods and goddesses of long-forgotten or underground faiths—were read out, and the passions of the flesh exalted. The workings of LaVey's ritual chamber were strongly focused on the psychological power of the Mass, yet, in stark contrast to the witches of old, the high priest and his congregation did not celebrate their rites in secret. Their Black Mass was forthrightly performed and well publicized; it was the Church of Satan's trademark.

The Church was definitely testing the edges of the acceptable. In an age where John Lennon's comment that The Beatles were "more popular than Jesus now" could spark a splenetic backlash,[4] mass burnings of the group's records, and international condemnation, Anton LaVey was openly proclaiming himself a Satanist and celebrating Black Masses in his suburban home. Pop stars dabbling with drugs and controversy were one thing; a Satanic congregation committing blasphemous paeans to the devil around an altar adorned with a naked woman, entirely another.

The neighbors were certainly worried: "There is definitely something going wrong over there. I just have a feeling I can't trust him [LaVey]. There are women there who are without clothes—naked. And the men wear a kind of black hooded robe. And sometimes from my window I can see a kind of red light and silhouettes like devils. And one silhouette, a big one, maybe it's him, standing over the whole crowd and preaching."[5] The neighbor was a woman interviewed in the diablomentary *Satanis: The Devil's Mass*, one of the numerous and evermore outrageous methods that the church was using to promote itself.

THE COUNTERCULTURE RELIGIOUS CLIMATE

These fiendish goings-on were hardly without precedent. The combination of sacrilege and self-indulgence had been practiced as long as Christianity had been the dominant cultural force in the Western world, preaching the perils of the flesh to the impressionable. In the 1960s, establishing a new religious sect was also reasonably common. Some were vague, perpetually stoned hippie dreamers living in communes. Some were vague, perpetually stoned hippie dreamers living in communes who preached apocalypse and massacred pregnant celebrities. Others, like L. Ron Hubbard a decade before LaVey, founded completely unique movements. Hubbard's legacy, the secular religion Scientology, has proved extraordinarily resilient and has succeeded in malingering into the twenty-first century. More popular than starting from scratch, however, was taking existing beliefs and reinterpreting them to create an original but recognizable synthesis.

The prime example of the apocalyptic synthesis school of religion is the Process Church. The Process originated in England in 1963, when founder Robert DeGrimston met ex-prostitute and future wife Mary Anne at L. Ron Hubbard's London Institute of Scientology. They married the following year, split from Scientology, and set up their own self-help system, Compulsions Analysis. Encouraged by early results and success in finding followers, the system developed into a spiritual quest and was renamed the Process Church of the Final Judgment. In 1966 they migrated to Mexico with 30 members in tow, and the charismatic DeGrimston began to realize that he was Jesus Christ. With his long hair and dreamy expression, he certainly looked the part. Enlightened, DeGrimston then revealed the truth of universe: the gods Jehovah, Lucifer, and Satan were the three principles of reality, each representing the respective qualities of wrath, harmony, and excessive physical indulgence. Beside these gods stood Christ, who served as the link to humanity. It was an apocalyptic vision that saw the end of the world fast approaching, when the Lamb and the Goat (Christ and Satan) would join together and all three gods would be reconciled, hearkening a new beginning.

The Process Church spread to America in 1968, where it quickly established itself as the largest quasi-Satanic cult of the times. Before long its members were trawling the hippie centers of San Francisco for donations and converts. Despite large differences, the Process Church was easily confused with the Church of Satan by observers. DeGrimston's followers existed in the same milieu, were equally dramatically dressed in long black robes, adorned themselves with intimidating Goat of Mendes badges, worshipped both Christ and Satan, and had a similar frighteningly Satanic edge (although the Process was far more apocalyptic). Both were suspected of harboring Nazi sympathies. The Process in particular flaunted a swastika-like mandala and openly courted neo-Nazi affiliations. At one point, DeGrimston's cult approached LaVey proposing a union of sorts, which LaVey dismissed immediately—unsurprisingly, given his open contempt for flower child spiritualism. Like the Church of Satan, the Process became associated with Charles Manson, although again far more directly. Manson was a one-time neighbor of the group who, it is claimed, adapted parts of the Process cosmology and portentous vision to his self-serving theological mélange. The connection was to dog the church, eventually spelling its demise. By 1974, DeGrimston's reign as messiah was over.

The Process Church was indicative of the era and the search for alternate forms of religious belief and practice. Gurus, visionaries, and charismatic leaders—like DeGrimston, LaVey, and Manson—abounded, feeding on the openness of the times and the spiritual hunger of the counterculture, releasing a wave of new religious groups. With his budding church, LaVey was paradoxically in step with the times yet completely outside the parameters of the counterculture. But, of all the churches and ideologies established in the 1960s, LaVey's is one of the few to have persisted. Within three years of Walpurgisnacht 1966, LaVey's church had not only grown in numbers and reputation, it also had a founding text. A bible. A *Satanic Bible*—and occult best-seller.

THE ADVERSARIES

Naming your new religion "Satanism" and the organization the "Church of Satan" may seem like an open request for negative attention, and the young organization certainly had its share. Journalists and mainstream religious leaders lined up to express their disapproval. LaVey, however, had his reasons:

> "Satanism is based on a very sound philosophy" say the emancipated. "But why call it Satanism? Why not call it something like 'Humanism' or a name that would have the connotation of a witchcraft group, something a little more esoteric—something less blatant." There is more than one reason for this. Humanism is not a religion. It is simply a way of life with no ceremony or dogma. Satanism has both ceremony and dogma.[6]

LaVey's rationalization was a partial explanation but certainly not the full story. Consider the response his contemporary and influence Ayn Rand gave in *The Virtue of Selfishness* when asked why she similarly chose a term with negative connotations to promote her philosophy:

> The title of this book may evoke the kind of question that I hear once in a while: "Why do you use the word 'selfishness' to denote virtuous qualities of character, when that word antagonizes so many people to whom it does not mean the things you mean?"
>
> To those who ask it, my answer is: "For the reason that makes you afraid of it."[7]

LaVey's reasons are no doubt similar. "Humanism" wasn't going to get the press that "Satanism" would. The term did not mean to him what it meant to the vast majority of people, and he reveled in the mistakes and presumptions they made about his church. Shock value was an exceptionally good means of generating publicity, as the million-plus readers of *The Satanic Bible* attest.

Nonetheless, it is (or was) a troubling name. Accordingly, definitions of modern Satanism inevitably begin with a number of disclaimers about what it is not, rather than what it is. Satanism does not endorse mutilating or sacrificing animals, rape, desecrating or burning churches, robbing graves, exhuming corpses, ritual murder, or cannibalism. Though *The Satanic Bible* states this without ambivalence, LaVey was to lament nearly 20 years later: "[W]e've wasted far too much time explaining that Satanism has nothing to do with kidnapping, drug abuse, child molestation, animal or child sacrifice."[8] The common name for those who commit such crimes in the devil's name is "generational satanist"—an underground group that today is either infinitesimally small or nonexistent.

Modern Satanism is an ideology of the self, one that holds that individuals and their personal needs come first. It is not the belief in and worship of Satan as a supernatural personal being, or even as an impersonal force or energy, except in a metaphorical sense. Satanists do not commune with the devil, regard him as a living entity, nor try to summon his essence. The name is employed as an archetype, a figure that embodies certain principles—individualism, nonconformity, rebellion, and pride. *Satan*, in its Hebrew origins, simply meant "accuser" or "opposer." The term used in the Book of Job is *ha-satan* or "adversary," a designation that bears none of the opprobrium later associated with the devil. It is adopted by modern Satanists as an oppositional standard, a symbol of antipathy towards conventional beliefs, morality, and practices. Far from being an occult-obsessed order that aims to summon demons, LaVey's version of Satanism is materialistic, Darwinian, and atheistic. It is a body of beliefs that is more philosophical in flavor than religious, although it incorporates a religious, ritualistic aspect, primarily for its psychological potency. Satanism's true heritage is a selective reading of the works of Machiavelli, Thomas Malthus, Herbert Spencer, Friedrich Nietzsche, Aleister Crowley, and Ayn Rand, among others.

With a basis in antipathy and resolute individualism, Satanism is hardly a soft, friendly creed. It is dedicated to the dark side of the psyche, with a strong focus on humanity's carnal nature and the recognition of man as an animal. A major characteristic is its antagonistic us-against-them stance toward society as a whole. Satanists consider themselves to be an elite, a rare breed who have raised themselves above the herdlike nature of the mass of humanity. They eschew traditional views on altruism and self-sacrifice, believing them to be the basis of an antilife and antirational philosophy. Satanism, by contrast, is a realistic, unembellished look at the world the way it is. As the hastily prepared *Satanic Bible* states, "Satanism has been thought of as being synonymous with cruelty and brutality. This is so only because people are afraid to face the truth—and the truth is that human beings are not all benign or all loving."[9] This pessimistic outlook exposes the most worrying aspects of Satanism. The unremitting focus on social elitism, appeals to force, and scorn for egalitarian principles make Satanism strongly reminiscent of the doctrines of Nazism, a criticism which has dogged the creed. As *Newsweek* observed in 1971, if there is anything fundamentally diabolical about Satanism, it stems more from the persistent echoes of Nazism in its theories than from the shock-horror pantomime of its name and image.[10]

This book is concerned with modern Satanism, which specifically refers to the form established by Anton LaVey in 1966, promulgated and jealously guarded ever since by the Church of Satan. LaVey's appropriation of a term that already had a rich history of its own creates difficulties, but any use of the terms "Satanism" or "Satanic" in a post-1966 context can hereafter be assumed to refer to the modern religious/philosophical movement, not its traditional meaning of devil worshipper. (For any more general post-1966 usage, "satanism" or "satanic" will be used.) The ideology is best exemplified by LaVey's writings, but other interpretations or recastings of the central ideas have developed over the past four decades. A large number of independent Satanists and even other Satanic organizations have been heavily influenced by the form first espoused by LaVey, and his doctrines are axiomatic to many Satanists, LaVeyan or not. *The Satanic Bible*, his landmark 1969 work, remains the central text. The issues of magic and the occult have become a dividing line between different sects, with the Church of Satan—eventually—placing itself firmly on the skeptic's side. Yet even LaVey's staunchest critic would not deny his influence. He is a don of sorts; not unchallenged, but widely respected. This achievement is itself a testament to his authority, given the constant running battles of words, doctrines, and egos within the Satanic community.

The antecedents of modern Satanism are legion. While alive, Anton LaVey referred to authors and thinkers he felt an affinity with as Satanic, even if it was often highly unlikely they would define themselves as such. John Milton, Tom Paine, Jack London, H. G. Wells, W. Somerset Maugham, Ben Franklin, Mark Twain, and others were retroactively bestowed with the esteemed title. Satanism finds allies and precursors scattered throughout history, often lurking on or beyond the fringes of acceptable society. This ideological promiscuity has resulted in a genealogy that is more akin to a mosaic of associations rather than a tidy, linear heritage. Nonetheless, a bloodline of sorts can be mapped. Satanism owes its existence to three historical traditions within Western culture: it begins in the religious story of Satan, is emboldened greatly by the literary heritage of the modern period, and eventually adopts a number of the theories of philosophical/scientific tradition as it enters the contemporary era. Although there are devil figures in a variety of cultures, Satanism is very much a Western cultural phenomenon, and its origins are very much in the Western—especially Christian—tradition. As LaVey acknowledged, "we are living in a culture that is predominantly Judeo-Christian."[11] This account of contemporary Satanism will therefore be, for the most part, limited to this territory, beginning with the history of its infernal namesake.

Contemporary attitudes towards Satan range from the millions of people with deeply held religious beliefs who believe in the literal existence of the devil to secular figures who consider it an archaic myth to be laughed at openly or exploited for shock value. On one side, we have evangelists openly proclaiming the horrors of the devil:

> Satan's plan is to destroy God's creation. Satan's entire purpose is to steal, kill, and destroy. Satan lies in order to conceal our true identity as children of God from us; to cause us to believe that there is no God...The Devil wants us to believe that Man, along with all life on earth, was an accident that crawled out of a slimy ocean 4.5 billion years ago, and gradually became men and women who could choose to love God or deny He even exists.[12]

On the other side, there are people like Mark Twain who find it amusing to write letters to Saints Michael and Gabriel, letters ostensibly penned by the devil:

> Man is a marvelous curiosity...he thinks he is the Creator's pet. He believes the Creator is proud of him; he even believes the Creator loves him; has a passion for him; sits up nights to admire him; yes, and watch over him and keep him out of trouble. He prays to Him, and thinks He listens. Isn't it a quaint idea?[13]

Twain has, unsurprisingly, been accepted by modern Satanists as one of their own.

It is no surprise that the devil arouses such a range of responses. With the help of apostle, church doctor, heathen, and heretic alike, Satan has emerged from his long genesis as one of our most evocative cultural icons. Widely referenced by religious leaders, writers, artists, filmmakers and heavy metal bands, the depth of Satan's character enables him to embody a great many principles: to the religious figure, he is source of all evil, the tempter and betrayer; to the artistically inclined, the embodiment of heroic rebellion and creative liberation; to the Satanist, the benchmark for individualism and self-reliance. That all of these interpretations—and many more—come from the same mythology indicates both the richness of the devil's story and its ability to be bent to the individual's needs. Whether he represents unmitigated evil or unsurpassable freedom, the devil just won't go away. Many don't really want him to—he's just too interesting.

The Morning Star: On the Origins of Satan

…rejoice, you heavens
and you who dwell in them!
But woe to the earth and the sea,
because the devil has gone down to you!
He is filled with fury,
because he knows that his time is short.

—Book of Revelation, 12:12

It was Christianity which first painted the Devil on the world's wall;
it was Christianity which first brought sin into the world.
—Friedrich Nietzsche, *The Wanderer and his Shadow*, §78

Satan has by far the richest genealogy of any religious or mythological figure. With a history that stretches more than 3,000 years into the past, the biography of the great beast reaches further than written accounts, passing through the poems of nineteenth-century French poets and English Romantics, hedonistic eighteenth-century Hellfire clubs, renaissance witch hunts, secret societies and medieval knights, dark age heretical sects, Papal edicts, early Christian splinter schools, and biblical scriptures—both apocryphal and canonical. Ultimately, the grand deceiver fades cipherlike into the mists of Roman, Greek, Persian, Hebrew, and Egyptian mythology, taking his leave in uncharted prehistory.

Satan's ancestry is the result of an elaborate cross-breeding of traditions that has spanned millennia. Numerous faiths and folklores have contributed to his bloodline as it has passed through history, creating a figure rich in resonance and lore. Though widely regarded in the present day as a single supernatural entity, the preeminent embodiment of evil, Satan is actually a reduction or hybridization of a number of individual demons and mythical beings. The list of his progenitors, kinsmen and co-conspirators includes Lucifer, Mephistopheles, Beelzebub, Belial, Azazel, the Devil, various lesser devils, Ahriman, and even the Egyptian deity Set (Seth). This impressive gallery of seducers, liars, and destroyers gradually coalesced into the grand figure of the archfiend as he is now known, the great adversity of God and humanity.

EARLIEST ORIGINS

The Western conception of the devil has its beginnings in the faiths of the Middle and Near East. The beliefs of the Egyptians, Canaanites, and Persians abound in demonic figures that both represented and accounted for the harshness of their environment. In Egyptian mythology, the desert god Set is associated with desert caravans and sandstorms. Often colored red and variously depicted as a serpent, crocodile, or black pig, Set's animosity toward Horus (and Osiris) is recounted in a number of gruesome tales of attempted drownings, rape, castration, sodomy, and assorted fraternal strife. Set was later associated with Baal, the Canaanite fertility and storm deity, a name that is in turn synonymous (in the Bible at least) with Beelzebub, Lord of the Flies. Baal is the most difficult deity of this period to pin down, as the name literally means "lord" and can refer to any god or gods of the Semitic tribes. The Bible presents Baal as an evil god, but this is most likely the result of later prejudice as the name was earlier used by the Jews to refer to their God. The exact genealogy of Satan's prebiblical heritage is almost impossible to derive from this tangled demonic pantheon, but it is assumed that all of these figures made their contribution to his creation.

While the various myths of ancient Egypt and Canaan were undoubtedly influences, the main pre-Hebrew origin of Satan is found in the Persian religion Zoroastrianism. Founded by Zoroaster, a Persian prophet born around 660 B.C.E., Zoroastrianism is a unique development in the history of religion, as it is the first formed around a doctrine of ethical dualism—the eternal opposition of good and evil. Though Zoroastrianism has only one absolute deity and representative of truth, Ahura Mazda (later known as Ohrmazd), through whose will all things have come into being, the might of this supreme ruler is not unopposed. Balanced against him is Angra Mainyu, or Ahriman, a destructive spirit around whom all evil is concentrated. Described as a serpent, Zoroastrianism's proto-Satan is credited as the author of a vast catalogue of calamity, with plagues, snakes, locusts, lusts, witchcraft, and a stunning 99,999 diseases attributed to his ceaseless machinations. Around these two figures the forces of good and evil face off in constant battle, until the final judgment where legends tell Ahura Mazda will triumph.

Zoroastrian teachings entered Hebrew thought as a result of Jewish misfortune—their defeat at the end of a bloody and drawn-out war against the Babylonian King Nebuchadnezzar. During their captivity in Babylon (597–537 B.C.E.) Jewish scholars encountered Zoroastrian beliefs firsthand. They saw in its doctrines the answers to a number of troubling theological issues, in particular the problem of evil. Once released, they returned to Jerusalem with a new perspective on their own faith. As a result of this contact, Zoroastrianism is commonly seen as the means by which the idea of an evil opposing force or devil entered the Judeo-Christian tradition. Other correlations reinforce this claim. The snakelike Angra Mainyu inhabited a "House of Lies," an ill-smelling abyss where the dead who failed judgment by Ahura Mazda were sent for eternal torment. This Hell-like void was a major influence—in conjunction with the Greek Hades—in changing the Hebrew Sheol, a bleak underworld where both good and bad souls resided, into something more akin to the later Christian conception of Hell.

THE BIBLICAL SATAN

With Satan's earliest mythological origins uncovered, the ancient Hebrew texts are the logical place to conduct a serious search for the devil. Yet strangely, the Bible is not the best place to find him. There is no single passage that clearly sets out the history, nature, and role of the devil.[1] Rather, the story is (and has been) reassembled by scouring the scattered references from Genesis to Revelations, and reading them in light of supporting legends and theological doctrines. In the works of the Hebrew Bible, Satan barely makes an appearance. There are admittedly a variety of devils, demons, and dark spirits, but the being now regarded as Satan is almost completely absent. Satan's fabled debut as the serpent in the Garden of Eden is a false sighting. The snake is, in the Jewish tradition, just a snake. The interpretation of the infamous tempter of Adam and Eve as Satan—or an agent of Satan—has been applied retrospectively, most likely through early Christian translation and interpretation of the Torah. The association, though widely accepted by contemporary Christians, is entirely unsupported by the original Hebrew text.

Aside from his falsely accredited entry into the Garden of Eden, the devil's most notorious appearance in the Hebrew Bible is the temptation of Job, the first of the two famous biblical temptations. In the Book of Job, Yahweh's loyal servant, a "blameless and upright man," is subjected to a series of misfortunes by Satan (known as ha-Satan), who spends his time "roaming through the earth and going back and forth in it."[2] Arguing that humanity is

only loyal because of the rewards Yahweh provides, the accuser wagers that
without these rewards, Job will abandon his Lord:

> "Does Job fear God for nothing?" Satan replied. "Have you not put a hedge
> around him and his household and everything he has? You have blessed the
> work of his hands, so that his flocks and herds are spread throughout the land.
> But stretch out your hand and strike everything he has, and he will surely
> curse you to your face."[3]

Satan is presented in the Book of Job as a member of God's divine council, a
lawyer who seeks out humanity's sinfulness and then acts as its accuser. Satan
subjects Job to a battery of misfortunes: his servants are slaughtered, his livestock is destroyed by fire, his camels are stolen by a raiding party, and finally a fierce wind brings down his house, killing his sons and daughters.
Job complains bitterly of his fate but does not betray his Lord and the testing
concludes.

The temptation of Job is the first major introduction of Satan. Throughout, it is clear that Satan is loyal to Yahweh, acting wholly under his
jurisdiction—even as he kills an innocent man's family. As the accuser, Satan's status never exceeds that of Yahweh's agent for evil; it is necessary for
him to petition the Lord when he wishes to visit further torments upon Job.
This subservience to the Lord and quasi-legal role is mirrored in the Book of
Zechariah: "Then he showed me Joshua the high priest standing before the
angel of the Lord, and Satan standing at his right side to accuse him."[4] In this
passage, there is again nothing demonic about Satan—he operates entirely at
the discretion of Yahweh, seeking out the evil in men and putting them on
trial for their transgressions. There is, however, a hint of exuberance in the
Lord's prosecutor, and his accusations against an innocent man anger his master: "The Lord rebuke you, Satan! The Lord, who has chosen Jerusalem, rebuke you! Is not this man a burning stick snatched from the fire?"[5] Satan, one
hopes, bore the dressing-down with dignity; there was far worse to come.

The second biblical temptation occurs in the New Testament. Following his baptism, Christ is led into the desert where he fasts for 40 days and
nights. In the depths of hunger, the "tempter" comes to him and says, "If you
are the Son of God, tell these stones to become bread." When Jesus refuses,
the devil tries to convince him to throw himself from the top of the temple,
as the Lord's angels "will lift you up in their hands." Refusing once more, Jesus
is tempted for a third and final time:

> Again, the devil took him to a very high mountain and showed him all the
> kingdoms of the world and their splendor. "All this I will give you," he said, "if
> you will bow down and worship me."

Jesus said to him, "Away from me, Satan! For it is written: 'Worship the Lord your God, and serve him only.'"[6]

Who is tempting Christ in this passage, Satan or a/the devil? The term used is *diabolus*, Greek for slanderer or false accuser. Only the Gospel of Mark identifies the devil as Satan—Christ's use of the term "Satan" has the generic meaning of accuser/tempter. Nevertheless, this episode shows an important confusion and mingling of the Bible's various devils with Satan and their shifting status: in the Old Testament temptation of Job, Satan is the adversary and tempter of humanity under the command of the divine; in the New Testament temptation of Christ he is the rival of God and actively campaigning against his plans.

The change of status is revealing. Satan is far more prominent in the New Testament. In contrast to his minor role in the Hebrew texts, Satan's role is significantly amplified by the books of the New Testament, authored in the 70–80 years following the death of Christ. In contrast to both Judaism and Islam,[7] the Christian scriptures contain a widespread outbreak of demonic activity. In the Christian Bible, Satan is mentioned by name at least 30 times, and is associated with a vast number of other figures: the devil (also more than 30 references), Beelzebub,[8] Belial,[9] and the Serpent or Dragon throughout Revelation. If modern Christian tradition is consistent in one thing, it is unifying a number of disparate references and names into one unique figure. A prime example is the inclusion of the morning star in the Satan mythology. In the Book of Isaiah, the following passage has gained immortality:

How you have fallen from heaven,
O morning star, son of the dawn!
You have been cast down to the earth,
you who once laid low the nations![10]

The morning star is the planet Venus, a heavenly body rich in mythological resonance from prehistoric times. While this passage is undoubtedly a depiction of overreaching pride that leads to a fall, the morning star represents Nebuchadnezzar, the King of Babylon, who is named in the same chapter. In Saint Jerome's fifth-century translation of the Bible from Greek into Latin, the Greek term "heosphorus" (literal meaning: "dawn bringer," a sobriquet for Venus) is rendered as "Lucifer," Latin for "light bearer" and an astrological term for the morning star. The term "Lucifer" already had a potent mythological and literary history, having been used by the Latin poets Ovid and Virgil; similarly, "heosphorus" appears in the Greek classics of Homer and Hesiod, as well as being associated with the legend of Prometheus, the stealer of light. The outcome of Jerome's injudicious translation is that later

Christian figures interpreted Isaiah 14:12 as referring to a rebellious archangel, Satan, and his fall from grace, rather than an arrogant king and the fall of Babylon. The name Lucifer was given biblical authority by Jerome and entered the Christian tradition as being synonymous with Satan, while simultaneously associating it with a preexisting literary and mythological tradition.

As a direct result of these and other emendations, Satan emerges from the Christian Bible as an almost godlike embodiment of evil, retroactively associated with the Fall of Adam and Eve. This interpretation is held by a number of biblical scholars and recent biographers of Satan. Henry Kelly, author of *Satan: A Biography* (2006), is entirely unambiguous: "Satan as the rebel against God was not in the Bible. He's just doing his job, he's been appointed as governor of the world...He's not the enemy, he's not some sort of a villain."[11] For early Christians, however, Satan was established as the adversary of both believers and God. The briefest comments in the Bible, such as "I saw Satan fall like lightning from heaven" in Luke,[12] were taken as reinforcement of the grand mythology of the eternal adversary, as Satan had become. Just like Ahriman in the Zoroastrian tradition, Satan works as a lightning rod, drawing criticism for evil away from God, when in fact it is God, the supreme being, that allows evil into human existence. The itinerant Satan from the Book of Job is still abroad in the New Testament world but is no longer merely an agent of God's order, having become a wild beast yearning for prey: "Be self-controlled and alert. Your enemy the devil prowls around like a roaring lion looking for someone to devour."[13]

By the composition of the Book of Revelations (circa 95 C.E.) the identification of the devil and Satan as one entity was complete, along with the link to the Fall, with Isaiah's seven-headed "Leviathan, the coiling serpent" thrown in for good measure.[14]

> And there was war in heaven. Michael and his angels fought against the dragon, and the dragon and his angels fought back. But he was not strong enough, and they lost their place in heaven. The great dragon was hurled down—that ancient serpent called the devil, or Satan, who leads the whole world astray. He was hurled to the earth, and his angels with him.[15]

How did Yahweh's legal adjutant come to "lead the whole world astray"? How did he become the evil mastermind preached from the medieval pulpit? Acknowledging the long composition period of the books of the Bible gives some perspective—over six centuries separate Satan's debut in the Book of Zechariah from the serpent's downfall in Revelation (Zechariah is an older text than the Book of Job). By the end of this lengthy evolution, Satan was firmly installed as the implacable foe of God's creation, ever plotting the destruction of the Church and humanity. As debates over Christian doctrine were waged in the following centuries, it became standard practice to label heretics—or simply anyone with whom one disagreed—as being in the thrall of the devil, the ever-present seductive whisperer beckoning the righteous to damnation.

In addition to the overt narrative of Satan's history, there is a sub-rosa mythos exerting its influence. The Christian Bible was not organized in its current form until the fourth century, when the texts now known as the apocrypha vied for position in the canon—the nightmarish Book of Revelation was one of those that walked the razor's edge between scriptural immortality and textual oblivion. One that didn't make the cut was the Book of Enoch. Enoch is relevant to Satan's biography because it recounts the legend of the Watchers, a group of angels who descended to Earth and, as mentioned in Genesis, coupled with human women: "[T]he sons of God went to the daughters of men and had children by them."[16] Their offspring were a race of savage giants, the Nephilim, who began to wreck havoc and devour humanity. God sent Raphael down to stop the giants. After watching their children being killed, the Watchers were imprisoned inside the Earth, and God sent down the flood to cleanse the corrupt Earth. With its tale of wayward angels, it is entirely unsurprising that the story of the rebellious Watchers was later associated with that of the greatest rebel of them all, Satan. The Watchers became identified as the angels who had mutinied alongside Satan, and they entered the lore of early Christianity until being unceremoniously ejected by the Church Fathers, who were appalled by the thought of angels taking corporeal forms and copulating with humans. The stories persisted however, although the forbidden Book of Enoch was little more than a legend for over a thousand years until it was rediscovered as part of the Ethiopian church's Bible in the eighteenth century.

EARLY AND MEDIEVAL CHRISTIANITY

His lineage assembled, Satan entered the nascent Christian era bearing the heritage of the Angra Mainyu, Set, Baal, the Hebrew ha-Satan, Lucifer, Prometheus, and any number of minor deities and demons, a mosaic of different traditions reduced into one figure. From this point, developments in the history the devil largely follow those of early Christianity, with the devil becoming evermore associated with the evils of the physical world. But the efforts of the early Christians to blame the still-ambiguous figure of Satan for the world's ills had an unforeseen effect—the influence on the philosophical and spiritual movement now known as Gnosticism.

Widespread in the second and third centuries, Gnosticism was an amalgam of concepts borrowed from Greek (particularly the philosopher Plato), Christian, Zoroastrian, and Judaic sources. The Gnostic Christians, most notably Marcion of Sinope (circa 110–160), took the Zoroastrianism-derived ethical dualism a step further than their more orthodox brethren, although no one was truly orthodox in such heterogeneous times. The Gnostics claimed that the entire physical realm was created and held under the thrall of evil. Yahweh, the creator God of the Old Testament, was in fact a cruel, merciless force known as the Demiurge, who had created the physical world, including humanity. The just God of love and mercy, revealed by Christ, existed in a purely spiritual plane, apart from the temptations of the physical. The Demiurge and the Christian God were eternally opposed principles of good and evil. The former had created the world and humanity; the latter, supreme deity, was righteous and just.

The Gnostics' dualist system was a logical extension of the separation of the spiritual and the physical begun by the disciples. Sects such as Marcion's were important in the development of Christianity as they forced early Christian thinkers to clarify and codify their own beliefs and doctrines. Christianity itself was evolving fast, being legalized by Constantine in 313, further standardized by the Nicene Creed of 325, and made the official religion of the (soon to crumble) Roman Empire by Theodosius in 383. The scriptural canon was also compiled in the same period. Gnosticism's direct influence on mainstream Christianity may have been quickly countered in the third and fourth centuries, forcing it into the periphery of theological discussion, but it continued to remain influential in various forms long thereafter and continued to throw challenges to the Church.

One of the principle figures in the defeat of Gnosticism and other dualist doctrines was Augustine of Hippo (354–430). St. Augustine's battle was as much personal as theological, having for nine years been a follower of Manichaeism, a dualistic religious philosophy that combined elements of Zoroastrian, Christian, and Gnostic thought. He later converted to Christianity and wrote about his spiritual journey in the classic *Confessions*. Fortunately for Augustine, the hedonism of his early life gave him plenty to confess, having kept a mistress for 15 years and fathered a child out of wedlock. Acknowledging his own sinful and immoral life, and seeking to resolve the doctrinal challenges facing Christianity, he sought to explain how evil could be present in God's creation. Satan and the Fall were central to this issue, and the convert asked in his *Confessions*, apropos of the devil: "whence…came in him that evil will whereby he became a devil, seeing the whole nature of angels was made by that most good Creator?"[17] Augustine's response was that all works of God are good, and are made evil only by action of free will. As he wrote in another classic, *City of God*:

> not even the nature of the devil himself is evil, in so far as it is nature, but it was made evil by being perverted. Thus he did not abide in the truth, but could not escape the judgement [*sic*] of the Truth; he did not abide in the tranquillity [*sic*]

of order, but did not therefore escape the power of the Ordainer. The good imparted by God to his nature did not screen him from the justice of God by which order was preserved in his punishment; neither did God punish the good which He had created, but the evil which the devil had committed.[18]

Moral evil, then, issues from the choices that God's creatures make. It is not, as dualists argued, a necessary or eternal aspect of the world. Rather, it is a perversion of nature. In his arguments, Augustine reaffirmed the world as God's creation and humanity's privileged place within it. "God...placed the human race upon earth as its greatest ornament." He argued against the view of a flawed universe created by a malevolent being, highlighting the abundance of "good things adapted to this life," and stressed that the individual's choices determine his destiny: "[E]very man who made a good use of these advantages suited to the peace of this mortal condition, should receive ampler and better blessings, namely, the peace of immortality...but that he who used the present blessings badly should both lose them and should not receive the others."[19]

The intellectual achievement of Augustine imposed order on the diversity of religious doctrines within the Roman Church and assured the marginalization of opposing creeds. Augustine's systematic and comprehensive vision became dominant. At the same time, official acceptance of hosts of devils seeking to pervert humanity—such as Satan in the Garden of Eden—was established as fact. The perennial association of sex, sin, and the devil was in no small part the result of Augustine's puritanical reaction to his own early excesses.

With medieval Christianity and the rising power of the papacy based on the intellectual bedrock of Augustine's writings, the Church began its steady expansion. Christianity's missionaries spread the faith through Europe from the fifth century, an advance that accelerated into conquest by force when Charlemagne reclaimed the Holy Roman Empire in 800 C.E. Christian holidays were superimposed on pagan holidays, the faith's pantheon supplanting or merging with local Gods such as Loki, Thor, and Woden.

Church Doctors continued to add to the intellectual tradition, with Saint Anselm (1033–1109) contributing an important essay on Satan, *De Casu Diaboli* (*The Fall of the Devil*). Anselm needed to answer how the fallen angels—in particular Satan—could believe it possible to attain equality with God, as their superior intellect would have caused them to see the impossibility of achieving their desire. Although predominantly concerned with the metaphysical and theological lessons to be drawn from Satan's fall, Anselm's treatment of the topic as a serious issue in the study of Holy Scripture reasserted its centrality in Christian theology.

By the time of the high Middle Ages, the Church was solidifying its position. The Catholic Church recognizes the Fourth Lateran Council (1215) under Pope Innocent III as the authoritative teaching in regard to the devil. Echoing Augustine, it charges—in the very first paragraph of the document— that the fallen angels began as innocent, angelic creatures that damned themselves by their actions: "The devil and the other demons were indeed created by God good by nature but they became bad through themselves; man, however, sinned at the suggestion of the devil."[20] Satan and his host were pure spiritual beings that did not possess bodies, contrary to the by then long-forgotten Book of Enoch. In the Catholic catechism the devil's great sin was desiring independence from, and equality with, God. Pride, arrogance, and failure to submit to the Almighty led to the Fall. The council also explicitly accepted St. Jerome's interpretation of Isaiah 14 ("O morning star, son of the dawn!"), reaffirming the canonical identification of Lucifer with Satan. The once multidimensional devil had finally been formally defined.

THE GNOSTIC VISION

The Church may have issued its definitive word on the matter, but Anselm and other scholastics were not the only ones concerned with Satan. Dualist creeds, though marginalized, had not disappeared. Rome may have converted Europe, but Manichaean doctrines were still widespread in Asia. They spread into Europe in the tenth century through the Bogomiles, a group of sects active in Bulgarian and Slavic lands. The Bogomiles believed that Satan and Jesus were the sons of God, with the elder Satan rebelling and being cast out of heaven. As an outcast, Satan's realm was the material world, forever tempting and corrupting humanity through physical means. In contrast to the increasing theological sophistication of Christianity, the dualist beliefs were attractively direct. As one medieval historian notes, "Dualist beliefs have the strong superficial attraction of simplicity; they present a clear cut world picture to an ignorant convert, or one passing from paganism, and they appear to provide a solution to the perennial theological problem of evil in a world created by a good God."[21]

The rationale of Gnosticism was straightforward: evil was simply too prevalent and too woven into the fabric of the material realm to be excusable. In discarding the assumption that the world was God's creation and attributing it to a purely evil entity or force, the problem of evil was overcome without the need for complex theological maneuvering, such as that of the Church Doctors. The complete separation of spiritual and physical realms posed a clear solution to the convert—renounce the corruptions of the flesh and escape the thrall of the devil. The dualists' claims for two deities, each reigning over their separate sphere of influence—the material and spiritual realms—were bolstered by their reading of Christian scripture. The actions of the tempting Satan in both Old and New Testaments, the stark contrast between earthly and heavenly planes, Christ's assertion that Satan was "the prince of this world,"[22] the apostles' repeated condemnation of the flesh—all were seen as justification of the dualist vision. Christians countered that, rather than solving the problem of evil, dualism merely crudely acknowledges two opposing principles. From the perspective of each, the other was fundamentally flawed and utterly damned.

The Church and the dualists were on a collision course. The Bogomiles' teachings reached Italy in 1030 and quickly spread into France, becoming particularly strong in the southern regions. By the time of Pope Innocent III, the need to root out heretics had become paramount. Labeling Christianity's enemies as agents of Satan had long been standard practice—the various Gnostic groups said the same of the Church—but had seldom gone beyond denunciation from the pulpit. In the first three centuries Christianity was only one of a number of sects jockeying for influence. Sustained persecution of heretics or opposing creeds could only come after the consolidation of Roman Catholic authority. By the thirteenth century this consolidation had been achieved. The Holy Roman Empire and its new pope's power were unparalleled. With the weight and unquestionable authority of the Roman Catholic Church to draw upon, the need to extirpate agents of the devil with pure force became inevitable. The persecution began in earnest in 1209 when Pope Innocent III called together the first crusade within the Christian empire, against the heretical Cathars of Southern France.

The Cathars, or Albigensians, were adherents to a form of Gnosticism similar to Marcionism and Manichaeism. They believed in a strident dualism in which the physical world was the creation of the evil Old Testament God, with the true God of good residing only in the spiritual realm. The Cathars had an immensely strong vision of Satan and his powers. He was responsible for luring angels from heaven, imprisoning them in clay bodies, creating the physical world, leading all humanity away from Christ, and plaguing the world with natural disasters. The Cathars believed in reincarnation, thus their beliefs were focused on breaking free of the devil's creation through strict rejection of all material elements—sex, possessions, worldly appetites—in order to enter the domain of pure spirit. The fleshly body was so corrupted by original sin that even the institution of marriage was viewed as advancing the designs of Satan. The Cathars did not discriminate between martial relations, adultery, premarital sex, or incest. All were equally pernicious.

The Cathars were put down in one of the most infamous military operations of medieval times. At the French town of Béziers in 1209, when posed with the question of how to determine heretic (Cathar) from Roman Catholic, the Cistercian commander of the Church's forces is said to have replied, "Kill them all, the Lord will recognize His own." The town was completely destroyed and an estimated 20,000 people indiscriminately slaughtered. The savagery continued for a further two decades. In 1244, the remnants of the outlaw faith were finally cornered and defeated at their mountain stronghold at Montségur on the Spanish border. Hundreds of Cathars paid the price of challenging orthodox Christian views and were immolated on an enormous pyre at the base of the castle.

The Cathars were consigned to history as the most famous victims of Christian intolerance and oppression. In the wake of the Albigensian massacres, nonconformist believers went underground in order to avoid persecution. The Church became more frequent in its use of force and the Papal Inquisition to stamp out heretical sects. The Waldensians, a Christian denomination that espoused poverty and austerity, were denounced like the Cathars and subjected to a prolonged persecution throughout the thirteenth and fourteenth centuries. The Luciferans were another Gnostic group, but one that put a new twist on the dualist vision of the universe: the supreme God was Lucifer, the light-bearer; the God of evil was the Christian God, a deceiver who had made the world believe he represented good. Confessing—presumably under threat of torture—to be devil-worshippers, the Luciferans confirmed the worst fears of an increasingly paranoid Church.

The trend became predictable. Anywhere that sectarian or unconventional groups sprang up, the Church responded with accusations of demonic allegiance and seldom restrained hostility. The Church's fanaticism in rooting out evil had inevitably led it to turn against groups within Christian lands. Eventually, it led it to turn against one of its own orders, in this case the monk-warriors of the Knights Templar.

THE PERFIDY OF THE KNIGHTS TEMPLAR (AND OTHER POPULAR FABLES)

The Knights Templar had been established in the wake of the First Crusade to protect pilgrims traveling to the Holy Land. As a Catholic military order answerable only to the pope, they received vast donations of money and land and became widely involved in finance and business. They quickly attained great fame and wealth. Their political stock fell drastically following the loss of Acre, Christianity's last foothold in the Holy Land, in 1291, and many suspect the order became the scapegoat for the Crusades' failure. The smear campaign waged against the Templars (1307–1314) by Philip IV of France reflects the French king's brazen opportunism more than any supposed perfidy of the Knights. Philip, deeply in debt to the wealthy Templars, recognized that accusing the order of devil-worship, blasphemy, and homosexuality was an easier option than repaying his loans. His sustained offensive of vilification and character assassination reached its denouement with mass arrests, confessions extracted by torture, and at least 50 knights burnt at the stake as heretics. The trial of the Templars saw them besmirched and broken. The order was disbanded, its wealth confiscated, and it has ever since been associated with the darker side of Christianity, the much heralded hidden history of the Templars. Rumors of fearful secrets—Black Masses, worship of an idol named Baphomet, possession of the Holy Grail or Ark of the Covenant—abound to this day although little, if any, corroborating evidence exists.

The trial of the Templars is the most blatant misuse of the Church's by then well-honed antiheretical apparatus, but by no means the last. The Beguines, Beghards, and mystics of northern Europe all faced similar persecution. The Inquisition gained stature and authority with every guilty judgment, feeding off its own success, no matter how flimsy the evidence or implausible the cases may have been. The logic was simple and self-perpetuating: the more people found guilty, the more palpable the threat of heterodoxy and the greater the necessity for vigilance. When two Dominican Inquisitors wrote the *Malleus Maleficarum* ("The Hammer of Witches") in 1485, they helped set off the series of witch trials that lasted for 250 years. The book documented, in lurid detail, the ways the devil works through witches to perpetrate evil. The logic underlying their claims is evident in the following passage, which is itself a citation from book 5 of Augustine's *City of God*:

> It is a very general belief, the truth of which is vouched for by many from their own experience, or at least from hearsay as having been experienced by men of undoubted trustworthiness, that Satyrs and Fauns (which are commonly called Incubi) have appeared to wanton women and have sought and obtained coition with them. And that certain devils…assiduously attempt and achieve this filthiness is vouched for by so many credible witness that it would seem impudent to deny it.[23]

The existence of lecherous devils thus proven—who doubts the word of Augustine, Christianity's greatest Doctor?—the *Malleus Maleficarum* was used to justify the waves of witch hunts that followed, campaigns that claimed thousands of lives. Belief in similarly fantastic accounts were not merely the domain of puritanical clergy. Late medieval Europe was highly superstitious and still largely unenlightened, as historian William Manchester describes:

> Scholars as eminent as Erasmus and Sir Thomas More accepted the existence of witchcraft. Conspicuous fakes excepted, the Church encouraged superstitions, recommended trust in faith healers, and spread tales of satyrs, incubi, sirens, cyclops, tritons, and giants, explaining that all were manifestations of Satan. The Prince of Darkness, it taught, was as real as the Holy Trinity. Certainly

belief in him was useful; prelates agreed that when it came to keeping the masses on the straight and narrow, fear of the devil was a stronger force than the love of God.[24]

With a cynical clergy and credulous populace, tales of pacts with the devil were also popular in folklore. In these tales, an individual makes a deal with the devil in which his soul is traded for diabolical aid, usually in the form of knowledge, esoteric power, juvenescence, or wealth. The scriptural authority is Isaiah 28:15, "We have entered into a covenant with death, with the grave we have made an agreement," with "grave" also translated as "Hell" or "Sheol." The most notorious pact with the devil is that of Faust. Most likely based on the life of late fourteenth-century German alchemist and magician Dr Johann Georg Faust, a trickster of exceedingly poor repute, the legend is a cautionary tale of the perils of what a poet might label vaulting ambition. Faust's desire to commune with the devil led to a successful summoning and a contract written in blood: the devil would serve Faust truthfully for a period of 24 years, after which time Faust's body and soul would be ceded to his infernal confederate. The deal struck, the ambitious scholar lived in luxury with ever-increasing knowledge, power, and perversions of taste until, the story goes, a near quarter-century later, when wild screams were one night heard coming from his home. The good doctor's mutilated corpse was found the following morning, amid a scene of bloody destruction.

The legend of Dr. Faust's terrible fate became famous all over Europe, eventually being immortalized by playwrights Christopher Marlowe and Johann Wolfgang von Goethe. Evidence of real devil worshipping is, however, in short supply. Clergy may have railed incessantly about the threat of the archfiend—Martin Luther in particular was completely obsessed with the devil, believing Satan to have a pointed interest in his bowels—but most common people were too genuinely scared of the dangers to flirt with the profane. Constantly informed that the devil was the source of all evil, and possessing a profoundly limited knowledge of the workings of the natural world, the general public found the terrible message issuing from the Church all too believable. Carnality, lust, self-importance, rebelliousness, impiety— the path to Hell was clearly marked. The devil's great pride and challenge to the lord of heaven had led to his downfall; the misplaced arrogance that had dared to challenge the omnipotent creator. Humility and subservience to clerical authority were, the priests assured, the only credible option.

Yet rumors of apostasy and subservience to satanic authority abounded. One of the most infamous examples was the fifteenth-century aristocrat Gilles de Rais. De Rais had fought alongside Joan of Arc and was one of the most powerful men in France. He was also the most notorious sexual predator of the medieval period, responsible for the deaths of between 8 (that he confessed to) and a fabled 800 children. A singularly vicious pederast, de Rais had his staff scour the villages near his estates for children to feed his perversions, obtaining them by abduction or purchase from impoverished parents. Once in his grasp, the children were subjected barbaric indecencies, frequently sodomized while impaled on hooks or being strangled. De Rais preferred boys, but would use girls in a similar fashion if necessary. A methodological killer, he kept the blood of his victims in copper vessels, carefully labeled with the date of death. The decapitated heads of attractive boys were also made into souvenirs. De Rais' depravity and sadism were seemingly boundless—one of his pleasures was to stab his victims in the neck and masturbate on them as they slowly bled to death. He even had plans to kill the child still in his wife's womb. She later testified against him.

The abuses continued for a number of years. As de Rais indulged himself and steadily frittered his wealth away, he became involved with an alchemist named François Prelati. The contriving Prelati convinced de Rais he could summon a demon named Barron, who could in turn provide gold to bolster the nobleman's ailing coffers. Prelati was a confidence man of the highest order, providing his gullible master with a litany of fantastic tales of successful conjurings. De Rais was, however, a coward who, despite his awful transgressions, was fundamentally a God-fearing Christian, refusing to sign a pact with the devil as Prelati encouraged him to. During his trial, de Rais fully expected God to exonerate him. Nevertheless, after he was tried and burnt at the stake, rumors of a vast catalogue of satanic ritual slaughter abounded, resulting in the legend of 800 victims. The popular escalation of de Rais' crimes is easily understood: when an individual is already proven to be a mass-murdering, child-molesting sadist, it is not a great leap to the status of full-blown devil-worshipper, especially in the eyes of a superstitious and poorly educated populace. Given the hysterical fear of black magic and dark forces that the Church actively promoted, it could almost be expected—the acceptance of such phenomena was fostered within the framework of orthodox belief. As Aleister Crowley noted in his 1930 "Banned Lecture" on the case: "Whenever questions arise with regard to black magic or black masses, invocations of the devil, etc., etc., it must never be forgotten that these practices are strictly functions of Christianity."[25]

Another equally famous case was that of the Affair of the Poisons involving numerous members of Louis XIV's court. At the time, love potions, charms, so-called inheritance powders (i.e., poison), and black magic were popular within the aristocracy. The 1776 trial of the Marquise de Brinvilliers for poisoning members of her family launched a widespread controversy. De Brinvilliers and her lover, the army executioner La Voison, were burned at the stake. The accompanying investigation led to accusations of witchcraft among the fortune tellers and alchemists. The investigation halted when

Louis XIV's mistress the Marquise de Montespan was implicated for her earlier involvement with La Voison. Jealous of the king's other mistress, de Montespan reportedly enlisted the help of black magic to gain his favor. With a priest contacted by La Voison, de Montespan had a number of Black Masses practiced over her body, rites that allegedly included the sacrificing of a human infant. The blood of the child was mixed with flour to make the host, which was then consecrated and inserted into the de Montespan's vagina. The conspiracy was eventually discovered but, fearing controversy, Louis allowed de Montespan to escape prosecution.

THE IMPACT OF THE ENLIGHTENMENT

Monsters like Giles de Rais and social climbers like the Marquise de Montespan were aberrations, not evidence of widespread demonology. With the revival of skepticism in the sixteenth century and the rise of science in the seventeenth, attitudes towards Satan began to change. The horrid figure used to scare peasants into conformity began to be mocked by the less-superstitious intellectual classes. The Enlightenment's triumph of reason and sustained attack on Church authority started to tell. Deism began to replace traditional theology—it fit better with the Newtonian model of the natural universe. Voltaire, one of the most famous writers of the time, was implacable in his opposition to religious hypocrisy and corruption. "[Christianity] is assuredly the most ridiculous, the most absurd and the most bloody religion which has ever infected this world" he wrote to Frederick the Great.[26] Asked on his deathbed if he renounced Satan and all his works, the writer reportedly replied: "Now, now my good man, this is no time for making enemies."

Voltaire's attitude is indicative of the times. The propensity to mock—rather than fear—the Christian devil took hold in sections of the intellectual classes. Hellfire clubs, first founded in England and Ireland in the early 1700s, began to openly align themselves with the devil. In truth, these clubs had little to do with the dark arts and everything to do with drunkenness and sexual excess, but as drunkenness and sexual excess were the traditional specialties of the devil, the association was inevitable. In the members' self-conscious rebellion, parodying Church sacraments and rites took a central role. As a horrified witness of a club meeting reported in a 1721 newspaper:

> The Purport of their Meetings was to ridicule, in the most audacious manner, the Person and Power of Almighty God, the Father, Son, and Holy Ghost, together with all the Sacred Mysteries of Religion, Blaspheming and Impugning the same in a manner very unfit to be here mention'd; some of them assuming the Names of the Patriarchs, Prophets, and Martyrs, mention'd in Holy Writ, making them the Subject of their Blaspheming Mirth and Pastime.[27]

The most famous Hellfire club was a small group established by Sir Francis Dashwood in 1746. It adopted François Rabelais' creed "Do what thou wilt" as its modus operandi. In irregular meetings on occasions such as Walpurgis Night in 1752, it conducted elaborate and blasphemous ceremonies. Rafts were floated down the Thames with members dressed in monk's robes. The group's private abbey was adorned in inverted crosses and lit with dark candles, and a Black Mass was conducted with the naked body of an aristocratic lady serving as an altar. Masked, naked nuns were also involved, most likely prostitutes shipped down the Thames from London.

With the advent of Hellfire clubs, disparagement of Christian convention became more common. Black Masses had long been reported to have been practiced by groups such as the Cathars, the Knights Templar, and witches' covens, though scant evidence survives. The most famous modern example of a Black Mass is the dramatization in Frenchman J. K. Huysman's 1891 novel *La Bas*. Huysman claimed that he had witnessed masses and that it was a genuine representation of such. In his vivid account, a congregation assembles in a private chapel and a priest praises Satan as the true God. When the celebrant defiles the host, the ceremony degrades into a vast orgy, "a monstrous pandemonium of prostitutes and maniacs."[28] Huysman's Black Mass—and other fictional accounts, including those in the Marquis de Sade's novels—have been widely influential in later Satanist organizations, forming the basis for contemporary rituals. Even the scarlet cap worn by the priest in *La Bas*, with two horns rising from the crest, was to reappear in later ceremonies.

Hellfire clubs and practitioners of Black Masses seldom accepted the existence of the devil; rather, they were using his image for a twofold purpose—to mock religious ceremony and justify hedonistic excess. In doing so they displayed that, for certain small segments of society, the ideal of the devil as eternal bogeyman was no longer effective. The modern, increasingly scientific vision of the world that was eroding the Church's power was also subduing the devil. No longer a beast on the prowl for prey, he was simply a convenient way to dramatize one's opposition to the dominant religious and social orthodoxy. Certainly, there were still large numbers of people who did believe in Satan's existence—as there always have been—but there were significant numbers who felt comfortable to laugh at, or with, him. Even the most blatant cases of supposed diabolical allegiance can be questioned. In the case of the various devil-worshipping sects throughout history, many of these had a different conception of the devil than the orthodox Christian view. Their beliefs were frequently based in Gnostic tradition, where the devil represented the natural order, rather than the embodiment of evil as in orthodox Christian teachings. There are very few cases of outright devil-worshippers, as most people would understand the term.

Satan was necessary for a monotheistic premodern religion such as Christianity, for it needed to find a way to explain the presence of evil to its followers. Complex arguments on the nature of free will may have satisfied church intellectuals, but they weren't particularly effective on illiterate peasants. By elevating and elaborating Satan's role in biblical sources, Christianity absolved its God of evil. It found—created—its scapegoat. As a consequence, Satan is associated with a number of very real, very human desires and emotions. It's no coincidence the Seven Deadly Sins are all sins of self-indulgence: lust, gluttony, greed, sloth, wrath, envy, and pride. In so closely aligning the devil and his fate with the temptations that ordinary people felt, the Church was warning its flock of the dangers that lurked beyond its protection, lest they meet the end of a misguided wretch like Dr. Faust.

Satan's role as scapegoat and association with all-too-human desires had the effect of making him attractive to marginalized members of society and helps explain the small pockets of (purported) devil-worship throughout history. Any individual who feels a weakness to more earthly desires, to fleshly pleasures, is automatically aligned with Satan. The Bible explicitly placed the spirit and the flesh in opposition:

> But I say, walk by the Spirit, and you will not gratify the desires of the flesh. For the desires of the flesh are against the Spirit, and the desires of the Spirit are against the flesh, for these are opposed to each other, to keep you from doing the things you want to do…the works of the flesh are evident: sexual immorality, impurity, sensuality, idolatry, sorcery, enmity, strife, jealousy, fits of anger, rivalries, dissensions, divisions, envy, drunkenness, orgies, and things like these.[29]

For anyone who wished to escape the repression of the dominant teachings, invoking the devil as a justification of natural desires was a logical and predictable step.

The repression itself resulted in a legitimization of the dissident groups and sects. The persecution of unorthodox views stimulated interest in these groups, resulting in a self-perpetuating and frequently circular mythology. As Richard Cavendish writes, "The principle beliefs and rituals of medieval witches seem to have come from the Cathars, the Luciferans and other sects accused of worshipping the Devil…It is also likely that the persecutions of Satanist sects and the witch trials themselves stimulated the activities they were intended to suppress."[30] Cavendish's assessment is convincing. The Cathars, for example, were accused by the Church of indulging in Black Masses and depraved orgies (in complete contradiction to their stated beliefs), and these rumors became the basis and justification of later practices. In the age-old spirit of recognizing the common enemy, all of these groups—the

Cathars, the Knights Templar, witches, Luciferans—have been claimed by modern movements as spiritual ancestors. The marginalized of today identify with their historical counterparts, and see in the persecution their antecedents faced the condemnation they feel today.

As the next chapter will show, Satan became increasingly attractive to artists—poets, writers, painters—in the modern era. As Western society developed and the Church's influence slowly eroded, it became acceptable to bring Satan further out from the shadows. Satan's close association with sex, and the obvious connection between sex and creation, became a powerful formula for modern artists. His outsider status made him a perennial favorite for those dwelling on the fringes—or, in many cases, beyond the fringes—of acceptable society. Just as the apostles and Church Doctors used the devil to warn of the dangers of the flesh, modern figures began to invoke his name with increasing frequency and bluntness to *celebrate* the joys of the flesh. Hellfire clubs were only the beginning of the co-opting of the devil.

Baleful Eyes: The Archfiend Gets an Entourage

It would be difficult for me not to conclude that the most perfect type of masculine beauty is Satan,—as portrayed by Milton.
—Charles Baudelaire, *My Heart Laid Bare and Other Essays*, p. x

In Satan, Christianity created an irresistible symbol. As the only being that could come close to disputing the omnipotence of its God, the fallen archangel held an unrivalled position. That his fabled insurrection had failed and he had been cast out of heaven seemed irrelevant. He had, after all, taken a third of the population of that hallowed principality with him. Satan was the only one who had launched a legitimate challenge to the authority of God, a challenge that His temporal representative—the Church—openly acknowledged and obviously feared. Given his unequalled antiauthoritarian legitimacy, it was inevitable that Satan would become a standard for many who wished to question or defy authority. Whether as a worldly presence or as a figurehead, Satan's standing was assured. Christianity had created its antithesis, and he wasn't going to go away.

In the European artistic tradition, painters were quickest to recognize the power of demonic imagery. Medieval depictions of the devil focused heavily on his mouth and the Gates of Hell, which were often combined into the terrifying and pervasive image of the Hell-mouth. The medieval Hell-mouth arose from yet another combination of biblical passages, this time associating the great serpent, Leviathan, with the terrible fate Moses describes in Numbers for those who have spurned the Lord: "the earth opens its mouth and swallows them, with everything that belongs to them, and they go down alive into the grave."[1] Countless images of a grotesque mouth devouring the unfortunate who have fallen from grace were soon inscribed on church stone and depicted in the stained glass of churches throughout Europe. People didn't so much go to Hell as be consumed by it. Even Satan, when he was shown anthropomorphically, frequently had more than one mouth, with gaping jaws in his stomach or rear. Often half-human, half-animal—or fully animal—he was as far from the grace of God as could be imagined.

The era's other representation of Satan was as a goat, which has both biblical and pagan origins. In the Jewish scapegoat ritual described in Leviticus, Aaron is instructed to "lay both hands on the head of the live goat and confess over it all the wickedness and rebellion of the Israelites—all their sins—and put them on the goat's head."[2] The goat, with the evils within it, was led into the desert and thrown over a cliff. The negative connotations for the goat were not forgotten, especially not when combined with the cult of the satyr Pan, the half-man, half-goat Greek god. Kissing the anus of the he-goat became a symbol of submission to the devil, and appears in numerous renaissance-era paintings and woodcuts. In a time of widespread illiteracy, images such as these had a profound influence in forming people's conception of the devil, easily rivaling the Bible in influence. After all, prior to the Reformation the holy book was only directly accessible by the clergy.

SATAN AND THE LITERARY TRADITION

The devil may have been well served by medieval painters, but his appearance in great literature was delayed until the fourteenth century and Dante Alighieri's *Divine Comedy*. The work's legendary warning, "All hope abandon ye who enter here," fails to deter the fictional poets Dante and Virgil, who pass through the Gates of Hell into the horrors of the *Inferno*. The nine concentric levels of Hell, described in detail by Dante, house those individuals damned by their earthly vice. Descending through ever-worsening punishments and torments for ever-worsening transgressions, the poets' journey culminates at the center of the earth, where the Inferno's master resides. What they find is representative of the era's depictions of the devil. Lucifer, when finally introduced, is a gigantic static brute, immersed to the chest in a lake of ice.

> The Emperor of the kingdom dolorous
> From his mid-breast forth issued from the ice;
> And better with a giant I compare
> Than do the giants with those arms of his;
> Consider now how great must be that whole,

Which unto such a part conforms itself.
Were he as fair once, as he now is foul,
And lifted up his brow against his Maker,
Well may proceed from him all tribulation.[3]

His angelic beauty long since faded, the shaggy three-headed Emperor of
Hell says nothing, perhaps fully occupied chewing the famous traitors in each
mouth: Brutus, Cassius, and Judas. His size may be impressive, but there is
something of an anticlimax to Dante's Lucifer. The monster's role is passive
and minimal, notably devoid of personality. Dante's devil is a broken, spent
figure. The major demonic presence of the *Inferno* is Hell itself, not its frozen, immobile lord.

The effective marginalization of the devil by the great writers of this period is common. The work of the titan of English literature, William Shakespeare, while filled with numerous characters driven by devilish passions and
frequently mentioning him in passing, is largely devoid of references to Satan
himself. There are many allusions, but they usually serve to describe the negative qualities of an earthly character: "Not in the legions / Of horrid hell can
come a devil more damn'd / In evils to top Macbeth."[4] Shakespeare, it seems,
was far more concerned with fate and human nature than the temptations of
the devil. His contemporary, playwright Christopher Marlowe, came closer to
a true introduction of the diabolical with *The Tragical History of Doctor Faustus* in 1589. Yet despite Marlowe's acclaimed reworking of the widespread
legend, his Faustus merely strikes a deal with a devil, Mephistopheles, not
the devil. Echoing the intermittent appearances of his early biblical career,
the archfiend's major entrance into high literature was somewhat delayed.
Shakespeare mostly ignored the devil. Dante and Marlowe gave him bit parts
but certainly didn't give the devil his due. What Satan really needed was his
name in lights, the leading role that would define his career and launch the
diabolical into the big time. It came in 1667.

John Milton (1608–1674) was an unlikely man to immortalize Satan. A
deeply religious man, he sought to compose an epic poem that would stand
beside the works of Homer or Virgil. The stated aim of *Paradise Lost* was to
"justify the ways of God to men" by covering the central lore of Christianity: the expulsion of the rebel angels from heaven, the serpent's tempting of
Adam and Eve in the Garden, and Satan's residence in Hell.[5] It is a milestone
both in literature and the biography of the archfiend. It presented for the first
time a powerful evocation of the Satanic figure, imbued with psychological
depth never witnessed before. In *Paradise Lost*, Satan is no longer the bogeyman of the inquisition or the silent brute of Dante. He is an iconoclastic rebel
cast out from heaven, complete with complex desires, emotions, and flaws.

The flaws in particular make him an entrancing character, as he seethes with the ambition and self-regard that prompted his downfall:

> round he throws his baleful eyes
> That witnessed huge affliction and dismay
> Mixed with obdúrate pride and steadfast hate.[6]

Vanity and ambition have contributed to his fate, but most predominant is the pride that saw him rise in rebellion. It is the fatal flaw that Saints Augustine and Anselm had stressed, but as Milton's Satan regroups from his heavenly expulsion, rebelliousness looks suspiciously like a virtue:

> Here at least
> We shall be free; th' Almighty hath not built
> Here for his envy; will not drive us hence;
> Here we may reign secure; and in my choice
> To reign is worth ambition though in Hell:
> Better to reign in Hell than to serve in Heav'n.[7]

The renegade angel declares his independence and places himself in an explicitly adversarial relationship with God, whose authority he resents. There is an undeniable vitality in his insurgence; Satan may be disfigured, but he is unbowed:

> yet shon
> Above them all th' Archangel: but his face
> Deep scars of thunder had intrenched, and care
> Sat on his faded cheek, but under brows
> Of dauntless courage, and considerate pride
> Waiting revenge.[8]

It was an enormously powerful and influential characterization. Milton, above all, made Satan attractive, both physically and as an ideal. The defeated angel has fallen, but there are traces of beauty and splendor in his fate. He reigns, "Majestic though in ruin," his heroic energy evident in the strength of "Atlantéan shoulders fit to bear / The weight of the mightiest monarchies."[9] *Paradise Lost* may conclude by damning its protagonist, by then an embittered serpent that retreats to Hell, but few readers can rid themselves of the portrait of the noble, tragic Satan presented in the first two books. Like Dante's treatment of Hell before him, Milton took Satan far beyond the scarce details of the Bible. It is the rich detail of this vision of a humanized Satan that has persisted. The poet's gift was psychological strength, nobility, beauty, and undaunted self-belief. As a result of this gift, the popular conception of Satan today owes a far greater debt to Milton's epic than to the Bible.

Despite Milton's achievement, interest in the devil temporarily subsided in the face of Enlightenment rationalism. Yet the changes that the period witnessed were to be important to his development. The authority of both the Christian church and monarchal government came under increasingly heavy attack by the forces of secularism and reason. The philosophical principle that common people should have a greater role in determining their political fate took hold across Europe. In 1776, America rose up against its colonial masters and claimed its independence. More shocking however, were the seismic waves produced by the French revolution (1789–1799). The French didn't just relieve their king of his political authority; they relieved their king of his head.

Another victim of the rise of reason was the Inquisition. With the widespread championing of science—Newton had very nearly eclipsed God in some quarters—and trumping of superstition, the populace was no longer credulous enough to accept the inquisitors' claims. As the French essayist Michel de Montaigne had commented, "it is putting a very high price on one's conjectures to have a man roasted alive because of them."[10] A critical shift in perspective had occurred, and when Satan reappeared in literature in the early nineteenth century, it was with renewed vigor. Interest rose in the wake of Matthew Gregory Lewis' Gothic epic *The Monk* (1796), and Satan was soon receiving a sympathetic portrayal again, although this time intentionally, from the Romantic poets.

THE ROMANTICS

With the Romantics and Satan, Milton's influence prevailed: William Blake and Percy Shelley were both deeply impressed and influenced by what they saw as the great poet's sympathetic portrait of Satan, interpreting the former angel as the lead character in *Paradise Lost* and viewing him as a heroic instigator of rebellion against a tyrannous heaven. Shelley was effusive: "Nothing can exceed the energy and magnificence of the character of Satan as expressed in [*Paradise Lost*] ... Milton's Devil as a moral being is far superior to his God."[11] Blake in turn declared he had divined where Milton's true allegiance lay: "The reason Milton wrote in fetters when he wrote of Angels & God, and at liberty when of Devils & Hell, is because he was a true poet and of the Devil's party without knowing it."[12]

The Romantics recombined the existing mythology with that of Prometheus, the Greek immortal who stole fire from the gods. Shelley's *Prometheus Unbound* (1820) is a fiercely revolutionary text, combining Milton's rebellious emblem with a defiant stance against oppression that sees the enslaver, in this case Zeus, deposed. Despite his admiration for *Paradise Lost*, Shelley felt Prometheus represented a purer figure than Milton's protagonist as he was free from vanity, envy, or desire for personal glorification. In Prometheus, Shelley coupled the political ideals of the time with Milton's unwitting liberation of Satan. Shelley's staunch atheism is pivotal in this marriage of influences, for he consciously used the existing mythology symbolically, divorcing it from religious doctrine. This development in the appropriation of the mythology was an important foreshadowing of things to come.

The apex of the Romantics' Satanic aspect is the life and work of the poet Lord Byron, forever defined by Lady Caroline Lamb's reproof/endorsement as "mad, bad, and dangerous to know."[13] Byron, a legend across Europe and exile from his homeland, was something of a one-man cultural phenomenon, his life a swirl of profligacy, drug use, scandal, and allegations of incest and sodomy. The author of *Childe Harold's Pilgrimage* and *Don Juan* created, through his life and odes to self-assertion and defiance, the ideal of the tragically flawed artistic hero. He embodies the Romantic who wants to know, wants to experience, and is willing to trample any taboo in order to do so, traditional notions of good and evil be damned. The Satanic/Byronic hero is the prototypical rock star, the timeless representation of hero-as-outsider. It encapsulates in one figure the Romantics' preoccupation with the complex relations between individualism, political authority, rebellion, and artistic creation. The appeal of the archetype has not waned: the fabled narrative of the life of Lord Byron saw him long regarded as one of the most Satanic figures in history, the poetic embodiment of the demonic, heroic, and radical.

As influential to the development of the Satanic tradition as Milton, the Romantics were such a challenge to the dominant tradition in art that they were dubbed "the Satanic School" by poet Robert Southey,[14] in stern disapproval of their pride and "audacious impiety." This condemnation was a reaction to the unorthodox views and frequently dissolute lifestyles of Shelley and Byron in particular. Later critics, most notably C. S. Lewis, lambasted them for their exclusive focus on the heroic Satan of Books I and II of *Paradise Lost* and failure to recognize his deep flaws. Yet Lewis's critique was of a fundamentally religious nature, and the Romantics were clear about the qualities that their much-maligned standard represented for them: protean creative energy, nobility and courage, principled rebellion, lack of respect for rank and privilege, intellectual freedom, and the overthrowing of oppression. They were Satanists, certainly, but for them the power of the Satanic tradition was in enabling liberation of the imagination.

The English Romantics were not exploring this territory alone. Germany's greatest genius, the polymath Johann Wolfgang Goethe, was contemporaneously challenging the religious orthodoxy in the context of Enlightenment advances. Though more restrained than his British counterparts, Goethe's work shared their subjectivity and defiance in the face of authority. He had insisted in the poem *Prometheus* (1773) that man's belief in God(s) would be better placed in belief in himself, fuming, "I know of nothing more wretched / Under the sun than you gods!" Though ostensibly set in the classical world, the message was equally applicable to monotheism:

> I pay homage to you? For what?
> Have you ever relieved
> The burdened man's anguish?[15]

In his concern with the individual, Goethe helped engender German Romanticism and influenced every major writer and thinker of the century to come. His two-part *Faust* drama (1808 and 1832) was so influential it was dubbed "the drama of Germans." Working with the same folklore that Marlowe had dramatized two centuries earlier, Goethe expanded the topic's scope to create an analysis of history, psychology, politics, and industrial society. Goethe's devil, however, is truthful, wise, and more philosophical than Marlowe's. His Faust is in turn presented as a secular post-Enlightenment student of science and theology who seeks out the antipodes of knowledge. He is a heroic, not tragic, character, stripping the legend of its traditional moral lesson. The shift in focus is also evident in the pact Faust makes: Mephistopheles does not automatically receive Faust's soul on his death, he receives it only if Faust ceases to strive for knowledge. In the post-Enlightenment Faust the devil is involved, at least symbolically, in humanity's quest for further knowledge— the same quest that was steadily undermining the authority of the Christian church.

The Satanic archetype remained in the artistic vanguard throughout the nineteenth century, due in no small part to the Romantics' resounding influence. The popularity of French poet Charles Baudelaire reaffirmed the perennial outsider appeal of the "grandest of Angels" in his 1857 *Litany to Satan*:

> O first of exiles who endurest wrong,
> Yet growest, in thy hatred, still more strong,
> Satan, at last take pity on our pain![16]

From the dawn of Romanticism onwards, Satan was consistently well represented in prose and poetry. The major development had been made: the transformation of Satan from religious standard for evil into a semi-legitimate, but highly effective, secular figurehead for rebellion. The artistic tradition, however, started to adopt a different flavor as it responded to the seismic changes of nineteenth-century scientific and philosophical advances, which produced radical changes in how the world was perceived. These changes were quickly harnessed by the literary world: Russian novels for example began to abound in a vast catalogue of nihilists, atheists, anarchists, and revolutionaries. Drawing Satan into this cultural mix was hardly difficult, as Shelley and Goethe had established the precedent of identifying Satan with social and scientific goals.

As noted in the introduction, modern Satanism draws from three historical traditions within Western culture: the religious story of Satan, the literary heritage of the modern period, and specific aspects of the philosophical/scientific tradition as it enters the contemporary era. In regard to modern Satanism, the eventual synthesis of these developments is of enormous importance. Though the discussion of certain figures in the third tradition and their relevance to Satanism may appear opaque at first, their relevance will assuredly emerge. Without the influence of Darwin, Nietzsche, London, and Rand there would be no modern Satanism.

THE INTELLECTUAL PRECURSORS TO SATANISM: POLITICAL PESSIMISM

Philosophers and social theorists have long concerned themselves with the complex relationship between human nature and the body politic. Renaissance writer Niccolò Machiavelli created a early form of political realism in his treatise *The Prince* (c. 1516), advancing a frighteningly pragmatic approach to leadership, "[I]t is better to be feared than loved if you cannot be both."[17] As a result, his work is often simplistically interpreted as an amoral justification of tyranny; the name Machiavelli and the term "Machiavellian" are now synonymous with unscrupulous, cunning behavior and expedient dishonesty. Shortly afterwards, British philosopher Thomas Hobbes's pessimistic view of human nature led him to argue that a strong political state (headed by a king) was necessary to protect society from descending into a so-called state of nature, where a "war of all men against all men" would occur.[18] Hobbes was convinced that human societies had developed as they are because having strong guidelines to interactions between individuals was for the benefit of all. Machiavelli and Hobbes became touchstones for countless later theorists with pessimistic views of human nature and society.

In his *Essay on the Principle of Population* (1798) English demographer Thomas Malthus announced that drastic measures were needed to curb population growth. Malthus claimed that, because population grows geometrically while food supply increases arithmetically, the great masses of humanity would suffer from limited supplies of food by the middle of the following century. To combat the looming specter of widespread famine, Malthus advocated limitations on reproduction—although only for the poor. That his analysis of human suffering focused exclusively on population and food supply did little to dampen enthusiasm for his ideas; neither did his failure to anticipate the growth of increasingly sophisticated and productive farming techniques. Yet, though repeatedly and comprehensively debunked,[19] the grim Malthusian vision still exerts its influence today. Historically, however, Malthus's *Essay* and its focus on the evolution of population had another unforeseen consequence: it made a young English naturalist think not just in terms of competition between different species, but competition between members of a single species.

Of all the scientific discoveries that have challenged religion's primacy, none has been as devastating as Darwin's theory of descent with modification. Charles Darwin (1809–1882), a naturalist and biologist, presented the fruits of his life's research in *The Origin of Species* (1859), later applying his findings directly to humanity in *The Descent of Man* (1871). Darwin showed that species evolve over huge periods of time, periods of time far longer than the biblical account of world history allowed for. Similar theories had been advanced previously, but Darwin, indebted in part to Malthus' underscoring of intraspecies competition in the "struggle for existence,"[20] provided the first account of the mechanism by which species evolved: natural selection. In any reproductive population, Darwin showed, favorable traits would tend to be preserved and unfavorable ones would tend to be destroyed. Over time, the population would evolve. It was a simple idea, but uniquely powerful.

The Darwinian revolution was too important to be limited to the natural sciences; it was also a philosophical revolution. It removed humanity from the center of creation, denied that nature was benevolent or designed, directly repudiated the Genesis creation story, and undermined (for many, eliminated) the role for a creator. The long-term implications for religious belief in particular were profound. Key processes in the natural world could be explained without reference to divine or biblical authority, and the anthropocentric assumptions of theism were shattered. By revealing the natural mechanisms that drive organic change, Darwin contributed enormously to the demystification of nature and is subsequently one of the most influential men in history, his name virtually synonymous with the vivid description of "nature red in tooth and claw," and the terms "evolution by natural selection" and "survival of the fittest." The philosophical implications of his work are still being debated today.

The phrase "survival of the fittest" was, however, not the formulation of Darwin but of his contemporary, the philosopher Herbert Spencer (1820–1903). Spencer was devoted to the general notion of evolution—particularly the earlier theory of Jean-Baptiste Lamarck—and social progress well before the publication of *Origin of Species*. For example, in his 1857 article

"Progress: Its Law and Causes," he argued that "[the] law of organic progress is the law of all progress," and applied its principles well beyond merely the biological realm:

> Whether it be in the development of the Earth, in the development of Life upon its surface, the development of Society, of Government, of Manufactures, of Commerce, of Language, Literature, Science, Art, this same evolution of the simple into the complex, through a process of continuous differentiation, holds throughout.[21]

With his belief in the parallel nature of biological and social development, Spencer is often regarded as the chief architect of social Darwinism, an early, misguided attempt at sociobiology. Though the theory was born in some of the Spencer's extensive writings—it was not a major theme of his—it was promoted most eagerly by late nineteenth-century capitalists and figures such as the American sociologist William Graham Sumner.[22] Social Darwinism is rooted in the nineteenth-century social engineering tradition of Malthus and others, although its advocates eagerly applied the enormous descriptive power of Darwinian terminology to social thought.

Social Darwinism claims that the fittest members of human society will naturally dominate, and that the weaker, less able to compete members will naturally be dominated. It further asserts that this stratification of society into those strong, worthy, and successful over those weak, unworthy, and unproductive is *morally* right, because it represents the natural development of society along evolutionary principles: not only *will* the strong dominate the weak, but the strong *should* dominate the weak. It is therefore morally wrong to assist someone weaker than oneself, for such assistance is unnatural and would be assisting the survival and possible reproduction of less desirable, parasitic elements of society. Sumner, echoing Spencer's fixation on progress, stated the central thesis bluntly:

> Let it be understood that we cannot go outside of this alternative: liberty, inequality, survival of the fittest; not liberty, inequality, survival of the unfittest. The former carries society forward and favors all its best members; the latter carries society downwards and favors all its worst members.[23]

The ethical implications of this theorizing became its most notorious legacy, especially when combined with another influential contemporary theory. Francis Galton, a geneticist and Darwin's half-cousin, coined the term *eugenics* in 1883 to describe the process of planned hereditary improvement of the human race by controlled selective breeding. Galton encouraged the use of eugenics to assist the so-called more suitable races or strains of blood in overcoming the less suitable; in practice, this entailed encouraging the breeding of those with supposedly noble qualities and the forced sterilization of the weak, disabled, or poor. Social Darwinism and eugenics were logical bedfellows and became popular with Western intellectuals. Winston Churchill, H. G. Wells, George Bernard Shaw, Alexander Graham Bell, and numerous American industrialists openly endorsed and applied the concepts well into the twentieth century. Their popularity led to enormously unjust eugenics programs in a number of countries, including America, and played a central role in Nazi racial policy. The use of social Darwinist and eugenic thought to justify mass exterminations during World War II showed all too clearly the moral failings of the theories, and both fields were almost entirely abandoned.

RADICAL INDIVIDUALISM

The principles of Malthusian pessimism and social Darwinism are, as will become apparent in later chapters, central to modern Satanism. Of equal importance, however, is a subversive body of thought that originates, in part, with one of the true radicals of philosophy, Max Stirner (1806–1856). Considered by his contemporaries to be little more than an intellectual barbarian and shunned as a result, Stirner is often seen as a forebear or influence for a number of different fields, including extreme individual egoism, nihilism, anarchism, and even fascism. Stirner's main work, *The Ego and Its Own* (1844), an unorthodox antiauthoritarian critique of Western society, led Friedrich Engels to label him the enemy of all constraint. Fiercely critical of morality, the state, religion, and all fixed ideas or absolute concepts, Stirner argued in favor of the complete autonomy of the individual. "I am my own only when I am master of myself, instead of being mastered either by sensuality or by anything else."[24] In this radical vision, "anything else" included religion, laws, educational systems, or any aspect of society that encroached on the individual. By combining this emphasis on total freedom with self-empowerment at the expense of others, Stirner advanced a vision that often veers to the extreme right. "My intercourse with the world, what does it aim at? I want to have the enjoyment of it, therefore it must be my property, and therefore I want to win it. I do not want the liberty of men, nor their equality; I want only *my* power over them, I want to make them my property, *material for enjoyment*."[25]

Echoes of Stirner's dissident individualism can be found in the anti-Christian polemicist Friedrich Nietzsche (1844–1900).[26] Nietzsche is one of the most recognizable figures in philosophy, and easily one of the best philosophical stylists; his iconoclastic writings have been extraordinarily influential in the Modernist age, reaching through art, science, philosophy, and literature.

Convinced that he lived in a time of cultural sickness and decay, of widespread dehumanization bought on by mass industrialization, Nietzsche championed a new focus on creative energies to counter the modern over-reliance on rationalistic thinking and promoted an elitist philosophy that shifted the focus away from the heavens and afterlife onto the joys of existence.

Nietzsche's work comes from a strong vein of anti-Christian—and frequently stridently atheistic—German writing. But whereas Goethe's antireligious paean of a century earlier, *Prometheus*, could only name ancient Greek gods directly, by the end of the nineteenth century Nietzsche has no such constraints:

> I *condemn* Christianity...The Christian church has left nothing untouched by its corruption; it has turned every value into an un-value, every truth into a lie, every integrity into a vileness of the soul...I call Christianity the one great curse, the one great innermost corruption, the one great instinct of revenge, for which no means is poisonous, stealthy, subterranean, *small* enough—I call it the one immortal blemish of mankind.[27]

Nietzsche's vitriol stemmed from his assessment of otherworldly religious doctrines as life-negating rather than life-affirming. Viewing religious observances as dangerous and misplaced pieties, he first made his most notorious statement, that "God is dead," in the 1882 work *The Gay Science:* "Whither is God?...I will tell you. *We have killed him*—you and I. All of us are his murderers." Humanity had engendered the collapse of the Christian worldview and the divine; all that was left was to acknowledge it. "Do we not hear anything yet of the noise of the gravediggers who are burying God? Do we not smell anything yet of God's decomposition? Gods too decompose. God is dead. God remains dead. And we have killed him." Christianity, he proclaimed, was simply obsolete. "What are these Churches now if they are not the tombs and sepulchers of God?"[28] Nietzsche's meaning—entirely metaphorical in intent—was not that God had literally died, but that the *idea* of God was dead. In the modern world, the concept was simply untenable and could no longer offer existential consolation or a basis for morality to humanity.

As he had renounced transcendent conceptions of morality, Nietzsche instead identified two historical moral codes at work in Western culture: that of the ruling class (master morality) and that of the oppressed class (slave morality). By Nietzsche's account, the oppression of the Romans—representing a philosophy of might, strength, and power—had caused the early Christians to respond by making virtues of their weaknesses. Thus, egalitarianism, pity, and brotherly love were extolled as honorable, though they were little more than the values of the spiritually and physically weak, the triumph of mediocrity as a virtue. In order to rise above this repressive slave (i.e., Christian) morality that corrupts society, Nietzsche called for a "revaluation of all values."[29] He wished to move beyond the false dichotomy of good and evil, a product of the so-called slave revolt in morality, toward a realization that life is something amoral—moral judgments are both arbitrary and subjective.

To respond to the crisis of values he had diagnosed, Nietzsche presented in *Thus Spake Zarathustra* (1883–1885) the concept of the Superman (*Übermensch*), a higher type of man who had moved beyond both Christianity and nihilism. The Superman turns away from the heavens and towards the earth, embracing creativity, life-affirmation, and the possibility of becoming more than human. "Man is something that shall be overcome."[30] Central to this development is the idea of the will to power, the deep-set instinctual growth of all life toward an accumulation of forces, of *power*:

> What is good?—Everything that heightens the feeling of power in man, the will to power, power itself.
>
> What is bad?—Everything that is born of weakness.
>
> What is happiness?—The feeling that power is growing—that resistance is overcome.[31]

Like so much of Nietzsche's writing, this passage is pregnant with ambiguity—the exact form of power being discussed is never clarified. Nevertheless, the central thesis of his work is clear: dominant Western (Christian) morality and values—pity, repentance, sin, guilt—are false and must be discarded. All forms of mediocrity have to be forsaken, and creative, expansive tendencies encouraged. Weakness of any sort is condemned, as his books contain frequent scathing attacks on conformity and acquiescence in the general populace, which he dubbed herd mentality. In *Thus Spake Zarathustra*, castigation of the "herd," the "all-too-many," the "superfluous," and the "rabble" is unending. His pitiless, elitist vision held scorn for the vast majority of humanity, honoring only those who excelled and rose above the masses.

Nietzsche's contemporary influence is almost unsurpassed. There are many reasons for his continued attractiveness to modern readers. His fierce, combative intellect and flamboyant writing style are certainly factors, as are the passionate nature of his critique and fervent irreligiousness. There is also the simple chance of birth: he lived in a point in time where it was just becoming possible to advance a radical critique of Western society's fundamental values and be widely influential. Earlier writers who had advanced broadly similar ideas—especially Max Stirner and the Marquis de Sade—were long regarded as unwholesome or uncivilized, effectively confined to the margins of intellectual discourse.[32] Following the concerted assault on the Christian worldview by Darwin and Marx, soon after joined by Freud, the intellectual world was, in many ways, ready for Nietzsche.

A LITERARY SYNTHESIS

The burgeoning interest in Nietzsche in the 1890s led to the reissue of Stirner's *The Ego and Its Own* in 1893 after half a century in the philosophical wilderness. Combined with the influence of Darwin, and the Spencerian appropriation of Darwin, these iconoclastic theorists sent shock waves through the intellectual and artistic circles of the period. One of those reading this incendiary new philosophy was American novelist and adventurer Jack London (1876–1916). Heavily influenced by Nietzsche and Spencer, and a personal favorite of Anton LaVey, London figures prominently in the development of modern Satanism because of his impressive fusing of the Luciferian poetic heritage with radical nineteenth-century philosophy.

In the novel *The Sea Wolf* (1904), London's ocean-borne exploration of social Darwinism at its most elemental, the bookish Humphrey Van Weyden finds himself held captive on a sealing ship captained by a vicious, primal tyrant. Slowly, Van Weyden begins entering into philosophical debates with the unexpectedly well-read Wolf Larsen, "enslaver and tormentor of men."[33] Larsen in turn submits Van Weyden to progressively higher levels of physical and psychological brutality. In their increasingly frequent discussions, Larsen counters Van Weyden's urbane humanism with an ideology of crude, militant materialism: "Might is right, and that's all there is to it. Weakness is wrong. Which is a poor way of saying that it is good for oneself to be strong, and evil for oneself to be weak."[34] Larsen's savage worldview— "The earth is as full of brutality as the sea is full of motion"—leaves no space for common civilities: "Life? Bah. It has no value. Of cheapest things it is the cheapest."[35]

The world of the *Ghost*, the ship on which *The Sea Wolf* unfolds, is an overtly social Darwinian microcosm, a high-seas Hobbesian state of nature ruled by an explicitly Satanic tyrant. The tension builds toward a critical confrontation between Van Weyden and the captain. Larsen begins "preaching the passion of revolt" and declares his allegiance to Milton's vision of the fallen Archangel:

> He led a lost cause, and he was not afraid of God's thunderbolts...Hurled into hell, he was unbeaten. A third of God's angels he had led with him, and straight away he incited man to rebel against God and gained for himself and hell all the major portion of all the generations of man. Why was he beaten out of heaven? Because he was less brave than God? Less proud? Less aspiring? No! A thousand times no! God was more powerful, as he said, Whom thunder hath made greater. But Lucifer was a free spirit. To serve was to suffocate. He preferred suffering in freedom to all the happiness of a comfortable servility. He did not

care to serve God. He cared to serve nothing. He was no figurehead. He stood on his own legs. He was an individual.

To this, the ship's sole female whispers: "You are Lucifer."[36]

Wolf Larsen's "defiant cry of a mighty spirit" concludes with Milton's paean in praise of individuality at any cost, "Better to reign in hell than to serve in Heav'n." His speech is a powerful articulation of Lucifer's heroic defiance, though Larsen's rebellion is directed not at the creator but at the world in general. Milton's classic poem had been taken up as a standard of rebellion many times before, but few had given the Luciferian spirit such open and forceful voice. London's stated aim for the novel was to use the character of Wolf Larsen to explore the concept of the Nietzschean Superman. In doing so, he was able to draw on resources of the modern era that were unavailable to earlier writers—a Darwinian perspective on both nature and society, and radical nineteenth-century social criticism.

London's *The Sea Wolf* represents the most explicit point where, in regard to Satanism, the literary tradition intersects with the philosophical. The philosophical strand of the Satanic/outsider ideal can be traced back to Sade or further. This strand favors, and frequently exalts, the primacy of the individual and importance of self-reliance, and is marked by explicit hostility to collectivism and religion (sometimes specifically Christianity, sometimes any form of spiritualism). As shown in London's Wolf Larsen, a harsh though nonetheless valid interpretation of Nietzsche's focus on power combines with pitiless theories of social selection to form the imperative "Might is right, and that's all there is to it."

EGOISM REDUX

Half a century after London, a philosophy of radical individualism once again came to prominence in English fiction, though in a more urbane and palatable form. Russian-born Ayn Rand (1905–1982) became a best-selling author in America in 1943 with her philosophical novel *The Fountainhead*, repeating her success in 1957 with *Atlas Shrugged*. Both books argued relentlessly in favor of the nobility of man, limited government, and the primacy of the individual. Rand attacked all forms of mysticism, by which she meant any religious or supernatural beliefs, and exalted reason and individualism as morally superior to sacrifice (altruism) and collectivism. Rand, however, flatly rejected might-is-right philosophy, claiming that there are no conflicts of interest between rational agents. She similarly rejected its inherent ethical nihilism, maintaining that there is an objective basis for morality—the morality of reason. For Rand, the individual's happiness is the moral purpose to life. In her highly optimistic assessment of modern industrialized society, the interests of rational individuals exist in harmony.

The centerpiece to Rand's philosophy is the 50-page-plus speech by the character John Galt in *Atlas Shrugged*. The dominant theme is repudiating the sacrifice of individual autonomy and product. Galt begins his speech, "I am the man who does not sacrifice his love or his values."[37] Galt's life is self-defined and focused solely on his happiness, irrespective of others: "Just as I do not consider the pleasure of others as the goal of my life, so I do not consider my pleasure as the goal of the lives of others."[38] These principles formed the basis of Rand's philosophical system, dubbed Objectivism. Developed in the nonfiction work *The Virtue of Selfishness* (1964), Rand declared that the concept of selfishness had been grossly maligned. "In the popular usage 'selfishness' is a synonym of evil…[Y]et the exact meaning and dictionary definition of the word selfishness is: *concern with one's own interests.*"[39] Rand's central argument is that humans *are* selfish, therefore they *should* be selfish. Altruism is unnatural as it contradicts the nature of the giver, is insulting to the autonomy of the beneficiary, and promotes dependence. Though her arguments are extraordinarily simplistic and frequently wrong, Objectivism has been widely influential in mainstreaming individual egoism and validating greed. Numerous prominent capitalists, industrialists, and economists find Rand's theories attractive, even if they have not had much influence with philosophers.[40]

The work of Ayn Rand brings us to the era of the LaVey's establishment of the Church of Satan. The figures that form the general intellectual background to modern Satanism are undoubtedly a heterogeneous group, but a number of core concerns can nonetheless be identified. When elements of each are combined, they form a radical, multifaceted critique of many conventional beliefs and values—the principles that LaVey championed certainly didn't arise in a vacuum. There are many other figures who could also be mentioned—Thomas Paine, Mark Twain, W. Somerset Maugham, H. G. Wells, Ben Franklin—but none would add significantly to those already covered. There is still one forebear who brings together aspects of the religious, literary, and philosophical traditions, even while sitting strangely uneasy with all them. An occultist, poet, seer, drug addict, and social provocateur, he stands on the margins of—if not completely outside—the tradition traced here.

AN OCCULT DIGRESSION

Aleister Crowley (1875–1947) was born to privilege in Warwickshire, England. He attended public (tuition-charging) schools and studied at Trinity College. Crowley's enviable position as the heir to his family's brewery fortune allowed him to follow any path he saw fit. He chose mountaineering, esoteric studies, poetry, (bi)sexual excess, and drug experimentation. A prolific writer and born adventurer, he traveled widely in search of arcane knowledge and higher mountains. He also became extraordinarily notorious for his personal conduct and sexual profligacy and cultivated a reputation as "the wickedest man in the world."[41]

Crowley became a member of the Hermetic Order of the Golden Dawn, a highly influential occult order, in 1898. His membership brought him into contact with S. L. MacGregor Mathers, W. B. Yeats, and other prominent occultists, propelling him to further travel and studies of tantric yoga, Buddhism, meditation, and ceremonial magic. Crowley's most famous work, *The Book of the Law*, was written in Cairo in 1904 while he was traveling under the name "Chioa Khan," literally "Great Beast." Over a three-day period, a spirit named Aiwass, apparently an emissary of the Egyptian god Horus, dictated its 220 verses to the scribe-priest Crowley. Dense, cryptic, allusive, and frequently incomprehensible (even Crowley battled to interpret it), the work is considered a sacred text of Thelema, the label Crowley appropriated for his system of occult philosophy. The name came from François Rabelais, Renaissance individualist writer, as did the work's central dictum, "Do what thou wilt shall be the whole of the Law."[42]

In 1914 Crowley became the head of the Ordo Templi Orientis (Ancient Order of Oriental Templars), a magical society that claimed the heritage of a number of esoteric orders, including the Knights Templar. At this point, he adopted the magical name of the Knights Templar's purported idol, Baphomet. The order's propensity to include sex in rituals suited Crowley perfectly. Sexual magic became increasingly important to his system, as he saw it as a way to harness physical and psychological energy, both internal and external. *The Book of the Law* strongly advocates sexual liberation, for male and female alike. Numerous passages address the nature of the so-called Scarlet Woman, through whom whoredom—in Crowley's eyes badly defamed by the Book of Revelation eighteen centuries earlier—will be redeemed. "Let her work the work of wickedness! Let her kill her heart! Let her be loud and adulterous! Let her be covered with jewels, and rich garments, and let her be shameless before all men!"[43] In practice, these sex magic explorations led to one of his most notorious acts: the 1921 ritual in which Crowley persuaded his Scarlet Woman, at the time Leah Hirsig, to have sex with a he-goat. The goat, however, did not perform, but Crowley substituted and the animal's throat was slit to complete the ceremony.

The system of magic that emerged from this life of study was dubbed "Magick," a synthesis of Eastern and Western mystical and esoteric traditions. Equally importantly, it was a quasi-scientific approach to spirituality and magic, with his ideas frequently presented in seemingly scientific language. The best example is his highly influential *Magick in Theory and Practice* (1930). "MAGICK is the Science and Art of causing Change to occur in conformity with Will."[44] With a strong focus on spiritual enlightenment, Crowley believed in advancement through the magical orders by development of will-power, self-control, meditation, and prayer. The central Thelemic creeds remained "Do what thou wilt" and "Love is the law, love under will."[45]

Crowley's philosophizing was not limited to only mystical and magic(k)al concerns. He had an aristocratic social outlook, and often echoed Nietzsche and other radical social critics strongly, particularly in his calls for a revaluation of all values and contempt for Christian slave morality. He had a dismissive attitude toward traditional moral limitations, writing to a friend in 1905, "I want blasphemy, murder, rape, revolution, anything, bad or good, but strong."[46] *The Book of the Law* is repeatedly punctuated by a disdain for humanitarian virtues—"Mercy let be off; damn them who pity! Kill and torture; spare not; be upon them!"[47]—that later found voice in stock social Darwinist and anti-Christian rhetoric:

> Nature's way is to weed out the weak. This is the most merciful way, too. At present all the strong are damaged, and their progress hindered by the dead weight of the weak limbs and the missing limbs, the diseased limbs and the atrophied limbs. The Christians to the lions!
>
> We must go back to Spartan ideas of education; and the worst enemies of humanity are those who wish, under pretext of compassion, to continue its ills through the generations. The Christians to the lions![48]

While no satanist himself—he abjured black magic and stood too far outside the Christian tradition to be any kind of devil-worshipper—Crowley prefigures the modern Satanist in a number of ways: his contempt for Christian piety, pity, and sexual repression; the focus on sexual freedom and sexual magic; strong elements of social Darwinism; use of ceremonial magic and ritual; and emphasis on attaining higher levels of consciousness. Combined with his quasi-scientific (effectively demystifying) explanations of magical theory, Crowley's legacy proved a potent mix that is second only to LaVey in its influence on modern Satanism. His prolific writings, at once abstruse and open to interpretation, continue to attract attention, and his position as a widely reviled figure both in life and death has only strengthened his appeal to self-conscious outsiders. A strong dose of notoriety does one's legacy wonders.

THE MANY FACES OF SATAN

Notoriety also came to be the original archfiend's strongest asset. From his humble beginnings in the sands of Egypt, the mountains of Persia, and as a member of the supporting cast in the Bible, Satan and his bad name have been propelled through Western history by a variety of sources: the early Christian drive to account for evil, medieval fear of the unknown, clerical need for a scapegoat or spook, and the need of artists to articulate their rebellion, individualism, and nonconformity. Gradually, a marginal biblical character was elevated to a status of enormous theological significance, accompanied by a hopeless blurring of the source mythologies. The adoption of a Satanic stance by revolutionary literary figures, and the raising of Satan as a standard to wage war on the dominant culture, merely increased the ideal's potency. The radical atheistic philosophical tradition of the nineteenth century does not invoke Satan but can be seen—and certainly is by modern Satanists—to champion Satanic ideals: elitism, egoism, rebellion, social upheaval, and overturning of Christian values.

The philosophic, literary, and religious traditions are equal creators in the foundations that modern Satanism builds on, although some are, as the saying goes, more equal than others. The importance of the philosophers and social theorists included in this overview indicates how far from the biblical devil Satanism has digressed. A number of the figures mentioned here are decidedly nonsatanic, in the popular understanding of the word, that is, regarding devil-worship or issues that are explicitly wicked or evil. Objectivism, for example, appears completely divorced from any traditional satanic ideals. There is something of a paradox in this phenomenon: the closer we get to the birth of modern Satanism, the further from Satan we stray. The religious origins of the devil are important for their symbolic potency, but the real ideological power comes from other, far more secular sources that champion sexual liberation, psychological and ethical egoism, and elitist social doctrines.

As the counterculture movement of the 1960s made its bid to change the world for the better once and for all, all the ingredients for a darker, far less tolerant ideology stood ready. The major themes of Satanic thought were largely prefigured in the monomaniacal Wolf Larsen—an explicitly demonic figure, a tyrant who rules his kingdom by pure force, simultaneously drawing on the philosophical, scientific, and dramatic traditions to buttress his claims. All that was needed was an iconoclast, a latter-day conjurer who would weave together the separate strands of the existing traditions and formulate the ultimate outsider's credo.

The Black Pope:
The Making of a Myth

I'd rather have my background shrouded in mystery.
> —Anton Szandor LaVey, quoted in
> *Rolling Stone*, September 5, 1991

Whatever else may be said of him, no one can accuse Anton Szandor
LaVey of being uninteresting.
> —Michael Aquino, review of *The Secret Life*
> *of a Satanist* in *Church of Satan*

Everyone sees what you appear to be, few experience what you
really are.
> —Niccolò Machiavelli, *The Prince*, p. 58

Anton Szandor LaVey was born Howard Stanton Levey to Michael and
Gertrude Levey in Chicago on April 11, 1930 (not Anton Szandor LaVey
to Joe and Augusta LaVey as he long claimed—more on this later). The
majority of knowledge of LaVey's early biography comes from his own accounts, and are unsupported by external sources. Unsurprisingly—given his
ultimate calling in life—he relates his childhood as the story of a go-it-alone
outsider, "something of an offbeat child prodigy," more interested in passing
the days immersed in "music, metaphysics and the occult" than spending
time with the jocks and the scholars.[1] His teachers were Bram Stoker, Mary
Shelley, and H. P. Lovecraft; his companions horror stories, magic books,
and pulp magazines. He lived in the domain of fantastic worlds and esoteric

knowledge, far removed from the mundaneness he saw around him and in his peers. The fact that he didn't fit in with his peers even manifested itself physically. He reported having a prehensile tail that had to be removed in his early teens, no doubt a powerful indicator of his animal nature.

"Tony," as he was called then, developed a talent and love for music at an early age, playing the oboe in the San Francisco Ballet Symphony Orchestra. The drudgery of high school held little interest for him, and he dropped out at 15 in favor of pool halls and the company of hoodlums and petty criminals. He became involved in the Clyde Beatty Circus as a cage boy in 1947, discovering an immediate affinity with the big cats. He quickly progressed to working with the lions and tigers in live shows, his natural rapport with the animals apparently extending to sleeping in the cage with them. He learnt valuable lessons from the cats, especially when cornered by their rough play. "You have just one defense left: willpower. Any good cat trainer has to learn how to use it, how to charge himself full of adrenalin, to send out gamma rays to penetrate the brain of the cat. That's when you really learn power and magic, even how to play God."[2] That year Tony toured the Pacific coast with the circus, resting the gamma rays and employing his musical ability by substituting as a calliope (steam organ) player under the moniker "The Great Szandor."

Once introduced to the circus life, he settled into a life on society's fringes. In the years that followed, Tony recalled working with a number of carnivals—the circus' less reputable, down-market substitute—developing his repertoire and skill on the calliope and organ. Apparently on the lam from an undisclosed altercation with the law, The Great Szandor sought companionship among other outcasts and lived the seemingly ideal lifestyle for a runaway. Yet, amidst the festival atmosphere, he was apparently shocked by hypocrisy he witnessed:

> On Saturday night...I would see men lusting after half-naked girls dancing at the carnival, and on Sunday morning when I was playing organ for tent-show evangelists at the other end of the carnival lot, I would see these same men sitting in the pews with their wives and children, asking God to forgive them and purge them of carnal desires. And the next Saturday night they'd be back at the carnival or some other place of indulgence. I knew then that the Christian church thrives on hypocrisy, and that man's carnal nature will out no matter how much it is purged or scourged by any white-light religion.[3]

In later conversations and writings, LaVey frequently referred to his so-called carny days, recounting tales of his experiences with flea circuses, Tasmanian Devils, live sex shows, fortune tellers, sword swallowers, and freaks of all stripes. They were undoubtedly formative years for LaVey, teaching him the power of show business, and how the weaknesses, quirks, and foibles of the public could be exploited to one's gain. He discovered that people wanted to be entertained, that the bizarre, forbidden, and ribald held a strong attraction for many.

> Through his carny experiences, he learned how much people would demand, and pay, to be fooled—how ghouls looked for always ghastlier thrills; how voyeurs wanted newer, more prurient treats; how the lonely and the sick wanted miracles—and how they only hate *you* when they're not fooled enough. The carny magician knows there aren't any miracles—there is only what you make happen in your life yourself.[4]

A central tale from LaVey's youth is reported to have occurred during the carnival's off-season in 1948. A stripper at the Mayan Burlesque Theatre in Los Angeles became entranced by the Svengali gaze of the accompanist, and a passionate if short-lived affair ensued, with the young couple moving into a rundown motel together. The stripper was, it is claimed, a young Marilyn Monroe. The Svengali, an 18-year-old Anton Szandor LaVey. Marilyn was apparently entranced by the mysterious organ player, "fascinated with Anton's stories of his life in the carnival and his ever-deepening study of the Black Arts." By LaVey's account, it was a difficult period in the life of the troubled actress, who "always wanted to hear more about occultism, about death—to explore the provinces of the strange and bizarre that Anton was becoming more and more familiar with."[5] He later related the episode in an idealized, semimythical tone—two drifters on the high seas of life taking safe harbor together for a time. She was a vulnerable, down-on-her-luck thrill-seeker with a taste for sex in cemeteries, in open awe of her precociously cultured and worldly young lover. He liked pale blondes.

LaVey tired of Los Angeles and drifted back to San Francisco. His life there followed a similar pattern of odd jobs in seedy strip bars, but for two important exceptions: he met his first wife, Carole Lansing, at an amusement park; and the Korean War caused him to enroll in college to avoid the draft. Burton H. Wolfe, a journalist who met LaVey in the late 1960s, recounted the importance of this period in his oft-quoted 1976 introduction to *The Satanic Bible*:

> After LaVey became a married man himself in 1951, at age twenty-one, he abandoned the wondrous world of the carnival to settle into a career better suited for homemaking. He had been enrolled as a criminology major at the City College of San Francisco. That led to his first conformist job, photographer for the San Francisco Police Department. As it worked out, that job had as much to do as any other with his development of Satanism as a way of life.

"I saw the bloodiest, grimiest side of human nature," LaVey recounted in a session dealing with his past life. "People shot by nuts, knifed by their friends; little kids splattered in the gutter by hit-and-run drivers. It was disgusting and depressing. I asked myself: 'Where is God?' I came to detest the sanctimonious attitude of people toward violence, always saying 'it's God's will.'"[6]

The endless parade of homicides, rapes, vehicular carnage, and arbitrary savagery took their toll, forever coloring the young man's previously sanguine view of humanity. Fortunately, the S.F.P.D were pleased with his work, and within a couple of years LaVey—now with a daughter, Karla—had been moved over to investigating the reports of strange occurrences that flooded the police department. His domain had become weird noises, UFO sightings, and unexplained phenomena. Though the position fit well with his natural predilections for the bizarre and macabre, by 1955 he was nonetheless ready to conclude his respectable police job and devote himself full-time to even more suitable occupations: exorcisms, hypnotism, and, once again, organ playing—this time as San Francisco's official city organist.

The following year he reported making one of the more important decisions of his life, purchasing the foreboding hilltop house at 6114 California Street, San Francisco. The 13-room residence had a history checkered enough for its new owner—constructed in 1887, it had been a brothel and Prohibition-era nightclub and was riddled with secret panels and trapdoors. LaVey immediately set about modifying the house to suit his personality. He lived at the property, dubbed the Black House, until his death. The house was developed into a physical manifestation of its owner's unique personality and interests.

From the outside, it is an unlikely looking Vatican. Apart from the electronically controlled, barbed-wire-topped gate barring uninvited visitors, the three-story gray Victorian house from the outside appears little different from its neighbours. The interior, however, is a different story.

The living room contains such arcane bots of furniture as an Egyptian sarcophagus, a sled-chair once owned by Rasputin, and a coffee table made from a yogi's bed of nails. In the den, a wall of shelves lined with books on every esoteric subject imaginable—from the carnival to cannibalism—is, in reality, a secret passage that opens into an adjoining sleeping chamber decorated with ceremonial masks. The entire house, in fact, is honeycombed with secret passages, left over from its days as a bordello and speakeasy. The fortunate visitor might even be taken down the staircase behind the fireplace and into the old speak, now the Den of Iniquity, a private saloon created by the master of the house, the so-called Black Pope—Anton Szandor LaVey.[7]

Replete with his new castle, the king was ready to hold court. The late 50s and early 60s were the years of cocktail parties at the Black House, with the LaVeys developing an eclectic social clique of eccentrics, artists, savants, and nonconformists. The evenings developed in more formalized nights of seminars and occult investigations, with the regular participants eventually forming Anton's Magic Circle, the forerunner to the Church of Satan. In 1959, he started seeing the 17-year-old Diane Hegarty, and soon after divorced Carole. Diane—whom LaVey never married, but stayed with until 1984—took Carole's place as the hostess of the parties. At $2.50 a head, members of the public were treated to lectures on vampires, ESP, werewolves, zombies, love potions, fortune telling, voodoo, the black arts—anything that freed people from their workaday lives and transported them to a world of the bizarre, inexplicable, and fantastical.

LaVey was slowly gaining notoriety as a black magician. He took a black leopard named Zoltan as a pet, deriving great pleasure from frightening onlookers as he strolled through San Francisco parks with the animal on a chain. The leopard, eventually killed by a car, was replaced by a Nubian lion named Togare. LaVey was an intriguing figure, with his imposing reputation and suburban gothic residence—complete with a roaring 500-pound lion to keep the neighbors awake.

MYTH AND HISTORY

Without doubt, Anton Szandor LaVey's account of his early biography is colorful and varied, perhaps even a little too colorful. The aforementioned biographical details stood mostly unquestioned for over a quarter-century, until the imposition of journalist Lawrence Wright in 1991. In the course of fact-checking an article on LaVey for *Rolling Stone* magazine, Wright started to uncover some inconsistencies in the oft-repeated official story. There was, for example, no record of a San Francisco Ballet Symphony Orchestra operating during LaVey's teen years, making it difficult for the 15-year-old to have played second oboe for such an ensemble, as he claimed.

Eventually, Wright revealed a catalogue of embellishments, half-truths, and straight-out lies relating to LaVey's longstanding biography. On the day of his birth in Cook County, Chicago, there were no records for an Anton Szandor LaVey, only a Howard Stanton Levey (a name he later acknowledged). The San Francisco Police Department had no records of anyone bearing either his given or adopted names working for them; likewise, the City College had no record of a Levey or LaVey studying criminology. San Francisco didn't have an official city organist either. Paul Valentine, who had run the Mayan Theater in Los Angeles in the late-1940s, denied that the club was ever a burlesque and that either Marilyn Monroe or Anton LaVey had worked for him. Most telling of all, LaVey never purchased the house at 6114 California Street; it was a gift from his father. Mike and Gertrude Levey (not Joe and Augusta LaVey, as named in his biographies) bought the property when they moved from Chicago shortly after Howard's birth in 1930. The Leveys moved to another San Francisco house in the 1950s, allowing their son to live on the property. In 1971, Michael Levey transferred joint owner-ship to Anton and Diane. Interestingly, all authorized biographical material fails to mention that LaVey's parents were living in a large 13-room San Francisco house during his wandering, self-sustained carny days. It seems likely that his late-teens return to San Francisco wasn't simply because, as his hagiographer claimed, "he knew the prospects could be no better or worse than in L.A."[8]

When Wright originally presented his findings to LaVey, however, the response was surprisingly passive:

> "I don't want the legend to disappear," LaVey told me anxiously after I con-fronted him with some of the inconsistencies in his story. "There is a chance you will disenchant a lot of young people who use me as a role model." He was especially offended that I had tracked down his eighty-seven-year-old father in an effort to verify some of the details of LaVey's early life. "I'd rather have my background shrouded in mystery. Eventually you want to be recognized for what you are now."[9]

Wright's article, "It's Not Easy Being Evil in a World That's Gone to Hell," was published in *Rolling Stone* in September 1991. The inconsistencies he uncovered have been contested vehemently by the Church of Satan ever since. However, lacking anything substantive to back up LaVey's history—employment records, tax records, and so forth—the response has been limited to a sustained gainsaying of Wright's findings and presentation of inconclu-sive documentation: photos of LaVey, dressed in a suit, standing next to two circus staff; a photo of a car wreck; a nude calendar purportedly signed by Monroe, and so forth. The absence of any solid evidence to counter these claims undermines the many other tales he relates. For instance, *The Secret Life of a Satanist* states: "his photos attracted a fair amount of attention. He exhibited some of his work, sold a few photos to magazines, and won honors in a number of competitions."[10] Further information—specific names and dates of the magazines, competitions, or locations of the exhibitions—is not provided. As an indication of reliability, the same work devotes two pages to LaVey's 1956 discovery of the Black House and his dealings with the real estate agent, a quarter-century after his parents bought it.

The *Rolling Stone* exposé was not the end of the myth-breaking state-ments. After LaVey's death in 1997, Zeena LaVey, his daughter with Diane, claimed that the famed ritual head-shaving of Walpurgisnacht 1966 was nothing more esoteric than a home-hairdressing challenge, and reclassified the fearsome Zoltan from black leopard to large Burmese housecat. Togare, however, was a genuine lion that lived at 6114 until 1967, when LaVey was arrested and forced to donate him to the San Francisco Zoo.[11] Other accusations were not so benign, with charges that LaVey's control of Togare owed more to plentiful use of an electric cattle prod than natural affinity with big cats, and allegations of spousal abuse emerging in the court proceedings following Anton and Diane's 1984 separation.[12]

The central facts, or lore, of LaVey's biography are only important because the Church of Satan and Anton LaVey have made them so important. The mythology, aura, and image of Anton LaVey have been every bit as critical to the organization as the doctrines of *The Satanic Bible*. His dubious back story is related in two biographies, both written by close associates—Burton H. Wolfe's *The Devil's Avenger* (1974) and Blanche Barton's *The Secret Life of a Satanist* (1990). Every edition of *The Satanic Bible* has had an introduction that focuses heavily on the eventful life of Satanism's high priest,[13] and LaVey repeated the central claims throughout his many interviews. Image is also central to Satanism. All LaVey's books and most Church of Satan material bear prominent images of his instantly recognizable shaven head and Mephistophelean goatee. It is undoubtedly the aesthetic—the Baphomet, the nude women on altars, the outsider stance—that appeal to many of LaVey's followers, a fact that at times annoyed even him, when he wished people would take his philosophy more seriously. Yet his mythography was essential in creating the mystique on which the church has traded for decades. Dispelling the mythology only affects the doctrines of the Church of Satan to the extent that those doctrines are tied up with the legend of the elusive entity known as Anton Szandor LaVey. And they are, inextricably.

LaVey's exercise in self-mythologizing is in some ways impressive. That he was able to maintain his fantastical biography in the full glare of attention for over two-and-a-half decades is quite astounding. Why did so many people believe it? Most likely because they wanted to, and because LaVey had the ability to sell it. Whatever his background, LaVey either realized or was innately aware of people's ability and willingness to believe almost anything. As he noted, people will frequently demand to be fooled. Howard Stanton Levey indulged in a Gatsby-esque creation of a history to fit the persona he desired. In doing so he created the Platonic conception of Anton Szandor LaVey that his followers could revere and idolize, irrespective of more mundane truths.

Employing his regular strategy of remodeling anything he was accused of as a virtue, LaVey later admitted: "I'm one helluva liar. Most of my adult life, I've been accused of being a charlatan, a phony, an impostor. I guess that

makes me about as close to what the Devil's supposed to be, as anyone…
I lie constantly, incessantly."[14] Embellishing or completely fabricating his past
was hardly out of character. His avowed heroes—Rasputin, Aleister Crowley,
Count Cagliostro, Sir Basil Zaharoff—are hardly men known for their personal integrity or aversion to self-mythologizing. Rather, they are all known
for consciously creating an almost tangible air of mystery around themselves.

He was liberal with the truth, certainly, but LaVey was also—as almost
everyone who met him attests—a charismatic and entertaining figure. Visitors to the Black House regularly recount stories of staying up half—or
all—the night discussing philosophy, religion, and music. Especially music.
A keen organ player with knowledge of a vast catalogue of forgotten classics,
music was undoubtedly the primary passion of his life. LaVey bonded with
people over conversation and music, although he had a famous distaste for
the bombast of rock, favoring instead warmth, melody, and lyricism. Possessing a magnetic personality, he made friends and followers with ease, as
one-time follower Arthur Lyons attests:

> LaVey himself, whom I expected to be a bombastic, evangelistic carnival trick-
> ster, running about screaming that he was the Devil incarnate, actually is a
> personable, highly intelligent man. Although he cuts a rather awesome figure,
> sporting a shaved head and a rather devilish Van Dyke beard, in conversation
> he is uncommonly perceptive and displays a keen sense of humor…Despite
> his accusers, he is a sincere and dedicated man, demanding sincerity and dedi-
> cation from his members.[15]

Yet he was also a genuinely misanthropic man who was deeply alienated
from the rest of his species. His obsessive contempt for the mass of humanity
is the most prominent theme in his writing and interviews, and only grew
stronger as he grew older.

THE DEVIL'S CHURCH IS BORN

From the early-1960s onward, the history of both Anton LaVey and the
embryonic Church of Satan, and the lines between fact and fiction, are much
easier to track. The meetings at the Black House continued to bring LaVey
into contact with a range of characters. He met Kenneth Anger, who had just
published the gleefully salacious *Hollywood Babylon* (in French, the English
version didn't appear until 1975), a lurid recounting of the scandals of the
early decades of the entertainment industry. The two men formed a life-long
friendship, with Anger a frequent guest at 6114 California Street over the
following decades. An accomplished avant-garde filmmaker who influenced
Martin Scorsese and David Lynch, Anger made the occult classics *Invocation*

of My Demon Brother (1969), which starred and featured a soundtrack by Mick Jagger, and *Lucifer Rising* (1972), with an unused score by Led Zeppelin's Jimmy Page. A noted Crowley enthusiast and occultist, he restored and made a documentary of Crowley's Thelema abbey in Cefalù, Sicily (where the notorious goat incident had taken place).

Anger was one of those present on Walpurgisnacht 1966 when the Church of Satan was formed. The idea of building on LaVey's existing reputation and transforming the Magic Circle into the heart of an official Satanic church was suggested by friends, who urged LaVey to make the most of the resources he had at hand. Establishing a new religion was hardly unprecedented given the counterculture explosion of alternate religious practices, although setting up an openly Satanic church was certainly unique. Even the Process Church's apocalyptic eschatology was ultimately positive. But the Church of Satan was not actually *satanic*, at least not in the traditional sense. Nonetheless, a small piece of Satanic history was made on the night of April 30–May 1, 1966, when LaVey ritually shaved his head (well, maybe) and initiated Anno Satanas—Year One of the Age of Satan.

Ex-carny or not, LaVey displayed an unerring sense for self-promotion and instinct for what would push the public's buttons, infuriate the straight-laced, and, above all, attract attention. Following the founding of the church, a number of highly successful and dramatic publicity stunts followed in quick succession. In early 1967, Anton presided over the Satanic wedding of journalist John Raymond and socialite Judith Case at the Black House, joining them under the auspicious will of the archfiend. Shortly thereafter, the high priest conducted the world's first Satanic baptism. Unable to find a newborn child for the ceremony—the burgeoning Satanic community was evidently capable of some restraint—Anton and Diane's three-year-old daughter Zeena was chosen to serve as the beneficiary of the infernal blessing. The event, which can only be described as a media circus, was capped off with Zeena, sitting in front of an altar bedecked by a naked acolyte and framed by a large black Baphomet, receiving an invocation specially composed by her proud father for the occasion:

> In the name of Satan, Lucifer…welcome a new mistress, Zeena, creature of ecstatic magic light…in the name of Satan, we set your feet upon the left hand path…And so we dedicate your life to love, to passion, to indulgence, and to Satan, and the way of darkness. Hail Zeena! Hail Satan![16]

Zeena, by all accounts, thoroughly enjoyed the event, though decades later LaVey's biography made the interesting comment, "Today, LaVey probably would have been charged with Satanic child abuse—there were no such legal avenues in 1967."[17] LaVey, no doubt seeking to cap off his year of successfully inverting and perverting key Christian ceremonies, followed up the Satanic wedding and baptism with their logical successor—a Satanic funeral. Church of Satan member Edward Olsen, a U.S. Navy seaman, had died in a traffic accident on December 3 and his widow, also a member, requested the service in his honor. LaVey gladly agreed, and the resulting obsequies caused a minor outrage, including letters of complaint to the president. Unsurprisingly, press interest in each of these events was high; elaborate Satanic rituals made great copy in the midst of the Summer of Love.

Church doctrines were still loosely defined, existing as a variety of short essays on multicolored "rainbow sheets," but it was beginning to codify its beliefs, with the *Eleven Satanic Rules of the Earth* being released the same year.

1. Do not give opinions or advice unless you are asked.
2. Do not tell your troubles to others unless you are sure they want to hear them.
3. When in another's lair, show him respect or else do not go there.
4. If a guest in your lair annoys you, treat him cruelly and without mercy.
5. Do not make sexual advances unless you are given the mating signal.
6. Do not take that which does not belong to you unless it is a burden to the other person and he cries out to be relieved.
7. Acknowledge the power of magic if you have employed it successfully to obtain your desires. If you deny the power of magic after having called upon it with success, you will lose all you have obtained.
8. Do not complain about anything to which you need not subject yourself.
9. Do not harm little children.
10. Do not kill non-human animals unless you are attacked or for your food.
11. When walking in open territory, bother no one. If someone bothers you, ask him to stop. If he does not stop, destroy him.[18]

The rules—guidelines to Satanic etiquette, if you please—served to clarify what the church represented and offered reassurance that Satanists were not out to murder babies or sacrifice animals (for the latter, you still needed to follow Crowley's Thelema). The rules are mostly commonsense dictates, though couched in the high priest's characteristically idiosyncratic and overblown language.

In the early years, Satanists tended to be middle-class and middle-aged. Championing free sexual expression and exploring esoteric beliefs may have been in step with the times, but the strongly individualistic and compassionless nature of the church's creed did not appeal to the denizens of Haight-Ashbury and their commune-dwelling fellows. The Satanists were too heavily focused on the darker side of human nature to appeal to the idealistic flower-power set. Church members tended to be older, more financially secure, and shorn of the optimism that drove the counterculture. Many were ordinary people with stable jobs—police officers, university lecturers, artists, armed service personnel, and writers. They were drawn to Satanism out of distaste for the pieties of the Christian church and woolly ideals of the hippie movement. Membership numbers of the Church of Satan in this period is unknown, but estimated to be a couple of hundred (although the church was optimistically claiming 10,000 members by the end of the decade). Eventually, celebrities began to appear on the scene, with interest growing in the organization as its notoriety spread.

THE FAMOUS AND INFAMOUS

Among the curious drifting up the hill to find out what was really happening at the Black House was the late-1950s B-grade actress Jayne Mansfield. Mansfield was a busty Monroe clone with thespian aspirations, but her balmy public persona saw her forever typecast as a poor man's Marilyn. By the time she met LaVey, soon after Walpurgisnacht 1966, her film career had stalled and she was trading her fame for handsome rewards in nightclubs and talk shows worldwide. There is scant proof that Mansfield's involvement with the Church of Satan was anything more than the briefest flirtation, long enough for a couple of photo ops and little else. But LaVey, ever the able self-promoter, was not one to let scant proof impede a good story.

The Black Pope's version of events can be summarized, in character, as follows: Jayne fell under LaVey's spell. Like Marilyn before her, she was entranced by his magnetic personality, good looks, and command of arcane knowledge. She became dependent on him, emotionally and spiritually, barraging his citadel with phone calls. When Jayne's young son, Zoltan, fell afoul of a lion at a San Francisco zoo and was hospitalized, gravely injured, the busty blonde was desperate. By then, the starlet was involved in a highly-charged sexual relationship with the powerful conjurer. Again like Marilyn, she was nearly overpowered by the unquenchable fires of her primal lust. With a child in peril, LaVey didn't hesitate to act. Though there was a ferocious rainstorm, he sped to the top of Mount Tamalpais, the highest point in the area, and delivered an invocation in aid of the mortally endangered youngster. Picture, if you will, the sorcerer adorned in his black ritual cape, standing atop the mountain in defiance of the elements, thundering arcane words into the ether. Imagine, "as he held his cape out like great leathery wings against the raging wind, the rain beat hard on his face, and, summoning all the power within himself, LaVey called upon his Brother Satan to spare Zoltan's life."[19]

According to LaVey, the invocation prevailed and the child lived. Mansfield was indebted, and further enthralled by her lover. The relationship, however, was causing friction between the starlet and her attorney Sam Brody, who, in more dependable accounts of the starlet's life, was Mansfield's live-in lover. LaVey and Brody clearly detested each other. The animosity between them had been rising steadily, resulting in Brody being cursed by LaVey during a visit to the Black House, and afterwards being the target of a Satanic destruction ritual. When Brody and Mansfield were killed in car accident in 1967, with the latter apparently decapitated, LaVey was distraught. The night before their deaths, he had inadvertently cut the head off a photo of Jayne. The conjurer blamed himself; his powers had gone awry.

Reality is sometimes a little less dramatic. Mansfield was not decapitated, merely scalped. She earned for herself a permanent position in the lore of the Church of Satan, along with the title of priestess. Much has been made of the B-grade actress's flirtation with the powers of darkness. LaVey traded on the association for decades after, ever eager to pose in front of poster of the fallen idol. It was no doubt a chance for great publicity, the blonde Hollywood starlet meets—and couples with!—the devil's high priest. The episode and the tone in which it is related illustrates the carefully choreographed and frequently absurd nature of LaVey's self-mythologizing. The image of Anton LaVey as a man apart from normal men was clearly as important to the development of the movement as anything he wrote.

Hollywood, for its part, seemingly couldn't get enough of the devil. In 1968, Roman Polanski's *Rosemary's Baby* was filling movie theaters worldwide. The psychological/supernatural thriller can be interpreted as a 136-minute wide-screen advertisement for Satanism, which is certainly how the inhabitants of 6114 California Street saw it. The Black Pope was enlisted for publicity purposes, attending the San Francisco premier and scaring audiences almost as much as the film. LaVey eventually claimed to have worked as a technical advisor on the film and that he was the figure in the devil suit during the legendary love/rape scene, but there is no corroborating evidence. Interestingly, the other great satanic-themed horror film of this era, 1976's *The Omen*, is universally reviled by Satanists as nothing more than Vatican propaganda. *Rosemary's Baby*, it seems, presented a more palatable vision of urbane, civilized devil-worshippers colluding to beget Satan's spawn.

Already associated with two dead Hollywood icons (Monroe died in 1962) and a cinematic devil-child, the Church next became inadvertently linked to the most infamous crime of the decade (with the possible exception of the Kennedy assassination) through its contact with members of the Manson Family. Kenneth Anger's *Invocation of My Demon Brother* starred his handsome young protégé Bobby Beausoleil, but the two fell out and Beausoleil stole a large amount of camera equipment and irreplaceable footage of *Lucifer Rising*, Anger's work-in-progress. Beausoleil then fell in with Charles Manson, who had recently been released from prison. Manson was a career criminal with loose connections to the Process Church, which had in turn tried to form an alliance with the Church of Satan but had been rebuked by LaVey. In July of 1969, Manson sent Beausoleil and two females from his Family to the house of musician/drug dealer Gary Hinman. One of the women was Susan Atkins, a former topless dancer who had been a vampire in a Church of Satan performance titled "Topless Witches Review." Accounts of events at Hinman's house vary, but by the end of the day Hinman was dead, a crime for which Beausoleil was later arrested and convicted.

A few weeks later, for reasons that have never been fully explained, Manson sent members of his Family to 10050 Cielo Drive, the home of director Roman Polanski. On the night of August 8, 1969, members of the Manson Family, again including Atkins, brutally murdered five people The victims included Polanski's heavily pregnant wife, actress Sharon Tate, in whose blood the killers wrote on the walls. The following night, members of the Family killed supermarket executive Leno LaBianca and his wife in their home. Though he wasn't present at the Tate murders and didn't himself kill anyone at the LaBianca residence, Manson received the death sentence for orchestrating the crimes, later commuted to life in prison. In doing so he managed to become the icon for an era, one every bit at enduring as Marilyn Monroe. The Family's actions have been debated ever since, and Charles Manson has been reinterpreted by some as a kind of noble revolutionary, an antiauthority visionary who saw through the hypocrisy of society. To others he is just the guy with a swastika on his forehead. Nonetheless, Charlie remains, along with Che Guevara and Kurt Cobain, the icon of choice for disenfranchised youth.

There was no direct link between Manson and the Church of Satan, but the association alone was enough to be of concern, given the firestorm of publicity surrounding the case. The Church and LaVey weren't strangers to attracting the attention of disturbed individuals. Along with the journalists and police officers, a variety of unbalanced and bizarre flesh-seekers were being drawn to the door of the Black House. The Manson connection, however, was one the church was eager to distance itself from, lest it meet the same fate as the thoroughly vilified Process Church. There were obviously still limits to just how iniquitous an organization could be, an invisible line between LaVey's carnivalesque brand of diablerie and being seen to endorse or engender mass murder.

THE SATANIC BIBLE

In 1969, the husband of a woman at one of LaVey's Witches' Workshops made a suggestion.

> Fred [a recently published author] said I should write a book, and he felt sure it would get published. "Wait a minute," I said. "I'm not a writer, never have been, and never have had any aspirations."

"That's OK, don't worry about it," said Fred. "You can do it." He introduced me to his literary agent, Mike Hamilburg, who brought a man to see me. His name was Peter Mayer, a dynamic new editor at Avon Books. We talked a little, and Peter asked me, "How soon can you have it ready?"

The book may have arisen, like the church itself, haphazardly, but it would nonetheless serve a number of purposes: it would popularize the church, generate income, and clarify LaVey's philosophy. "I thought that after being taken as entertainment value, my book would straighten a few things out concerning Satanism."[20] He set about compiling the materials he already had—lecture notes, pamphlets, handouts, and assorted documents—into a presentable form. At the time, LaVey was contributing a weekly column, "Letters to the Devil," to the *National Insider.* Yet still, LaVey, assisted considerably by Diane, struggled to amass enough material under the deadline Mayer had set. He solved this problem by adding a Satanic translation of sixteenth-century occultist John Dee's Enochian Keys to the end of the book. Though comprising only 10 percent of the word count, the Keys command nearly half the pages.

The Satanic Bible reached the bookshelves in early 1970. It has since sold over 1 million copies and gone through dozens of reprints. Though the introduction has been changed many times, the central text has remained unaltered. Labeled a bible, the work obviously does not claim to be the revealed word of Satan in the way that the Christian Bible is the word of God or the Koran is that of Allah. Rather, it is the vehicle by which LaVey articulated the philosophical, ethical, and ritual outlook of Satanism, using "Satan" for its original Hebraic meaning: the adversary. He is not seen as "an anthropomorphic being with cloven hooves," but rather as "a force in nature."[21] Shorn of all theistic implications, modern Satanism's use of Satan is firmly in the tradition that John Milton inadvertently engendered—a representation of the noble rebel, the principled challenger of illegitimate power.

LaVey's *Bible* is divided into four separate sections, the books of Satan, Lucifer, Belial, and Leviathan. The first two articulate the ideology of Satanism, the third discusses the theory and practice of ritual, and the final book is mostly Dee's Enochian Keys. It has often been pointed out that the magical/ritual aspects of *The Satanic Bible* sit uneasily with the atheistic, materialistic doctrines that precede it. The preface indicates where LaVey's loyalties lay:

This book was written because, with very few exceptions, every tract and paper, every "secret" grimoire, all the "great works" on the subject of magic, are nothing more than sanctimonious fraud—guilt-ridden ramblings and esoteric gibberish by chroniclers of magical lore unable or unwilling to present an objective view of the subject.

The skeptical tone continues: "Herein you will find truth—and fantasy. Each is necessary for the other to exist; but each must be recognized for what it is."[22] So what is the truth, and what is the fantasy? In the first two books, those that contain the philosophy and social observations of the Satanist, LaVey expounds his position with uncompromising self-assurance. He is, at every point, making what he believes to be an objective statement about the world. There are no qualifiers when LaVey discusses human nature and the importance of the individual. By comparison, all discussions of ritual and magic place a large emphasis on the their aesthetic qualities and meaning for the practitioner. LaVey's view on magic is that its efficacy is primarily subjective and psychological, although he occasionally claimed specific magical abilities. From the mid-1970s onward, he became more vocal in his criticisms critical of magic and those he considered "occultniks." The Church of Satan eventually ceased its ambivalence entirely, bluntly denying the supernatural. In the early 1960s Magic Circle, LaVey was clearly willing to hedge his bets a little more.

The true focus of *The Satanic Bible*, that of celebrating humanity's carnal nature, was to be addressed in the prologue:

> This is the morning of magic, and undefiled wisdom. The FLESH prevaileth and a great Church shall be builded, consecrated in its name. No longer shall man's salvation be dependent on his self-denial. And it will be known that the world of the flesh and the living shall be the greatest preparation for any and all eternal delights![23]

Fortunately, the faux-King James Bible tone doth not prevaileth throughout. The exclamation marks, however, do: the work contains more than four hundred.

To the contemporary reader, some sections of *The Satanic Bible* are surprisingly commonsense. Despite the work's sensationalist tone and rumors of debauchery and profligacy surrounding the Church, the essay titled "Satanic Sex" firmly stakes out the middle ground between pious sexual repression and counterculture profligacy. "Satanism does advocate sexual freedom, but only in the true sense of the word. Free love, in the Satanic concept, means exactly that—freedom to either be faithful to one person or to indulge your sexual desires with as many others as you feel is necessary to satisfy your particular needs." Similarly, despite the book's stressing that humans are carnal animals, LaVey does not favor indiscriminate excess. "Satanism does not encourage orgiastic activity or extramarital affairs for those to whom they do not come naturally. For many, it would be very unnatural and detrimental to be unfaithful to their chosen mates...Each person must decide for himself what form of sexual activity best suits his individual needs."[24] The frequent interpretations of modern Satanism as primarily hedonistic are inaccurate. For LaVey, sexuality—as well as the other natural appetites—should not be denied, but must be satisfied in accordance with one of the prevailing mantras of Satanism, "Indulgence…not compulsion."

Other parts of the book are more predicable. It contains regular fusillades against Christian morality and authority, a relentless focus on the individual in opposition to the collective, frequent conscription of devilish pageantry and rhetorical overkill, a Nietzschean emphasis on temporal existence, and symbolic deification of the self in place of the fallen Christian God. LaVey's saw God as a cosmological projection of humanity's self-identity. "All religions of a spiritual nature are inventions of man. He has created an entire system of gods with nothing more than his carnal brain. Just because he has an ego, and cannot accept it, he has to externalize it into some great spiritual device which he calls 'God.'"[25] For LaVey, the converse is true. "Man, the animal, is the godhead to the Satanist."[26]

The final book of the *Bible*, the Book of Leviathan, is mostly composed of John Dee's Enochian Keys with brief descriptive notes. LaVey's supposed translation is largely an interpretation of the Keys with Satanic substitutions or augmentations for central phrases that completely contradict the original text, despite LaVey's insistence that he presents the only accurate, unexpurgated version of the Keys. For example, the final phrase of Dee's First Key, "true worshipper of the highest," becomes, with characteristic subtlety, "true worshipper of the highest and ineffable King of Hell!"[27] Similarly, the Second Key's "mind of the all powerful" is remodeled as "mind of the All-Powerful manifestation of Satan!"[28] With liberties such as these throughout the work, it is unsurprising that LaVey's low regard for occultists is returned in kind. Crowley's one-time protégé Israel Regardie had nothing but contempt for the "stupidity" of the bastardizations in the "debased volume," declining to even mention the author by name.[29]

The corruption of the Enochian Keys was not the new author's only indiscretion. *The Satanic Bible* was book ended by borrowings from earlier writers. The majority of *The Infernal Diatribe* from the first book was plagiarized from an obscure 1896 social Darwinist text titled *Might Is Right*. The book was published under the pseudonym Ragnar Redbeard, but was most likely written by New Zealander Arthur Desmond, although Jack London is another (highly unlikely) possibility. LaVey cited the original author— "Ragnar Redbeard, whose might is right"—as an influence in the original 39-name dedication page to *The Satanic Bible*, but he in no way acknowledged that this section of the work was not his. The brief dedication to Redbeard, an unknown writer, was removed from subsequent printings. The plagiarism stood unnoticed for nearly two decades, until it was revealed in the late 1980s. LaVey was unapologetic, eventually writing the introduction for a reprint of *Might Is Right*, praising its "blasphemy" and taking credit for popularizing it. In his final interview he stated, *"Might Is Right...is probably one of the most inflammatory books ever written...It was only natural that I excerpted a few pages of it for *The Satanic Bible.*"[30] The semantic gulf between "excerpt" and "steal" seemingly wasn't apparent to LaVey.

ENTERING THE 1970s

With *The Satanic Bible* in the bookstores, the Church of Satan entered the 1970s at its strongest point. The book was soon accompanied by the film *Satanis: The Devil's Mass* (1970) in the theaters. The flesh-heavy diablomentary had everything needed to further the Church's reputation—flagellation, a boa constrictor, a lion, a naked woman in a coffin, middle-aged exhibitionists, vague assertions of bestiality, and a half-hearted devil's kiss. It was another effective public relations exercise for the church—risqué enough to trouble the Mormons it interviewed, but seemingly not bothering LaVey's neighbors. LaVey is shown holding court dressed in a priest's uniform, delivering his standard rhetoric. "This is a very selfish religion. We believe in greed, we believe in selfishness, we believe in all of the lustful thoughts that motivate man because this is man's natural feeling. If you're going to be a sinner, be the best sinner on the block. If you're going to do something that is naughty, do it, and realize that you're doing something naughty and enjoy [it]."[31]

There were no more naughty publicity events, possibly because events were progressing well at the Black House. Church member Arthur Lyons' *The Second Coming: Satanism in America* (1970) appeared in print, providing a history of Satanism from earliest times and an extended account of LaVey and his associates. The church was also expanding through its grotto system. A grotto was a satellite of the central church run under the auspices of a Priest of the Church. All grottos were subordinate to the Black House, which became known as the Central Grotto. With the interest generated by the *Bible*, documentary, and publicity stunts, it was an effective way to enable the geographical spread of the church beyond its San Francisco base. By the early to mid-1970s there were grottos across America, including Boston, Detroit, New York, Los Angeles, and Louisville. Membership was healthy, though probably far short of the 10,000 members the church claimed. Between 200 and 500 at its peak is usually considered more accurate. Randall H. Alfred, a researcher who claimed to have infiltrated the church from April 1968 to August 1969, gives this indication of local membership: "At the church headquarters in San Francisco during 1968–69, attendance at the rituals of the Central Grotto was usually about twenty to thirty from a pool of about fifty to sixty members at any one time."[32] Michael Aquino, who as a senior member of the church would have had a clearer knowledge of nationwide figures, appears to support Alfred's observations, claiming a 1974 membership of two hundred and fifty.[33] Arthur Lyons generously estimated a 1970s peak "closer to 5,000."[34] The Church of Satan has never provided any documented or verifiable membership figures.

With the success of *The Satanic Bible*, LaVey continued to pursue writing as a means to circulate his ideas. In 1970 he produced *The Compleat Witch, or What to Do When Virtue Fails* (later renamed *The Satanic Witch*). Far from another ritual or Satanic theory text, it is a do-it-yourself magical guide for women to aid them in manipulating and seducing men, predominantly by means of exposing cleavage, and once more stressing that humanity's animal nature is the key to success. Topic headings "How and When to Lie," "Secrets of Indecent Exposure," and "Learn to Be Stupid" are a good indication of the main themes and content. The work also contains LaVey's most frequently lampooned idea, the salad dressing theory of masculinity. Apparently, a lot can be learned from a man's taste in salad dressing: opt for a sweet French or Russian dressing and you are obviously a strong masculine type; choose a strong blue cheese, vinegar, or Roquefort flavor and you are a submissive, feminine type or "passive *or* latent or active homosexuals." Why the difference? Because the former dressings resemble "the odor of a woman's sexual parts and therefore agreeable to the archetypical male," and the latter "is similar to the male scrotal odor."[35]

The Satanic Bible was followed by its companion volume *The Satanic Rituals* in 1972, a collection of nine rituals, each with its own short introductory essay. LaVey also used his essays in the church's monthly (later, quarterly) publication *The Cloven Hoof*, and in its 1990s successor *The Black Flame*, to put forth his opinions on Satanism, culture, music, and mannequins. Begun as an internal church newsletter in 1969, *The Cloven Hoof* soon developed into a full publication. Two collections of LaVey's essays from the 1970s to 1990s were later released, *The Devil's Notebook* (1992) and the posthumous *Satan Speaks!* (1998). The voice piece of the church was edited from 1971–1975 by Michael Aquino, an energetic serviceman who was to play an important role in the development of Satanism and a crucial role in the fortunes of the Church of Satan. This era also saw one of the more surprising developments of the church, when in 1973 Sammy Davis, Jr. became particularly involved, forming a friendship with LaVey and actively proselytizing for the church in Hollywood. Sammy made no secret of being down with the dark lord, eventually recording an album of diabolical tunes, *Satan Swings Baby!* (1974), including renditions of "Witchcraft," "Sympathy For Devil," and featuring the vocals and Wurlitzer organ of LaVey on "Devil in Disguise."

The founding era of 1966–1975 represents the prime years of the Church of Satan. The Black Pope reigned over the first openly Satanic church in history, even if it was a Satanic church that denied the existence of Satan. Though opponents lined up on all sides to discredit him or label him a charlatan and fraud, he had succeeded in establishing a unique organization and had become an iconic counterculture figure. His church struck traditional religious practitioners as one of the most troubling developments of the era, clear proof that a monstrous force for evil was at work in the world. More secularized figures simply saw it as an amusing entertainment and viewed its feeble pretensions of wickedness as little more than adolescent melodrama. A populist provocateur like LaVey is a rather poor terminus for the rich literary and philosophical traditions he drew on but, thankfully, many were able to identify a ritualistic Satanic baptism with no particular theological significance as the attention-seeking stunt that it was.

Yet there would always be a small minority who thought that a Satanic church was the most splendidly outrageous thing possible. In an overwhelmingly Christian culture, what could be more rebellious? What could strike deeper at the heart of the dominant outlook than taking up its greatest enemy, Satan, as a standard? It was by no means an original idea, but what had worked for the Romantic poets and Hellfire clubs still worked for LaVey...to an extent. The organization was certainly dramatic and audacious, but, beyond a few newspaper headlines, small membership, and general notoriety, its successes were modest. What LaVey did achieve can be attributed to a combination of his charisma, colorful (if fanciful) history and personality, knack for self-promotion, and the immediacy of ideas that he promulgated.

The latter cannot be underestimated, for once modern Satanism expanded beyond San Francisco, the doctrines set forth in *The Satanic Bible* became the most frequent portal into Satanism. Indeed, the vast majority of people who have called themselves Satanists never met the creed's founder. But if the history of LaVey and his church appears largely benign, it is the result of the frequent instances of amateur theatrics in the Church of Satan's history. However, it is also necessary to consider the thought that buttressed the overblown rhetoric and sensationalist antics. And, as we turn to the ideas that LaVey promulgated the story becomes, by necessity, considerably darker. The very aspect of Satanism that LaVey wanted to be respected for is that deserving the sternest criticisms. If there is one thing Anton LaVey was correct about, it is that the ideology of Satanism warrants much closer attention than it has generally been given.

Man, the Animal: The Doctrines of Modern Satanism

You must be creative. Take inspiration from the most sordid sources if necessary, but never imitate. Rip-off artists proclaim themselves divinities because they lack the originality or creativity to come up with some fresh ideas.

—Anton Szandor LaVey, *The Devil's Notebook*, p. 66

If someone were to ask me what I considered the single most contributing factor to my personality, I would have to answer: "Avoidance of the influence of other people."

—Anton Szandor LaVey, *Satan Speaks!*, p. 169

"I AM A SATANIST! BOW DOWN, FOR I AM THE HIGHEST EMBODIMENT OF HUMAN LIFE!"[1] It may not be the best place to look for humility, measured rhetoric, or stylistic restraint, but *The Satanic Bible* is undoubtedly the central text in modern Satanic literature.

Its influence is unquestioned. In the Church of Satan, acceptance of "the elegant architecture of Dr. LaVey's principles" is a prerequisite for being a Satanist.[2] The rival Temple of Set, despite three decades of animosity toward the original organization, still pays tribute to LaVey's work. Likewise, disgruntled ex–Church of Satan members typically have a dispute with Church of Satan hierarchy and organization, not with the founding text. Independent Satanists, too, openly acknowledge their debt, and their beliefs frequently diverge only marginally from LaVey's. For Satanic dabblers (those who are sympathetic to Satanism or identify with its doctrines, but do not actively pursue allegiance) a cursory reading of *The Satanic Bible* inevitably forms the basis of their identification. In fact, the only Satanists who dissent are the more extreme latter-day adherents that feel it is too mild or too humanist.[3]

The Satanic Bible is a broad work and not all of it—not even most of it— concerns the central creed. Of the four sections, the first two set out the core beliefs and ideology, the third concerns the practice of ritual magic, and the fourth and lengthiest is simply LaVey's bastardization of John Dee's Enochian Keys, with brief commentaries. Within the first two sections, which are the focus of this analysis, large tracts are extended rants against Christianity and its failings. These attacks bolster the position of the text's omnipresent Satanist by ridiculing Christian doctrine, deriding it as repressive and unrealistic. Satanism, by contrast, is depicted as the only religion that is suited to the true needs and desires of humans. To this end, the Seven Deadly Sins are inverted and posited as positive virtues. Other frequent targets of LaVey's scorn are so-called white light religions, by which he means Wicca and other modern pagan practices that have a basis in witchcraft or magic. LaVey, in contrast, places Satanism within the tradition of Hellfire clubs and historical practitioners of the black arts, framing his church as the heir to these movements.

The principles LaVey's work advances are regarded by many Satanists as its strongest point. Satanism is a life-affirming philosophy, similar to Nietzsche's, in that it focuses entirely on this world and does not embody any otherworldly beliefs—in God, gods, spiritualism, the afterlife, and so forth. Satanic ideology is therefore atheistic and materialistic. Though LaVey presents a few standard arguments against the existence of God, atheism is generally a presupposition that underpins the rest of the work. Its materialism is represented by an idiosyncratic interpretation of Darwinism that places heavy emphasis on the animal and carnal nature of man, simultaneously describing humanity as rational while focusing on unavoidable primal drives. A proviso is required, however, as the hedonistic aspect of Satanism is easily overstated. LaVey was staunchly opposed to drug use of any kind, and his opposition has remained the default position for the Church of Satan and many independent Satanists. And as noted previously, LaVey's approach to sexuality is generally progressive, advocating free, uncompelled expression of the individual's sexual identity, be it straight, gay, fetishistic, exhibitionist, or otherwise.

The central axioms of Satanism are based on LaVey's analysis of human nature and societies. *The Satanic Bible* and other writings are infused with a pessimistic Malthusian vision that sees the embattled inhabitants of an increasingly overcrowded world fighting for scarce resources. The individual agent is therefore pitted against others in a primitive battle for survival where only the strong will survive. Accordingly, *The Satanic Bible* endorses a form of strident individualism that radically downplays social responsibility in favor of psychological and ethical egoism. The individual has but one ultimate aim—his own welfare. Any sense of community or shared humanity with others is denied, replaced by a focus on isolated individuals who must by necessity focus on their own self-aggrandizement and survival. In this analysis all actions are, by necessity, self-regarding. All forms of altruism are summarily dismissed as unrealistic phantasms, and self-sacrifice for the benefit of others is forgone, with a single exception in the provision for love of select individuals—the Satanist's closest companions.

Satanism's championing of individual empowerment expresses itself in a number of ways: a Nietzschean condemnation of pity and compassion as weakness, suspicion of and hostility to any majority positions, frequent use of violent imagery, a ubiquitous contempt for egalitarian values, and a constant focus on negative emotions such as anger, hatred, and revenge. *The Satanic Bible* consistently emphasizes vengeance and hostility towards enemies, again explicitly inverting Christian values of compassion and forgiveness.

> Hate your enemies with a whole heart, and if a man smite you on one cheek, SMASH him on the other!; smite him hip and thigh, for self-preservation is the highest law! He who turns the other cheek is a cowardly dog! Give blow for blow, scorn for scorn, doom for doom—with compound interest liberally added thereunto! Eye for eye, tooth for tooth, aye four-fold, a hundred-fold![4]

LaVey's claims are presented as truisms and are often unsupported. The weakness of the arguments is obscured and counterbalanced by the text's highly emotional tone and use of loaded terminology. As a result, the psychological and rhetorical impact of *The Satanic Bible* is just as powerful, if not more so, than the content itself. The work constantly flatters the reader—now the Satanist—as being unique and having gained insights that the mass of humanity are unaware of. It fosters a self-conscious outsider status that is of central importance to the Satanist, and consistently ridicules popular values or social norms. Accordingly, the work abounds with catchphrases: "Indulgence...not compulsion," "Responsibility for the responsible," and "We are self-respecting prideful people—we are Satanists!" This superficiality is not unacknowledged. LaVey himself later admitted "*The Satanic Bible* won't strain people's intellects too far."[5]

The various constituents of Satanism—materialism, atheism, ritual magic, sensualism, humanity as rational being, humanity as mere animal, Malthusian pessimism—fit together only cosmetically. When submitted to analysis, various tensions, inconsistencies, and contradictions appear. As a result, Satanism is better described as an ideology than a philosophy. "Philosophy" generally indicates a mode of thought, a systematic and rational evaluation of argument and counterargument to arrive at a consistent, justified position. No such process is present in LaVey's writings. All external commentators are denied any right to comment on Satanism, and any attempts to do so are universally ignored. Within Satanism, LaVey's writing is uncritically accepted as revealing deeper truths about the world.

THE INFLUENCE OF THE EGOISTS

Ideologically, the most important part of *The Satanic Bible* is the short, strident "Book of Satan" and its *Infernal Diatribe* (quoted from in the previous chapter), which covers a scant six pages. This brief section outlines the basic doctrines that echo throughout LaVey's writings. The *Infernal Diatribe* is read out at performances of the Black Mass, and a recording made by LaVey remains popular.[6] Ironically, this section contains the bulk of LaVey's plagiarism. The entire contents are only lightly edited borrowings from the obscure late nineteenth-century social Darwinist text *Might Is Right*. Nevertheless, the doctrines it contains have received wholehearted endorsement by Satanists. After the plagiarism was discovered, LaVey and the Church of Satan promoted the earlier work as a paradigm of Satanic thought.[7]

Might Is Right is a polemic almost unmatched in its stridency. Bombastic and devoid of subtlety or restraint, it contains few original ideas but is set apart from comparable works by its sheer profanity and belligerence. *Might Is Right*'s central thesis combines Max Stirner's anarchic individualism with a uniquely militant reading of social Darwinism. As with Stirner, the individual is raised as the supreme measure of value, and as such has no responsibility to society at large. Naked self-interest is pursued by any means necessary, irrespective of the cost to others. Denying that the state has any valid authority, the work advances an open legitimization of violence through a consistent reduction of every social phenomena to simple power-relations. No matter what the question, the response of the pseudonymous author, Ragnar Redbeard, is the ruthless application of force, justified uniformly by the tyranny of nature. "The natural world is a world of war; the natural man is a warrior; the natural law is tooth and claw. All else is error. A condition of combat everywhere exists. We are born into a perpetual conflict."[8] Similarly, the work explicitly denies the existence of all moral values. Drawing heavily from Nietzsche, Redbeard repeats his theories of master/slave morality and herd mentality almost verbatim, except for recasting the former as a conspiracy that falls "from the lips of a feeble Jew."[9]

In addition to its militancy, *Might Is Right* is a profoundly racist, misogynistic work that frequently betrays a deep vein of anti-Semitic paranoia. It calls for the reinstatement of slavery on the grounds of the natural inferiority of non-Europeans, states "woman is two-thirds womb,"[10] and voices open disgust at the idea of "a Jew for a god," a "weeping, horse whipped Jew!"[11] Redbeard argues consistently for the innate superiority of the European races, asking at one point, "What power on earth can permanently keep the Negro on parity with the Anglo-Saxon?"[12] He continues elsewhere, "Our race cannot hope to maintain its predominances, if it goes on diluting its blood with Chinamen, Negros, Japanese, or debase Europeans. Panmixia means both death and slavery."[13] *Might Is Right* represents a worst-case scenario in the interpretation of individualist philosophy and social Darwinism, and is most accurately described as a proto-fascist white power manifesto.

Might Is Right is so outrageously unbalanced, and its caricatures of Darwin and Spencer are so misleading, that it has led to suspicions that the work is, at least in part, satirical (the fabricated references to Darwin present the retiring British naturalist as a bloodthirsty psychotic). The issue is, however, academic, for LaVey plainly regarded the text as authentic. It became the single greatest influence on his thought and, by extension, the doctrines of contemporary Satanism. LaVey stole selectively and edited lightly, avoiding the racist, anti-Semitic, and misogynistic sections, instead focusing on the omnipresent appeals to force. The following extract from *The Satanic Bible* differs from *Might Is Right* only by arrangement and interpolation of the terms "righteously," "cloven," and the final twelve words.

1. Blessed are the strong, for they shall possess the earth—Cursed are the weak, for they shall inherit the yoke!
2. Blessed are the powerful, for they shall be reverenced among men—Cursed are the feeble, for they shall be blotted out!
3. Blessed are the bold, for they shall be masters of the world—Cursed are the righteously humble, for they shall be trodden under cloven hoofs!
4. Blessed are the victorious, for victory is the basis of right—Cursed are the vanquished, for they shall be vassals forever!
5. Blessed are the iron-handed, for the unfit shall flee before them—Cursed are the poor in spirit, for they shall be spat upon![14]

The likeness of these doctrines to twentieth-century political extremism is by no means trivial, especially if one considers one of the Redbeard proclamations that LaVey chose not to include: "Cursed are the unfit for they shall be righteously exterminated."[15]

LaVey's debt to *Might Is Right* extends beyond the sections he plagiarized. Redbeard's heavily emphasized disdain for egalitarian values and the Golden Rule (treat others as you would like to be treated) echoes throughout *The Satanic Bible* and other works. Ideologically, there are few ideas in Satanism that aren't completely prefigured by the earlier work.[16] In an important 1989 essay, "Pentagonal Revisionism," LaVey declares Satanism "a life-loving, rational philosophy," before reaffirming its key doctrine:

1. *Stratification*—The point on which all others ultimately rest. There can be no myth of equality for all—it only translates to mediocrity and supports the weak at the expense of the strong.

The essay later devolves into a Malthusian condemnation of the "human locusts overrunning the world," the need to "isolate and evolve genetically superior humans," and the eventual relocation of "the herd" to off-planet "space ghettos"—hardly the most economically viable solution to global overpopulation, real or imagined.[17]

In addition to the Redbeard-filtered echoes of Malthus, Spencer, Stirner, and Nietzsche, Satanism at times closely parallels Ayn Rand's Objectivist philosophy. Consider LaVey's comments in a 1975 article: "Man is a selfish creature. Everything in life is a selfish act. Man is not concerned with helping others, yet he wants others to believe he is." And, "[I]t is a truism that every act is a selfish act...Rational self-interest is a virtue, but should be seen for what it is: self-interest. That is the predominant theme of Satanism."[18] "Rational self-interest" is also part of the core terminology of Objectivism, and the language here so closely mimics Rand's that it could be taken directly from Galt's speech in *Atlas Shrugged*.

The Church of Satan claims the primary difference between Satanism and Objectivism is that the former is a religion with the individual as Godhead. Yet, as LaVey acknowledges, Satanism's claim of a personal Godhead is not a transcendental claim. Atheistic, materialistic Satanism cannot make claims of this sort. Rather, it is a rhetorical device, a symbolic application in the same way that the use of Satan is symbolic. The Satanist's Godhead is merely a metaphorical restatement of the ethical egoism of Objectivism—the barometer for action is that which serves the needs of the individual agent.

The substantive difference between Objectivism and Satanism lies in their respective views of human nature and morality. Rand dismissed might-is-right philosophy without qualification. She argued that in an industrialized society rational agents acting in their own self-interest will work together, recognizing the mutual benefit in cooperation. In stark contrast, LaVey's Redbeard-derived vision simply sees humans as mere animals pitted against each other in a merciless struggle for survival. It allows for the exploitation of the weak by the strong, which Rand argued (poorly) was irrational and counterproductive. In regard to morality, Rand stated clearly that her vision of rational self-interest "is applicable only in the context of a rational, objectively demonstrated code of moral principles...It is not a license 'to do as he pleases' and it is not applicable to the altruists' image of a 'selfish' brute nor to any man motivated by irrational, emotions, feelings, urges, wishes or whims."[19] Objectivism may be atheistic, but it does not dismiss the reality of moral values, whereas the moral nihilism of the Redbeard/LaVey axis explicitly denies any objective basis for morality. The echoes of Objectivism in Satanism can therefore be dismissed as perfunctory formulations and rhetorical borrowings, employed to buttress the theory intellectually, but largely incommensurate with the former. The primary influence remains the primitive social Darwinism of *Might Is Right*.

ANIMALITY AND CARNALITY

Not only are LaVey's ideology and Objectivism ultimately incompatible, but his own Objectivism-inspired comments on rational self-interest are also hard to reconcile with his other statements on human nature. Satanism, again echoing Redbeard, dwells on man's so-called animal nature and animal logic, stressing repeatedly that man is simply another beast motivated largely by primal, animalistic drives. The influence of Darwinian theory is obvious, though implicit. There is only a single reference to Darwin in *The Satanic Bible*, whereas *Might Is Right* refers to either Darwin or Spencer on nearly every page (crucially, Redbeard makes no distinction between Darwin's biological theory and its contentious application to the social sphere). Nonetheless, the theory obviously has a deep underlying influence in Satanism, and it is here that the creed's most fundamental problems arise.

To identify these problems, it is important to distinguish what the Darwinian revolution does and doesn't mean. Darwinism's displacing of the supernatural account of human origins removed the chasm between humanity and other animals, revealing the strong biological similarities. Post–*Origin of the Species*, *Homo sapiens* was no longer above and apart from other living beings, no longer the divinely sanctioned beneficiary of the natural world, nor an immutable organism unchanged since the dawn of time. The Darwinian revolution revealed that humanity was embedded in the natural world and was itself the product of natural processes that did not require the presence of a cosmic benefactor. In acknowledging that common descent applies to humans as well as animals, Darwin established that "the difference in mind between man and the higher animals, great as it is, is one of degree and not of kind."[20] The long reign of supernaturally consecrated anthropocentrism was over.

Nonetheless, Darwin's overturning of the anthropocentric worldview did not make humanity simply another animal. As he noted, there is still a difference of degree. Despite shared evolutionary origins and strong biological similarities to other species, humans are nonetheless unique. First and foremost, humans are nowhere near as violent as other animals. The more aggressive nature of early hunter-gatherers was significantly tempered to allow the development of large settlements, cities, and eventually nations. Murder rates within other species of mammals are thousands of times higher than the most dangerous human cities.[21] Humans are the only animals that have developed true language, including complex grammar and syntax. With language we shape concepts out of words, and are able to pass on our accumulated knowledge and experience from one generation to the next. The development of concepts in turn means the ability to engage in conceptual and abstract thought, which has become the species' trademark. Humanity is the only species that has developed high intelligence, rich culture, highly sophisticated ethical systems, and scientific advancement. Stated bluntly, camels do not put other camels on the moon. Ants do not debate the philosophical ramifications of their natural subordination of the individual agent to the colony.[22] The predator in the wild does not formulate ethical justifications for killing its prey—they simply do so because they need to eat. The type of moral distinctions a human hunter can make—between killing for sport and killing for food—are absent in the animal world. Humans are an animal species, certainly, but a uniquely sophisticated, extraordinarily self-aware animal capable of levels of moral and abstract reasoning that other animals are not.

Satanism ignores these distinctions and enlists a pseudo-Darwinian framework in support of its ideological presuppositions. The simplistic reference to humanity's status as just another animal leads to the kind of statement made by current Church of Satan High Priest Peter Gilmore: "Man is an animal, and must go back to acting like one."[23] This claim displays a sophomoric understanding of both the lessons of modern science and the philosophical issue of what it means to be human. Mere biological similarities should not determine how we behave, especially not with the wealth of attributes and accomplishments that separate us from animals. Most humans do not let the toilet practices of apes and baboons determine their behavior, any more than they do the cannibalism of crocodiles. This reductive reasoning is technically known as the Fallacy of Mediocrity, or the "just" fallacy—the false claim that because we are *just* animals, we can only have the attributes that animals have.[24]

Ironically, Satanism's focus on humanity's animal nature buys into the caricature of Darwinism that modern Christian fundamentalists make—that Darwinism reduces us to the level of animals. A famous historical example is the 1860 Oxford University debate between Archbishop Wilberforce and T. H. Huxley. Wilberforce ridiculed evolution and asked Huxley whether he was descended from an ape on his grandmother's or his grandfather's side. The truth of course is neither. Apes and humans are different species that have are descended from a common ancestor, as Huxley pointed out with pleasure. Satanists and modern Christian fundamentalists, for their part, advance a reading of Darwinism every bit as misguided as that of Wilberforce, albeit a century later. To call modern Satanism's viewpoint Darwinian would be to insult the complexity and sophistication of even Darwin's mid-nineteenth-century writing, let alone the modern synthesis of contemporary evolutionary biology and genetics.

Hand in paw with the Satanic focus on humanity's animal nature is the emphasis on our supposed carnal nature, with LaVey even referring at one point to man's "carnal brain."[25] As with the previous claim, the focus on man as a carnal animal is compromised by its narrowness. A person's sexuality is, undoubtedly, a central part of their identity. As Nietzsche, prefiguring Freud, observed: "The degree and kind of a man's sexuality reaches up into the topmost summit of his spirit."[26] Even so, sexuality is not the full story. A married man's carnal brain may cause him to lust after a young female, but his higher brain functions will make him all-too-aware of the consequences of infidelity, and the moral and legal consequences of forcing his attentions on her. Subsequently, factors other than his carnal inclinations will have a strong bearing on whether or not he follows his natural instincts. LaVey partially acknowledges this with the dictum "indulgence, not compulsion," yet returns again and again to statements about the fundamentally carnal nature of humanity. Ultimately, the Satanic emphasis on carnal nature fails for the same reason as the emphasis on our animal nature. It presents a superficial account of human behavior that fails to acknowledge the complex web of interactions between culture, society, self-awareness and moral reflection.[27]

HUMAN SOCIETY: THE SATANIC PERSPECTIVE

If Satanism's assessment of human nature is desultory and frequently inadequate, its analysis of human society fares no better. Satanism is unabashedly elitist and discriminatory. The vast masses of humanity are, according to LaVey, the herd—a vast collection of apathetic, docile drones. Spurred on by his deep misanthropy and echoing Nietzsche, LaVey spent his writing career developing new pejoratives for the majority of humanity. Through constant reiteration of loaded terminology—herd, masses, rabble—LaVey convinces his readers that they are superior to the vast majority. In the privileged coven of Satanism, the main criteria for achieving nonherd status are simple: reading *The Satanic Bible*, recognizing your own innate superiority to the vast majority of humanity (i.e., non-Satanists), and acknowledging how fundamentally you agree with LaVey's critique.

The problem with these criteria is that they are completely arbitrary. The decision is subject to individual will or judgment without restriction—it depends entirely on the individual's discretion. A person can elevate themselves above the herd simply by stating, "I adhere to a philosophy that scorns the mediocrity of the herd and therefore I'm better than the herd." Anyone else can also escape his herd-status by reading *The Satanic Bible* or a similar tract, recognizing and proclaiming his own innate superiority, and scorning the mediocrity of the herd. Hopefully, the herd won't realize how easy the process is, or else soon there will be nothing but a vast, self-proclaimed elite with no herd to scorn. Which, unfortunately, would put everybody pretty much back where they started again. This circularity is a serious logical problem, one that even LaVey later acknowledged: "As a mass-market book, *The Satanic Bible* breeds pretentiousness in the inferior—everyone believes he is a superman."[28] Tellingly, LaVey could offer no solution to this problem, other than references to so-called true Satanists.

The vagueness of the term *herd* is another problem. Who are the people singled out by LaVey's mobile army of metaphors but never actually defined? Unoccupied pronouns—*they* or *them*—and nonspecific pejoratives—*the masses, locusts*—are hardly useful. If you attend a sports stadium, you are part of the herd. If you sit in a lecture theatre at college, you are part of the herd. In fact, if you do anything that large numbers of other people do (for instance, watch a popular television show) you are part of the herd. These are, of course, activities that almost none of us can avoid. As a descriptive term, it is worthless, for it is unlikely that anyone can avoid indulging in such activities. Use of the term elevates the Satanist at the expense of an ill-defined and perpetually shifting other, but beyond its rhetorical impact it has no value whatsoever.

The Satanists' claim to elite status and the view of a world of perennial strife they envisage is also problematic, as it creates opportunities for other, even more extreme adherents of similar ideologies. Let's take Satanic ideology out of the pages of *The Satanic Bible* for a minute and consider its implications. Imagine a rival sect setting up in late-60s San Francisco near the Satanists' headquarters. Having taken the Marquis de Sade a little too seriously, they call themselves "The Society of the Friends of Crime."[29] The Society of the Friends of Crime shares the Satanists' ruthlessly materialistic vision and are similarly staunch social Darwinists and moral nihilists. They are also just as assured of their superiority to the rest of society as the Satanists are. However, there are two major differences between the two groups: The Society doesn't have an ethical injunction against murder, and its members are really, really nasty. Not nasty in a *look-at-me-I-scorn-the-herd* way, but nasty in an *it's-time-to-start-slaughtering-the-herd* way. Seeing the Church of Satan as the most immediate threat to its success (yet more than a little herd-like in their moderation), The Society of the Friends of Crime launches a preemptive strike, storms the Black House during a Black Mass reading of the *Infernal Diatribe* and slaughters the entire Church of Satan hierarchy in a frenzied orgy of rape, torture, and killing. Not very neighborly, but it's a rough world—nature red in tooth and claw and all that.

How could other Satanists respond to this random, senseless violence? The tenets of extreme social Darwinism don't require anyone to play nice. Satanists find it in their rational self-interest to prohibit murder and obey the laws of their society; another group may find it in their rational self-interest to slaughter all Satanists. As LaVey notes, "If you create a new rule and it takes hold, you have made a Right for yourself, however self-serving. Whatever prevails, overwhelms, holds in thrall, disarms, terrifies, frightens, controls, constrains, enslaves…will always be accepted as Right."[30] LaVey endorses this position without qualification. All that The Society of the Friends of Crime has done is prove that it is better adapted to the realities of a cold, merciless world and more willing to follow its ideology through to its logical conclusions: no pity for the weak; might is right; the strong will survive.

Obviously, this scenario is a fantasy unlikely to occur in any stable democratic nation, primarily because of the protections and freedoms offered by a political system based on universal human rights and freedoms. Satanists effectively leech off the goodwill of the majority—who for the most part play by the despised egalitarian rules of Western democracies—and are thus enabled to adopt their demonic pose. But in an environment or society lacking such protections—would Iran or North Korea tolerate their pretensions?—the Satanists could soon be mopping up the blood of their fallen Satanic brethren (or festering in a state prison). The key point is this: there would be no part of Satanic ideology that would give them the right to complain. They cannot assert that The Society of the Friends of Crime's behavior is wrong or unfair, for such objections would be inconsistent with Satanic principles. In the words the Black Pope, "Good is what you like. Evil is what you don't like."[31]

There is obviously, therefore, something deeply, systematically wrong in the Satanist's understanding of both natural processes and social interactions. The root of the problem is its reliance on the tenets of social Darwinist thought, in particular, Redbeard's militant and nihilistic formulation. Social Darwinism makes a simple yet absolutely critical philosophical error in its attempt to derive ethical principles from the (supposed) natural facts of the world. It commits what is often referred to as the Naturalistic Fallacy, the claim we can go from a *description* of the world to making *prescriptions* (that is, rules) about how things should be; that whatever exists *ought* to exist, that whatever is natural cannot be wrong. The struggle for survival is seen as an accurate description of the world, therefore it is only right that individuals should struggle relentlessly against each other. The fallacy lurking within this reasoning is that there are many perfectly natural things in the world that we try to reduce or eliminate: disease, floods, avalanches, famines, and so forth. The Naturalistic Fallacy points out that the perceived *naturalness* of a phenomenon does not necessarily mean it is beneficial to us, nor that we should simply acquiesce to it. If a Satanist gets a tooth cavity, does she allow the tooth to rot out? After all, tooth decay is perfectly natural. Therefore, it is only right that the tooth should rot. Any interference from those meddlers who would go against the force of nature, commonly known as dentists, would be a denial of nature. Indeed, brushing one's teeth would also be taboo. This line of thinking is obviously flawed. You can't derive an *ought* from an *is* in such a simple manner. The hard facts of nature do not provide moral guidance so readily.

If the claim that might is right were true, then Satanism could easily be used to give a moral justification of, for instance, rape. As observed, Satanism places profound importance on sexual desires. It is "a religion of the flesh, the mundane, the carnal."[32] Accordingly, if a man desires a woman, why shouldn't he simply take what he desires by force? His desire is perfectly natural. Furthermore, the moral injunctions against rape are, by the reasoning of Redbeard/LaVey, nothing more than the arbitrary prejudice of Christian slave morality. By their logic, if a man desires something, the fact that the desire is natural means that the desire is morally right; if he is able to satisfy that desire by force, it is also morally right. It follows that, for the Satanist, rape is perfectly moral. In fact, it is *only right* that men should rape. To not do so would be a gross denial of their carnal nature. Obviously, this is an odious conclusion, but Satanists either have to accept that there is a fundamental flaw in their ideological claims, or accept that the ideology logically allows if not *requires* them to be rapists.

It must be acknowledged that *The Satanic Bible* explicitly prohibits rape: "Satanism encourages any form of sexual expression you may desire, so long as it hurts no one else…the Satanist would not intentionally hurt others by violating their sexual rights. If you attempt to impose your sexual desires upon others who do not welcome your advances, you are infringing upon their sexual freedom."[33] Reasonable sentiments, certainly, but this passage raises a perplexing question: where does this sudden interest in the other person's *freedom* and *rights* come from? After all, this is the same work that declares strength to be the ultimate arbitrator of justice, and in regard to human nature asks, "Are we not all predatory animals by instinct? If humans ceased wholly from preying upon each other, could they continue to exist? Is not 'lust and carnal desire' a more truthful term to describe 'love' when applied to the continuance of the race?"[34] How can these comments be reconciled with a condemnation of rape? Quite simply, they can't.

THRASYMACHUS VERSUS TIT-FOR-TAT

The core ideological beliefs of Satanism engage some of the central issues in our understanding of the natural world and, more importantly, how we should interact with it and each other. These are intrinsically philosophical issues; more specifically, they are issues that philosophers have proven central to all philosophical discourse. Consider, for example, the following famous passage from Nietzsche's *On the Genealogy of Morals*:

> That lambs dislike great birds of prey does not seem strange: only it gives no grounds for reproaching these birds of prey for bearing off little lambs. And if the lambs say among themselves: "these birds of prey are evil; and whoever is least like a bird of prey, but rather its opposite, a lamb—would he not be good?" there is no reason to find fault with this institution of an ideal, except perhaps that the birds of prey might view it a little ironically and say: "we don't dislike them at all, these good little lambs; we even love them: nothing is more tasty than a tender lamb."
>
> To demand of strength that it should not express itself as strength, that it should not be a desire to overcome, a desire to throw down, a desire to become master, a thirst for enemies and resistances and triumphs, is just as absurd as to demand of weakness that it should express itself as strength.[35]

Nietzsche advances what is by now a familiar argument: that strength *should* express itself as strength. In doing so, he clearly commits the Naturalistic Fallacy. He also unmistakably endorses moral relativism, in which the moral claims of the birds and lambs are relative to their subjective perspectives. The passage also clearly parallels his concept of master/slave morality. The lambs represent Christianity and the birds represent the values of the Romans. Underlying all of this is the view of the natural world as fundamentally antagonistic, with individual agents battling relentlessly to succeed, and the outcome decided by strength. Nietzsche accepts all of this without hesitation—he also refers to his vision of noble men as "beast[s] of prey, as triumphant monsters who perhaps emerge from a disgusting procession of murder, arson, rape, and torture, exhilarated and undisturbed of soul, as if it were no more than a student's prank."[36] In regard to rape, Nietzsche is, unlike LaVey, consistent.

Yet Nietzsche's parable only presents one aspect of nature, the combative. Compare the phenomenon the Greek historian Herodotus witnessed in Egypt in 440 B.C.E.:

> Because [the crocodile] spends its life in water, its mouth is filled with leeches. With the exception of the sandpiper, all other birds and animals run away from it. The sandpiper, however, is on good terms with it, because it is of use to the crocodile. When the crocodile climbs out of the water...the sandpiper slips into its mouth and swallows the leeches. This does the crocodile good and gives it pleasure, so it does not harm the sandpiper.[37]

When Nietzsche read this passage (which, as a formally trained classicist, he unquestionably did) did he pause to wonder why the crocodile did not make a quick snack out of the sandpiper, just as his own birds of prey feast on the lambs? Is it not strange to observe one of nature's most dangerous predators calmly allowing a tasty hors d'oeuvre to dance without fear in its mouth? Why doesn't the crocodile express its strength as a strength, as Nietzsche, Redbeard, and the Satanist insist?

The answer, we now know, is *reciprocal altruism*. First presented by Robert Trivers in 1971,[38] reciprocal altruism is a form of trade-off where one organism accepts the short-term cost of helping another being in expectation of a future, or sometime simultaneous, benefit. It describes what happens when two unrelated birds take turns to pick the ticks out of each other's heads, or when a blackbird alerts other blackbirds of a circling hawk, but in doing so puts itself at risk. It also explains the temporary placidity of Herodotus' crocodile. The birds both get their heads cleared of ticks, so long as the other doesn't renege. The blackbird, though placing itself in increased danger by warning its fellows, will be rewarded by an early warning when the behavior is reciprocated by another bird. The crocodile gets its mouth cleaned, the sandpiper gets a free meal without being eaten itself. In each of these examples, an organism helps another, but is fully compensated.

The fact that reciprocal altruism is not true altruism (i.e., the act is not performed selflessly, as a payoff is expected) is unimportant. The model does not intend to justify moral action. Rather, it provides a way of understanding how unrelated organisms can be induced to cooperate with each other. Now regarded as a key development in the further understanding of natural selection, it is a direct rebuttal of the simplistic view that the natural world is simply a place of continual and unlimited bloodshed. Cooperating with other organisms is a beneficial behavioral strategy that can aid success in the Darwinian struggle for existence, with no blood spilt.

Reciprocal altruism is also compatible with a more nuanced understanding of Darwinian selection. The idea of the survival of the fittest is an accurate description of Darwinian natural selection, but only if understood properly. *Fit*, in an evolutionary sense, means best adapted to the environment. It refers to the organism most likely to reproduce successfully and pass on its genes. An organism's fitness includes its ability to survive, prosper in its habitat, find a mate, and ultimately produce offspring. Being fit does not simply mean being the biggest, fastest, or strongest. An insect camouflaged to blend in with the surrounding flora, for example, is fitter in an evolutionary sense than one that is highly visible to predators. There is much more involved than simply killing all competitors. The remorselessly antagonistic, every-critter-for-itself model that Redbeard and LaVey endorse is too one-dimensional to be accurate or useful. Moreover, it is directly contradicted by the findings of modern evolutionary biology.

The social Darwinist program in social engineering is hardly unique to Satanists. Likewise, the attempt to reduce morality to the mere whim of the strong and dismiss any notions of cooperation or altruism is nothing new to philosophy. More than 23 centuries ago in Plato's *Republic*, Socrates asked for a definition of justice. The sophist Thrasymachus was quick to advance one: "Listen then,...I say that justice or right is simply what is in the interest of the stronger party."[39] Challenged by Socrates, Thrasymachus continued:

> You are not aware that justice or right is really what is good for someone else, namely the interest of the stronger party or ruler, imposed at the expense of the subject who obeys him. Injustice or wrong is just the opposite of this, and rules those who are really simple and just.[40]

Thrasymachus' position is a classic iteration of moral relativism—your evaluation of the moral quality of an action is dependent wholly on your perspective, and it is unnecessary to consider the consequences for others. Socrates, however, is quick to identify an important flaw. "Let's put it this way...The just man does not compete with his like, but only his unlike, while the unjust man competes with both like and unlike."[41] Socrates points out that the antagonistic stance of the resolute individualist is counterproductive. It makes everyone his enemy, when there are times he will need to cooperate. When the *Republic* was written, around 340 B.C.E., Socrates's argument was merely logical, and a minor point. Nowadays, it can be proven and is far more central to the debate.

Reciprocal altruism provides a model for how instances of altruism can occur in nature. Robert Axelrod, in his 1984 book *The Evolution of Cooperation*, took the emerging field of game theory a step further and showed how systematic cooperation could evolve in a world of egoists without the interference of central authority. In his famous analysis of the Prisoner's Dilemma, Axelrod posited a scenario whereby two individuals are arrested for a crime and offered a lesser sentence for ratting out their co-conspirator. In deciding their behavior, both prisoners are influenced by the decision the other makes. Rat out the other prisoner while they remain silent and you reap the benefits; remain a silent sucker while being ratted out and you are punished. Rat each other out and you are both punished, though not as heavily as if you were a sucker. However, if both prisoners cooperate with each other by remaining silent, they both receive a minimal sentence. Analysis of the problem shows that it is impossible for one individual to make a decision without considering the decision of the other, leading to a mutually dependent impasse. The best overall strategy—for both prisoners—is the final one, cooperation (in this case, by means of conspiratorial silence).

Axelrod ran a virtual tournament of different strategies in an iterated Prisoner's Dilemma—one where numerous competitors face off again and again.

The winning strategy was one called *tit-for-tat*, "the strategy that cooperates on the first move and then does whatever the other player did on the previous move." Therefore, if its opponent cooperates, tit-for-tat does so also. In the tourney, tit-for-tat was successful because of its key properties: "avoidance of unnecessary conflict by cooperating as long as the other player does, provocability in the face of an uncalled for defection by the other, forgiveness after responding to a provocation, and clarity of behaviour."[42] In fact, it and other cooperative strategies were overwhelmingly more successful that combative, cynical strategies. Axelrod's work formalized—and made scientific—Socrates's counterargument to Thrasymachus two millennia ago. Resolute antagonism is counterproductive.

The power of Axelrod's work in game theory is that it shows clearly how behaving cooperatively ultimately benefits self-regarding agents. The interdependency of their respective outcomes leads them to cooperate and coordinate their actions, in the process of which establishing moral norms. In providing a genuine explanation of the emergence and maintenance of moral and behavioral norms, the model has been enormously influential in political theory, economics, moral philosophy, and evolutionary biology. By focusing on the interdependency of individual action, no altruistic impulses are presupposed. Rather, Socrates's point is upheld: the ruthless pursuit of self-interest without the regard for the actions or interests of others is self-defeating. In fact, any society whose members pursue egoist principles may well all end up worse off than one whose members act cooperatively. In regard to the present topic, the relevance of these conclusions cannot be underestimated: Axelrod's work in game theory drives the final nail in the coffin of might-is-right philosophy.

Ironically, *The Satanic Bible* advances an idea that sounds superficially like the tit-for-tat strategy that dominated Axelrod's tourney:

> Satanism advocates practicing a modified form of the Golden Rule. Our interpretation of this rule is: "Do unto others as they do unto you"; because if you "Do unto others as you would have them do unto you," and they, in turn, treat you badly, it goes against human nature to continue to treat them with consideration. You should do unto others as you would have them do unto you, but if your courtesy is not returned, they should be treated with the wrath they deserve.[43]

Unfortunately, this passage is too vaguely formulated to be of much use. Once a person defects, will treating them with the "wrath they deserve" be maintained permanently (not a winning strategy) or temporarily? The former appears more likely, given the Satanic lust for enmity and disproportionate retaliation, negating any similarity to tit-for-tat (see the discussion of Lex Talionis in chapter 7 of this book). Furthermore, LaVey's modified Golden

Rule directly contradicts other parts of *The Satanic Bible* (and many other writings of LaVey) where he wholeheartedly endorses the ideology of power and dominance. Might, hostility, and combativeness are the dominant themes in Satanism, the modified Golden Rule yet another hazy formulation.

THE INFERNAL DIAGNOSIS

Modern Satanism obviously owes a great debt to the writers and theorists who preceded LaVey. John Milton, Niccolò Machiavelli, the Romantic poets, Spencer, Stirner, Nietzsche, Redbeard, Jack London, Aleister Crowley, and Rand all made contributions to LaVey's hurried 1969 pastiche. Far from being an original work, *The Satanic Bible* is a jejune blending of disparate influences dressed up in diabolical attire. LaVey can hardly claim to have invented an original philosophy when the most influential section—the *Infernal Diatribe*—is an act of wholesale plagiarism. His chief achievement is therefore as a synthesizer of ideas from the cultural and intellectual fringe, the melding of extreme social Darwinist thought with the European artistic tradition's appropriation of Satan as a standard of rebellion—an act itself prefigured in the work of Jack London.

The fact that the all-influential *Might Is Right* remains in print today is—as LaVey modestly points out—no doubt due to the interest in the work that its importance to modern Satanism has fomented. Yet Redbeard's work was itself in no way original. It comes from an era when numerous similar quasi-scientific tracts were being written, primarily to justify unbridled capitalism, repressive social policies, racism, colonialism, and the exploitation of non-European nations. Theorists of the late nineteenth and early twentieth century were eager to utilize the enormous descriptive power of Darwinian thought in nonbiological spheres, and in doing so frequently over-extended the reach of the theory. As biologist Stephen Jay Gould notes:

> [Natural selection] has a history of misuse almost as long as its proper pedigree. Claptrap and bogus Darwinian formulations have been used to justify every form of social exploitation—rich over poor, technologically complex over traditional, imperialist over aborigine, conqueror over defeated in war. Every evolutionist knows this history only too well, and we bear some measure of collective responsibility for the uncritical fascination that many of us have shown for such unjustified extensions. But most false expropriations of our chief phrase have been undertaken without our knowledge and against our will.[44]

Redbeard's achievement was the synthesizing of his own racist and misogynistic prejudices with the pseudo-science of social Darwinism and the philosophical rhetoric of Stirner and Nietzsche—a particularly egregious example of a thoroughly debunked body of thought.

What, though, of Satanism? Satanism is a contemporary movement that appeals to the very same theories, theories that have since been comprehensively disproven. *Might Is Right* bears a dubious distinction in being openly praised as a work of merit in the present day, long after its fellows were condemned to the dustbins of history. Social Darwinism was a popular, mainstream theory in the later nineteenth and early twentieth century. Today, however, you will not find a single scientist, social theorist, or philosopher who supports it. The only groups who still claim that social Darwinism is in any way *scientific* are far-right neo-fascist and neo-pagan organizations.

Analyzed objectively, the philosophical doctrines of Satanism collapse. There are clearly deep, systematic faults and inconsistencies within LaVey's formulations. In particular, Satanism makes a number of basic errors in its assessment of human nature and the interpretation of evolutionary theory. The Darwinian revolution did not reduce humans to the status of mere animals, in anything other than the strictest biological sense. Even animals are not as reliant on violent competition as Satanism implies; humans far less so. The phrase "survival of the fittest" does not mean slaughter or be slaughtered. If the world really were the way Redbeard and LaVey imagine it, it would be little more than one great gladiatorial circus. Furthermore, even if LaVey's hyperbole were an accurate description of the natural world, the logical fallacy of conflating *is* with *ought* explains why it could not serve as the basis or justification for social policy. The principle assertions of Satanism and social Darwinism therefore suffer from two critical flaws, one interpretive and the other logical, each independently sufficient to invalidate their claims.

Satanism, ultimately, is based on catchphrases and obsolete nineteenth-century social theorizing and pseudo-science. These doctrines may hold some interest for the historian of ideas, but basing a late twentieth-century ideology on them is indefensible. To write in 2006, as LaVey's successor Peter Gilmore does, that "There is a lasting power in Redbeard's writing, since [*Might Is Right*] is an accurate depiction of how human societies function" is to be guilty of profound ignorance, not to mention openly endorsing a viciously racist text.[45] As a depiction of how human societies function, as understood by contemporary social and evolutionary thinkers, *Might Is Right* is completely inaccurate, as is *The Satanic Bible*. Similarly, Gilmore's description of Satanism as a "common sense, rationalist, materialist philosophy" is demonstrably false.[46] Satanic ideology is, as shown, riddled with contradiction, largely superficial, and almost completely unscientific. It is not helped by the frequently ad hoc pronouncements of prominent Satanists. Gilmore, for instance, openly supports the Stirner-derived anarchistic individualism of *Might Is Right*, but writes in his own work: "Man is by nature a social creature and makes his social contract with his fellows, thus rules of conduct are established to allow maximum freedom for individuals to interact,"[47] a statement in complete contradiction to the dominant themes of both *Might Is Right* and *The Satanic Bible*.

Beyond its profound philosophical flaws and grave disservice to modern sociobiology, the ideology of Satanism promotes a dangerous social agenda. It is tempting to regard LaVey's bombastic comments as mere rhetorical overkill, but it is necessary to remember that his assertions are accepted as fact by Satanists and regarded as accurate descriptions of both human nature and society. It is therefore important to recognize that Satanism is not an innocuous, life-affirming philosophy. It is a discriminatory ideology of bigotry and intolerance that legitimates and glorifies violence. It systematically aggrandizes the believer, appealing directly to their vanity and feelings of superiority, while degrading and dehumanizing all non–group members. While *The Satanic Bible* explicitly prohibits any illegal activities, it provides no rationale whatsoever for this prohibition. Satanism is, quite clearly, directly opposed to the fundamental values and principles that underpin a healthy, stable modern society—the rule of law, recognition of basic human rights, protection of civil liberties, nondiscrimination, tolerance, pluralism, and equality. If Satanism is dangerous, and on the basis of this analysis it undeniably is, the danger stems not from the cartoonish employment of Satan as a figurehead for rebellion, but in its appropriation of extreme-right principles to endorse an antidemocratic, antihumanitarian ideology that is all too often directly analogous to the modern world's most notorious political creeds.

Satanic Legions: Spreading the Gospel of the Black Pope

Then Jesus asked him, "What is your name?"
"My name is Legion," he replied, "for we are many."
—Mark 5:9–10

If the Devil lives anywhere, it could be in San Francisco.
—*The Occult Experience* (1985)

There is possibly no more dramatic way to demonstrate your opposition to conventional values than to declare yourself a Satanist. LaVey's doctrines, despite their flaws, constituted an attractive package that flattered its adherents and preyed on their desire for status and recognition. By engaging one of society's most taboo topics and embellishing it with direct, muscular ideals, Satanism has never ceased to find an audience on the margins of society. The release of a bible to articulate his provocative ideology spread it far beyond the environs of San Francisco, eventually reaching a global audience. Inevitably, many drawn to the individualistic creed realized it could be adopted and adapted without joining LaVey's church—although most still acknowledged and respected him as its iconoclastic founder. Even within the original organization, it wasn't long before the geographically isolated members of the various grottos started breaking away from LaVey and going it alone.

The Church of Satan expanded quickly following the publication of *The Satanic Bible*. In 1970, a satellite was established in Detroit, the first outside San Francisco. Named the Babylon Grotto, it was headed by Wayne West, a defrocked British Catholic priest. The Ninevah Grotto was established the same year near Fort Knox, Kentucky, where the army had stationed Michael Aquino. The Lilith Grotto in New York, named after its founder Lilith Sinclair, was another important outpost, and one of the largest. Other grottos followed soon after, as did the inevitable complications of growing decentralization. West eventually departed the church, either cast out for incorporating his sexual preferences into church rituals or departing voluntarily in opposition to changes to the church magazine *The Cloven Hoof*.[1] He set up a short-lived splinter group, the Universal Church of Man. Similar episodes followed. In 1973 John DeHaven's Stygian Grotto in Ohio was disbanded after rumors surfaced regarding drug usage, dealing, and possession of stolen goods. Given the very real dangers of negative attention that a Satanic church was likely to receive, its hierarchy dealt with any violations of the law seriously. DeHaven, predictably, set up his own organization, The Church of Satanic Brotherhood. It lasted a year.

The next development was the open fusion of Satanism and neo-Nazism. Satanic ideology was clearly easily blended with the tenets of National Socialism, as two East coast members of the Church of Satan, Michael Grumbowski and John Amend, recognized in 1973. They broke away from the founding organization and started The Order of the Black Ram and the Shrine of the Little Mother. Grumbowski (aka Reverend Blackshire) was a former lieutenant of West's and the head of Detroit's Phoenix Grotto. The paramilitary-styled Amend (aka Seth-Klippoth) had forged contacts with Canada's extreme right racist Odinist Movement and began to include the blood sacrifice of chickens in his rituals. They remained in full support of the doctrines of *The Satanic Bible* but incorporated its principles with Nazi theories of racial supremacy.

Both Grumbowski and Amend were in close contact with neo-Nazi James Madole, an outspoken anti-Semite who headed the small, violent National Renaissance Party. Madole had a deep interest in Satanism and the occult, sporting a large Satanic altar in his New York apartment. His party courted links with the Church of Satan, with LaVey visiting their headquarters. Other groups from the racist right also attempted alliances, including The American Nazi Party and the militant United Klans of America. Satanism's elitist, discriminatory ideology and focus on power, vengeance, and hatred resonated with these groups' extremist agendas. The United Klans were willing to disregard their Christian beliefs long enough to consider an alliance with a group that supported similar social policies, even if it seems at first glance an unlikely mix. The conservative, authoritarian nature of LaVey's doctrines, his vocal support for a police state, and the Germanic overtones of Satanism's ritual practices were, when combined with their shared status as fringe organizations, clearly compelling enough to override any aversion to the symbol of Satan. Ultimately, LaVey turned all these groups down, preferring to remain independent, but not without acknowledging appreciation for their "camaraderie."[2]

The continuing defection of various grotto heads showed the difficulties of maintaining a geographically extended satellite network under central authority, and the ease with which the doctrines of Satanism could be employed without the direct sanction of their pioneer. As Aquino noted in reference to Kentucky's Ninevah Grotto, "In San Francisco there was no perceived distinction between the Church of Satan and the person of Anton LaVey. The Church was what he said it was…2,000 miles away in Louisville I found that we would have to create and operate a Church of Satan on our own—bound to 6114 by the ideas, not by the person of Anton LaVey."[3] Still respected as the wellspring of the movement, the Black Pope was, even by the early 1970s, no longer essential to anyone who wished to employ or adapt the teachings of *The Satanic Bible*.

SCHISM

Losing a few members of far-flung grottos was of little consequence, but 1975 saw a schism that nearly destroyed the Church of Satan and deeply affected LaVey personally. Trouble began with his 1974 biography, *The Devil's Avenger*, which was openly critical of a number of his own followers, as well as promoting a fantastical vision of the high priest's lavish lifestyle, dissatisfying certain church members. When LaVey made his chauffeur a church magister the following year, senior members resented the promotion of someone they saw as unqualified to be a Satanic priest. LaVey was also drawing away from the strong focus on the occult, an affront to those who took their magical practices very seriously, many of whom regarded Satan as far more than a symbol. The catalyst for the break, however, was the announcement in a May 1975 *Cloven Hoof* article that lower-level priesthoods in the Church of Satan were available in exchange for material contributions—gifts of money and real estate. LaVey had asserted himself as the absolute leader of the Church of Satan and declared that he alone set the rules, even if it meant selling priesthoods.

The priesthood, or parts of it, rebelled. Aquino was at the forefront, accusing Anton and Diane LaVey of prostituting themselves. He tendered his resignation as editor of *The Cloven Hoof* and member of the Church of Satan and, in an angry and pained letter, declared he could not be party to a debasement of the church's principles as "I am bound by my sacred oath to Satan."[4] He then circulated copies of the relevant correspondence throughout the church. A number of senior members and grotto heads also chose fealty to Satan rather than LaVey and lined up behind Aquino to establish a breakaway church.

LaVey, understandably frustrated at the difficulties coordinating an organization that was spread from the Pacific to the Atlantic, as well as washing
over into Canada, had clearly tired of the limited returns for his efforts. The
yachts, holiday houses, and lavish lifestyle detailed in *The Devil's Avenger* did
not exist. He had tired of the occultist posturing and had become increasing
antagonistic to how seriously black magic was being taken by other church
members. LaVey, it seems, was at heart a showman and opportunist, not an
occultist. Yet the near-collapse of his church deeply disturbed him. He disbanded the remaining grottos, retreated into the Black House, and ceased life
as a public figure virtually overnight. His disappearance act was so convincing
that Aquino was able to claim that the Church of Satan no longer existed, and
eventually rumors of the Black Pope's death started to circulate. Nowhere
is the completeness of LaVey's withdrawal more evident than in his second
official biography, *The Secret Life of a Satanist*, which contains virtually no
biographical details between 1975 and its publication in 1990, substituting
instead extended discussions of his books, philosophy, social views, and the
supposed Satanic influence of the Lone Ranger.

LaVey later referred to the crisis as a reorganization and presented it as entirely intentional. The Church of Satan officially denies that the breach was a
breach. "Aquino attempted to make interested parties believe that the entire
Priesthood of the Church of Satan followed him in departing...The departure of less than thirty members can hardly be called a schism." Whatever the
numbers, it was a serious blow to the church, for the defectors included many
of the most senior and active members. The truth about the events of June
1975 lies somewhere between the Church of Satan's assertion that "This was
in reality a welcome housecleaning of an element that had become less than
desirable"[5] and Aquino's comment that "Within days the Church of Satan
was dead."[6]

THE TEMPLE OF SET

Following the cataclysm/housecleaning, Aquino was faced with a quan-
dary, possessing as he did a priesthood and no church. Fortuitously, the forces
of darkness intervened. In an episode eerily reminiscent of Crowley's 1904
Cairo convocation with the spirit Aiwass, Aquino had his own encounter with
an ancient Egyptian figure. A magical working on the night of June 21, 1975
led him to write, over a four-hour period, "The Book of Coming Forth by
Night." The work was the word of the ancient Egyptian god Set (Seth), "the
Ageless intelligence of the Universe."[7] Satan, it was revealed, was actually Set,
a god who pre-dated Christianity by millennia. Set had appeared previously
to Crowley and dictated the *Book of the Law*, instigating the Aeon of Horus
(HarWer), and had later begun the Age of Satan through LaVey in 1966. Set's

timely intervention, and claim to theological supremacy to the Hebrew sha-man Satan, provided Aquino with the authority he needed. The ex–Church of Satan number two was established the Magus of the new Aeon of Set, thus supplanting LaVey by infernal fiat.

Aquino named his new church the Temple of Set, tattooed "666" into his scalp, replaced the grotto system with similar branches known as "py-lons," formulated an elaborate degree system based on Crowley's, and began. Though possessing a far more pronounced occult edge, the Temple of Set maintained the Church of Satan's core ideology and heavy emphasis on indi-viduality. LaVey's thought was regarded as an important first step. As Aqui-no's wife Lilith, prior head of New York's Lilith Grotto, later stated, "The Temple of Set is the Church of Satan grown up. The Church of Satan started out on a very self-indulgent, materialistic level." The new group was to con-tinue the work of the former, but with a far stronger emphasis on black magic and attaining a so-called higher self in conjunction with Set. "There is this sentient being, which is the Prince of Darkness, or Set, or Satan on a more privative level, but it is a relationship of mutual respect, rather than worship in the popular sense of the word." Other aspects of the new order remained standard Satanic rhetoric. "Yes, we regard ourselves very highly, because we feel we are superior beings, in the sense that we're not just little robots going around, punching our time clocks, getting up, going to sleep, and that's our existence."[8]

The focus of the Temple's magic is "Xefer" (pronounced "Khefer"), based on the Egyptian verb for "to become" or "to come into being." Setian magical theory delves much deeper into metaphysical philosophy than LaVeyan Satan-ism, drawing from Plato's distinction between the world as it appears to us and the hidden world of the forms, and from Nietzsche's focus on the importance of will in personal and spiritual development (an opportunistic amalgam, given Nietzsche's seething contempt for Platonism). As critic Roald Kristiansen notes, the two groups both aim to achieve a higher destiny, but they "disagree as to the means of how to achieve this goal. The Church of Satan pursues the goal in terms of 'indulging' (affirming) humanity's carnal nature, while the Temple of Set pursues the goal through philosophy and mysticism. Both use magic and ritual for their purposes, but the form and content of those rituals are then shaped according to how they envision their paths." There are also important differences in the purpose of ritual magic. "Church of Satan rituals emphasize the ventilation of emotional frustration and the satisfaction of car-nal desires, whereas the Temple of Set emphasizes the self's symbolic participa-tion in a higher reality through ceremonial magic."[9]

Beyond the increased focus on magic and mysticism, the Temple of Set's most important development is that its form of Satanism is theistic. Set is re-garded as a sentient being, not an archetype or figurehead. Aquino maintains that in the early years LaVey's organization had two faces—an atheistic, carnival blend of Satanism for public consumption, and a cult of legitimate devil-worship that took place in private. LaVey, he claims, was a devil-worshipper who lost his faith. Beyond Aquino's continued assertions—which were necessary to validate his own authority—there is little to support this view. There is even less doubt that the current Church of Satan is rigidly atheistic, and the two rivals have, over time, each settled into their own niches, with their degree of interest in the occult forming the primary dividing line.

Aquino has always been careful to pay due respect to LaVey. "He believed in what he was doing and...I sensed that there was an individual who did in fact have a new perspective on the human equation, on what humanity really is."[10] The temple continues to draw disgruntled ex–Church of Satan members, both the casualties of frequent infighting and those whose deepening interest in the occult is at odds with the increasingly anti-occult church. The temple's membership claims are far more modest than LaVey's, beginning with 50 ex–Church of Satan initiates in 1975, possessing a mailing list of 75 by the mid-1980s, and claiming 80 members in 2002.[11] The Temple of Set focus on a pre-Christian deity has also distanced it from the directly confrontational opposition to Christianity that its predecessor maintains. It also places far greater demands on its initiates, with its reading list alone growing to over 400 titles, covering topics as diverse as ancient Egyptian history and philosophy, occult studies, Crowley, H. P. Lovecraft, psychology, politics, and science.

One area in which the Temple of Set has courted controversy is its deep fascination with Nazi occultism. Michael Grumbowski, formerly of the neo-Nazi breakaway Order of the Black Ram, joined the early temple and became a magister and member of the central council. Nazi occultism played a central role in the temple's Order of the Trapezoid. The order was impressed by the Romantic and Germanic magical tradition and its influence on the near-mystical qualities of Nazism. "The uncanny attraction of the Third Reich—Nazi Germany—lies in the fact that it endorsed and practiced both dynamism and life-worship without restraint and to a world-shaking degree of success."[12] Eager to experience this dynamism himself, Aquino traveled to the former SS headquarters at Wewelsburg Castle in Westphalia, Germany in 1982. There he performed a magical working in its so-called Hall of the Dead, the ritual chamber where SS chief Heinrich Himmler had conducted ritual magic. By 1985 the authoritarianism and emphasis on Nazi occultism led to friction within the Temple of Set, with a small group departing to set up the rival Temple of Nepthys.

The interest in Nazism and Nazi occultism is also evident in the extensive Temple of Set reading list. The list includes *Mein Kampf* and a number of other books on Nazi thought, occultism, and racial theory, with commentaries that are uniformly uncritical. For Hitler's politico-biographical treatise, Aquino advises "Look for the discussions concerning the selection of leaders, control of the masses, and the justification for human social organization. You may be surprised what your discover."[13] The collection *Hitler's Secret Conversations 1941–1944* is described as "an impressive look into the mind of an individual whom the postwar world has been conditioned to dismiss as a crude, criminal, and unintrospective thug."[14] Alfred Rosenberg's *Race History and Other Essays* gets a snide, supercilious blurb: "Extracts from the major race-history writings of the Nazis' 'official philosopher'—with a finger-waggling introduction, of course. It's O.K. for this book to be in print; it has the appropriate editorial condemnation."[15] Madison Grant's infamous 1916 work of scientific racism, *The Passing of the Great Race*, receives a similarly indulgent commentary that devolves into undisguised apologetics.[16] This willingness to promote long-since debunked racialist pseudo-science and hate speech as valid reading material hardly alleviates concerns about the Temple of Set's deep interest in Nazism. It is difficult to see what legitimate purpose—beyond that of historical curiosity—the works of Rosenberg and Grant serve. Works of wishful thinking and propaganda, not science, both aim to support the social prejudices of their time, which, in Rosenberg's case, means the prejudices of Nazi Germany.

Ironically, the reading list also includes Richard Dawkins's *The Selfish Gene* and Carl Sagan's *The Demon Haunted World*, two classics of popular science. Together, these two books address a number of the problematic anthropological, social, and religious issues related to Satanic beliefs. A close reading of *The Selfish Gene*, particularly its discussions of reciprocal altruism and game theory, would pose serious questions for anyone who supports LaVey's skewed views on human nature, aggression, and social interaction. *The Demon Haunted World*, the reading list notes, is "a spirited defense of the scientific method and skeptical thinking. The occult world is a standing target for people wanting to sell bad thought for money."[17] Indeed Sagan, a inveterate enemy of the misuse of science and of New Age mysticism, would be the first to apply a little skeptical thinking to the notion of an ancient Egyptian god making its wishes known in the middle of the night in twentieth-century suburban California.

SATANIC DIASPORA

From the mid-1970s onward, the various Satanic groups proliferated. LaVey had brought the term into mainstream discourse, and different applications of it abounded. In addition to Church of Satan defectors, there were numerous Satanic groups that were never affiliated with LaVey and simply took his ideas as a springboard. Some were merely variations on a LaVeyan theme, some almost exact duplicates. The majority were either very small, very short-lived, or both. Estimating the membership and influence of the various groups is equally difficult, as it is de rigueur to overstate membership, influence, and diabolical importance. The most active and determined self-publicist can appear far more important than is the case, especially in a field as dramatic and attention garnering as Satanism.

As LaVey's daughters Karla and Zeena grew up, they slowly became involved in church affairs, each eventually becoming prominent Satanists in their own right. Karla traveled to Amsterdam in 1975 to act as an emissary to the Magistralis Grotto, established three years previously by Martin Lamers, a former actor. In 1976 Lamers converted a former church into the Walburga Abbey, an Amsterdam sex club of sorts where counterfeit nuns masturbated on a stage/altar. Eventually running afoul of the authorities (for tax evasion, not moral turpitude—it was the Netherlands after all) the Abbey was closed down and LaVey severed ties. Though short-lived, the episode raised the profile of Satanism in Europe. It has since become well established on the continent, particularly in Scandinavia, Germany, and Eastern Europe. *The Satanic Bible* was eventually translated into most European languages, including French, German, Swedish, Danish, Norwegian, Czech, Italian, Spanish, and Portuguese.

Another highly sexualized Satanist was American Paul Valentine, who had drifted from Wicca to Satanism after reading LaVey. Valentine set up the Church of Satanic Liberation in New Haven, Connecticut, in the mid-1980s, attracting a largely female membership to his derivative blend of sex-magic and anti-Christian shtick. It is difficult to define Valentine's Satanic thought beyond being a carbon copy of LaVey's creed combined with a narcissistic need for attention and promiscuous sex. "I'm into the Satanic philosophy because it works, it's cold hearted. It's survivalism." But, being far younger and more photogenic than the reclusive Black Pope, Valentine appeared extensively as the public face and voice of talk-show Satanism. He was honest—"I'm into this for power, my own self-gratification, and I'm in it for the money"—but ultimately represents Satanism in its most vacuous form, heavy metal album covers notwithstanding.[18]

Others drawn to the new creed were more interested in exploring the outer boundaries of alternative religion. LaVey and Aquino had, between them, breached a major cultural taboo. LaVey had introduced the idea of Satan as a symbolic emblem of rebellion into mainstream discourse; Aquino had further extended the boundaries of alternative religion by publicly endorsing the worship (or at least acknowledgement) of a sentient being, be it Set or Satan. Theistic Satanism—which is to say, devil-worship—was (re)born. (It is one of the great ironies of the topic that a special term is needed to identify Satanists who actually believe in the devil.) There are now a number of groups professing to be vehicles for pre-modern devil-worship. Some theistic satanists do not worship the traditional idea of Satan, preferring a gnostic religious vision with Satan representing earthly powers. Some refer to Satan as a vaguely defined force or presence in nature rather than a specific entity or being. Others take a pantheistic approach that acknowledges Lucifer, Satan, Azazel, and other figures as individual entities. Finally, there are also several groups that profess to worship Satan, as traditionally understood by the term *generational satanist.*

Though the idea of genuine devil-worshippers may be chilling, what cannot be overemphasized is just how small and marginal such groups are. Often little more than a Web site and a few members, they stand on the fringe of the fringe, an extraordinarily small proportion of a minority subculture. The widespread dark force of nature interpretation of Satan makes it difficult to differentiate between atheistic and theistic Satanists, as the former often employ identical terms. In addition, the motives of the more dramatic theistic Satanists can be questioned on a number of points. Any movement that thrives on sensationalism and its antagonistic stance towards mainstream values can be expected to move towards greater, more shocking extremes. Eventually the symbolic adoption of Satan simply is no longer dramatic enough, and the next development is entirely predictable. Yet the extent to which the doctrines of many of these organizations fail to develop beyond the standard themes of LaVeyan Satanism also points to a degree of superficiality—the difference is frequently little more that the resubstitution of a literal Satan for a symbolic Satan. Take for example The Cathedral of the Black Goat. Also professing to be a vehicle for traditional satanism, the terminology and ideas are very familiar: "[F]or a species to find a place in the Universe, there was but one law—kill or be killed. The rewards for the strong were survival and enhancement. The consequences for the weak were death and extinction." Modern society has become weak, and Christians, clearly, are to blame "for their attempts to aid the poor, cure the sick, feed the hungry and enrich the feeble-minded."[19] Devil-worship notwithstanding, the core values are all too familiar: exalting the laws of nature as normative values, decrying Christianity as the promulgator of supposedly unnatural values, entrenched hostility to egalitarianism, and an overriding focus on strength versus weakness.

Clearly, the values that Satan represents are of greater concern than his purported worship, as is evident in the continuing fusion of Satanism and the ideology of the extreme right within both atheistic and theistic groups. One notorious organization is The Order of Nine Angels, a secretive English devil-worshipping sect established in the late-1960s or early-1970s. Though its origins are obscured, it is believed that its main propagandist, Anton Long, is in fact eccentric neo-Nazi David Myatt—a claim the ideologically adventurous Myatt, now a militant Muslim, denies.[20] Eschewing its ceremonial trappings of LaVeyan Satanism, Long/Myatt authored a number of periodicals and books that articulated his explicitly fascist and strongly Nietzschean philosophy. Unlike larger organizations, The Order of Nine Angels does not flirt ambiguously with National Socialism. "Adolf Hitler and his movement...seemed to represent a Satanic spirit, an urge to conquer, discover and extend."[21] Incorporating concepts of Aryan superiority alongside pre-Christian pagan spirituality, it exhorts the value of natural energies and maintains a strong individualistic focus. This cosmic occultism is fused with the work of apocalyptic cultural theorists Oswald Spengler and his fascist post–World War II successor Francis Parker Yockey. The focus on a civilization and race in decline lead to its most controversial doctrine, the open support for human sacrifice. These so-called cullings are justified by social Darwinian principles; not only is it a character-building experience for the magician, it also removes detritus from the evolutionary pool. Between these policies and its unabashed racism and antidemocratic bile, The Order of Nine Angels was for a long time the most prominent and recognizable link between Satanism and the extreme right. Though now completely underground, if not defunct, it has influenced numerous other extreme Satanic subgroups throughout the world.

The National Socialism/Satanism fusion has proven popular with other fringe figures. New Zealander Kerry Bolton has been active in independent occult-political circles since the late 1980s. An ex–Temple of Set member, white supremacist, and ardent social Darwinist, his numerous underground zines trumpet a routine list of Satanic bêtes noires: democracy, slave morality, egalitarianism, and the wretchedness of the herd. These publishing ventures have established him as an important figure in the subculture's extremist fringe and connected him with other apocalyptic theorists, despite his geographical isolation. LaVey, Crowley, Nietzsche, and the evils of the purported global plutocracy figure large in Bolton's occult-fascist axis, and he is also active in linking Satanism to nascent European racialist neo-paganism. "Satanism and the heathenism from which it ultimately descends are themselves the products of the archetypes and differentiated psyches of nations and peoples, and they therefore spring from the same 'occultic' or mystical sources as nationalism itself. Nationalism is the political manifestation of a folk's collective unconsciousness; heathenism/Satanism is the spiritual manifestation."[22] His now obsolete international network the Black Order, established in 1994, was named after the SS occult research division, and like many neo-Nazi organizations adopted the Black Sun motif from Wewelsburg Castle as its emblem. He is an active promoter of National Socialist and anti-Semitic literature, including his own work defending the authenticity of *The Protocols of the Elders of Zion*.

Not all Satanists are so severe. In contradistinction to the extremist underground sects are some of the more comic figures of theistic Satanism. Darrick Dishaw (aka Venger Satanis) is high priest of the Cult of Cthulhu, and a specialist in provocative rhetoric: "If human sacrifice was somehow legal…trust me, we would be doing it…an entire Left Hand Path culture would be throwing bodies by the thousands onto ritual altars the size of aircraft carriers!"[23] An ex-Church of Satan member who was expelled in 2005 for his over-enthusiastic fascination with H. P. Lovecraft's Cthulhu Mythos, Wisconsin native Dishaw left amid a flurry of grandiose warnings. "Before the old guard is destroyed by the new (as it must be), the new guard offers its hand in friendship…which the old firmly denies."[24] He energetically promotes his occult treatise *Cult of Cthulhu*, declaring, apropos of the mystical Lord Cthulhu, "We must Awaken the Sleeper Who Dreams Beyond the Emerald Waves." *Cult of Cthulhu* represents the low-tide mark for both Satanism and Lovecraft fetishism:

> The Cult of Cthulhu is where dreamers worship and artists evoke; where unfathomable tentacles protrude into fragile souls, and black monoliths tower over mankind. There are places which surpass any logic; where entities drip ichorous bile from their reptilian flesh as eldritch green opalescent hues dance and murder on the cavern walls of our soul. When it comes to harnessing the Satanic lore within our consciousness, we are mere woefully underdeveloped ape-men. All men are asleep, and knowing this brings us one step closer to Awakening![25]

Events such as Dishaw's departure from the Church of Satan to establish a rival group are common. Amid the delicate egos of Satanism, schisms, vendettas, and bulletin board flame-wars are the norm, not the exception. These exchanges frequently betray a high incidence of narcissistic personality disorders and tenuous attachment to reality. Unsurprisingly, Satanists do not forgive and forget: the Church of Satan is still engaged in a war of words with Paul Valentine after 20 years, though they now make their accusations on Web sites, and he responds in kind using an online videoblog rather than obscure publications.[26]

THE INTERNET AGE

The greatest development within modern Satanism since its inception has without doubt been the rise of the Internet. As with other specialized groups, the Internet has been important to Satanists for its negation of geographic distance between members by enabling instant communication from any point on the globe. For a decentralized subculture with large concentrations of individuals in far-flung locations, it is of particular importance. The Internet has radically changed the landscape of Satanism, engendering an enormous proliferation of Web sites and enabling a small, decentralized subculture to develop into a large, heterogeneous online community.

At the time of writing, Yahoo Groups and the social networking service MySpace are hubs of online activity, along with numerous Web sites and private discussion forums. MySpace is popular, as profiles are highly customizable, catering to the importance given to aesthetic preferences. Satanists on MySpace face regular profile deletions, as the content of their avatars—especially the comments posted between users—frequently contravene MySpace user guidelines and attract complaints. In regard to Web sites, only a few are worth noting. English LaVeyan Satanist Vexen Crabtree hosts Satanism: Description, Philosophies and Justification of Satanism, possibly the best general introduction to the topic available online.[27] New York theistic satanist Diane Vera also hosts an extensively detailed Web site, Theistic Satanism.[28] The Church of Satan site also has a wealth of information available.[29] Web sites often include a large amount of information, as essays originally written for small zines are shared widely and hosted online. There are also a vast number of extremely poor sites. For all the benefits of the Internet age, it has, in regard to Satanism, also engendered a churning maelstrom of delusion and mediocrity. As individuals like Venger Satanis prove, the path to becoming a Satanic leader in the Internet age involves little more than setting up a Web site and declaring oneself a Satanic leader.

The Satanic groups that exist today are numerous and varied, ranging from occult-focused groups to hard line fascist and neo-Nazi organizations to devil-worshippers to vampire and werewolf cults. The most common are those generally in line with the main currents of LaVeyan Satanism. The Sinagogue of Satan, for example, adopts Satan as "the perfect figurehead for a revolutionary religion. His act of rebellion was the first allegory of freedom."[30] The doctrinal similarities also manifest themselves in other ways. Karla LaVey now runs the First Satanic Church, not to be confused with The First Satanic Church of Sydney, The First Church of Satan, The Reformed Church of Satan, or The Modern Church of Satan. The Church of Lucifer is, on the other hand, a theistic organization, as is Diane Vera's polytheistic Church of Azazel, the previously mentioned Cathedral of the Black Goat and its splinter group The Black Goat Cabal, Dark Doctrines, The Cult of Mastema, and the Brotherhood of Satan. Another theistic group is the public service–minded Joy of Satan, which, aside from standard adult religious practices, runs a "Teens for Satan E-Group" for 13–19-year-olds who want "to learn more about and establish a relationship with Satan."[31]

Ideologically extreme groups include Australia's Black Legion Party, an openly fascist yet nonracist organization (for undisclosed reasons fascism is considered acceptable yet racism not), the viciously anti-Semitic Satanic Skinheads and the Heinrich Himmler–dedicated Black Sun 666, the Order of Nine Angels, and Ordo Sinistri Vivendi (Order of the Left Hand Path). Numerous Left Hand Path magickal groups sit at the fringes of Satanism, such as the Ordo Templi Luciferi, OFS Demonolatry, the Church of Satan offshoots the

Therion Temple and the non–blood drinking Temple of the Vampire, the Luciferian Order (aka Ordo Luciferi), and the Lovecraft-oriented Satanic Reds. Nonetheless, even with this proliferation of Satanic groups it can be assumed that the majority of Satanists are not affiliated with any organization and simply adopt Satanic philosophy as their own guide.

Though some of these organizations augment key Satanic ideas with various occult practices and beliefs, many are little more than fresh imprints of the original template. One example is the recently established League of Independent Satanists, a largely Internet-based international society based in America with chapters in Australia, the Netherlands, and Germany. A moderate group, Satanically speaking, the League is a prime example of twenty-first-century Satanism. It still accepts LaVey's work but tries to expand on it with essays exhorting its brand of free thought and adversarial evolution. The results are predictable paeans to Satanically justified individualism, as witnessed by "The Adversary's Manifesto":

> The Writings of LaVey, while dated at times, still contain intense and real truths. You use what you need to use. You are truly Satanic, truly an Adversary, and an Adversary of more than just what you are expected to be Adversarial with. You stand in opposition to ANY form of herdism, any form of mental slavery. You have found in your life what works and what doesn't, you wear what you wish, Read what you wish, Watch or Listen to what you wish, all for the glory of yourself. You don't allow others to dictate anything to you, anything at all.[32]

After 40 years of diabolical theorizing, the primary diagnosis remains unchanged: either enjoy the liberating individualism of Satanism, or remain a dronelike member of the herd. Nonetheless, the League of Independent Satanists had begun to make an impact with its loose confederation approach when it collapsed in mid-2006. One of its founders made the mistake of using his own mailbox as the public contact for the league. He resigned after being targeted by a mail bomb from a religious fundamentalist who had previously bombed an abortion clinic. The league, after making an energetic start, was dissolved and joined The Church of Satanic Brotherhood, The Order of the Black Ram, and countless other short-lived churches in the footnotes of subculture obscurity. Its members went on to form the more secretive, less explicitly Satanic Coven of Janus.

THE BLACK POPE STEPS ASIDE

While the post-1975 Satanic groups proliferated, the movement's architect remained largely unseen. The grottos were gone, *The Cloven Hoof* ever-diminishing in size until its 1988 demise, interviews rarely given. LaVey's next book, a collection of short essays titled *The Devil's Notebook*, did not appear until 20 years after *The Satanic Rituals.* In 1985, LaVey went through a messy court case arising from his separation from Diane (not a divorce, for they were never married). Court documents listed them as "equal partners in establishing, promoting, and operating the business known as the Church of Satan."[33] Diane received a share of the royalties from his book sales for her contribution to their composition. When Diane later sued for failure to honor their separation agreement, LaVey lost the Black House and filed for bankruptcy. During this period, LaVey's new live-in girlfriend and later biographer Blanche Barton (Sharon Densley) took charge of *The Cloven Hoof* until its eventual demise. New Yorker Peter Gilmore and his wife Peggy Nadramia started a new Satanic journal in 1989, *The Black Flame*, which later replaced *The Cloven Hoof* as the equally intermittent official mouthpiece of the Church of Satan.

During the height of the Satanic ritual abuse scare in the late 1980s, LaVey remained on the sidelines. Zeena, then high priestess of the Church of Satan, appeared as his proxy alongside Aquino in the infamous *Geraldo* special episode "Devil Worship: Exposing Satan's Underground." Zeena and her husband Nikolas Schreck quit the Church of Satan in 1990, eventually joining the Temple of Set. Henceforth, Zeena referred to LaVey as her unfather. The unfather became a father for the third time in 1993, with the birth of his only son Satan Xerxes Carnacki LaVey, known as Xerxes. A documentary of the same year, *Speak of the Devil*, shows LaVey as a nostalgic recluse, entranced by the prank books of his childhood and indulging his longstanding fascination with "artificial human companions" (mannequins). In stark contrast to the lively scenes at the Black House in earlier footage, LaVey performs his rituals in an empty house with a single assistant. The company of the mannequins in his Den of Iniquity, he freely admits, is preferable to that of humans. This increasing estrangement from society is reflected in the dire, pathologically misanthropic collection of later essays, *Satan Speaks*. The collection is notable mainly for its attempt to top the salad dressing theory of masculinity with a poem condemning panty shields. LaVey died in 1997, but even his death resulted in controversy, with accusations that his death certificate was altered to make it appear he had passed away on Halloween.

Following LaVey's death, the Church of Satan passed into the control of Barton. She was initially assisted by Karla LaVey, who departed in 1999 to establish her own church. In 2001, a private agreement was reached regarding "the business known as the Church of Satan," and Barton moved aside to allow Peter Gilmore to assume the role of high priest, with Peggy Nadramia later assuming the role of high priestess. The new leadership has undoubtedly reinvigorated the church, and it is once more the dominant voice of Satanism. Now based in New York, the church is energetically promoted, its leadership and members having established an array of magazines, Web sites, podcasts, discussion forums, electronic music groups, and an online store for church-related paraphernalia. These are accompanied by a veritable cottage industry of Satanic publications, mostly collections of previously published essays of long-term members. This recent development has been assisted by the establishment of a press, Scapegoat Publishers, founded by two church members and thus far dedicated to church-related publications. Combined, these endeavors make the Church of Satan again the largest, most active, and high-profile Satanic organization by a considerable margin.

As the high priest of the Church of Satan and heir to LaVey, Gilmore is undoubtedly the most prominent contemporary Satanist. As Magus, Gilmore is media-savvy and takes any opportunity to promote and further legitimize the church through print, television, and radio interviews. A friendly, polite speaker, this surprisingly mellow spokesman is slowly repositioning Satanism, publicly at least, as "skeptical Epicurean atheism." He takes pains not to conform to the expected stereotype of a sulfurous, combative Devil's advocate, and routinely presents Satanism as an exercise in harmless dramatics. "We're [religious organizations] all good showbiz folk, although we're the only one's to admit it." The devil himself is merely "a symbol of freedom, liberty and pride,"[34] and Satanic ritual "a way of ridding yourself of negative feelings…it's self-transformative psychodrama."[35] Expounded by Gilmore, Satanism takes the form of a benign self-help philosophy with a hint of rebellious, fist-to-the-heavens individualism. "We are the adversaries for all the spiritual creeds and all the people who would say you have to take your cue from somebody else, you have to obey. We create a heaven and hell here, in our own existence, and it's completely on it's own shoulders how it's going to come out."[36] Satanism, these interviews affirm, is nothing more than Baphomet existentialism, a harmless creed of atheistic self-reliance augmented by a dash of theatrics.

In 2007 the new high priest released a collection of essays, *The Satanic Scriptures*, through Scapegoat Publishing, assembled from two decades of underground magazine writing and church pieces written during his incumbency.[37] Markedly different in tone from his public appearances, the essays are permeated by an air of relentless, irritable misanthropy. The themes are predictable permutations of LaVeyan topics, dominated by strident declarations of the intellectual and genetic superiority of Satanists, and angry denunciations of the amorphous entity known as the herd. Essays composed since his establishment as high priest are unified by their reactionary nature: Gilmore is largely preoccupied fighting a rearguard action against Church of Satan critics and splinter groups within the—mostly online—Satanic community (although he denies such a community exists). Elsewhere, the heavy emphasis on social Darwinism and crypto-fascism that typified LaVey's thought from the 1980s onward is continued. The central message of *Might Is*

Right is upheld, eugenics programs championed, democracy and egalitarian-ism maligned, and the vast (non-Satanist) majority of humanity systematically belittled and dehumanized.

None of these issues, of course, are raised in mass-media interviews. Gilm-ore's public appearances and published writings clearly cater to two different audiences. To outsiders, the Church of Satan is presented as a mixture of le-gitimate religious practice and innocuous theatrics; internally, it advances an extremist agenda of authoritarian politics, discriminatory demagoguery, and simplistic moral nihilism. The contrast between the two faces of Peter H. Gilmore highlights two issues: Gilmore's desire to publicly protect his in-terests in the Church of Satan, and public ignorance of the topic. Given the opprobrium the name "Satanism" attracts, interviews rarely proceed beyond preliminary discussions of what modern Satanism represents, and that it does not entail devil-worshipping. As a result, the topic and its high priest are often introduced in a light-hearted fashion, as if it would be passé to be concerned about Satanism. Of Gilmore's many interviews as high priest only one—by the science-and-secularism-promoting Centre for Inquiry—has attempted to examine the ideology in any depth and challenged the doctrines of Satanism, with the host noting pointedly: "Game theorists, I think, would have a hey-day with the ethics espoused by Satanists."[38]

SATANISM TODAY

Despite its four-decade existence, Satanism remains a marginal subculture and is not widely understood. In many cases, the general public is unaware of its existence. As such, the difficulties arising from the adoption of the terms *Satanism* and *Satanist* have never ceased. By choosing the name of Western society's primary symbol for evil, LaVey intentionally created a lightning rod for vilification and negative press. Though atheistic Satanists—which is to say, the majority—complain of being repeatedly deemed devil-worshippers, it is extremely disingenuous to expect the world to follow LaVey's redefini-tion of a word that has borne a clear meaning for centuries. If LaVey had declared on Walpurgisnacht 1966 that, henceforth, *child abuser* simply means "someone who says nasty things to children," would his followers really ex-pect nonmembers of the Church of Child Abuse to follow his lead? Obviously not, for the term already has a clear existing meaning, and a single figure cannot arbitrarily redefine a controversial term based on his own authority. Heavily loaded terms such as "child abuser" and "Church of Child Abuse" will mean only one thing to the majority of English speakers, just as "Sa-tanist" and "Church of Satan" do. In all matters semantic, the majority—aka the *herd*—gets the final say. It can only be expected that the term *Satanism* will be associated with worship of the devil.

Another line of defense that Satanists employ when faced with the pre-sumption that they worship the devil is to seek refuge in the term's Hebrew origins. *Satan*, they claim, following LaVey and Gilmore's lead, means "ad-versary" in Hebrew. The proper definition of Satanist is therefore something like "adversary of mainstream values," not "devil-worshipper." This reason-ing is again based on a simple error. A word's origin—its etymology—does not define its meaning today. Words are defined by the way they are used by in a present day context. The term *gay*, for example, experienced a late-twentieth-century shift in meaning, *nice* does not mean "silly" as it did in old French, and *meat* is no longer a general term for "food." The use of the origi-nal meaning of a word as its current meaning is known as the etymological fal-lacy. It is an erroneous focus on word origins and failure to take into account semantic change, the simple fact that, over time, the meanings of words shift. *Satan* no more means "adversary" today than it means "chief prosecuting at-torney," another of its biblical usages. *Satanist* means, in common English usage, "devil-worshipper." The terms *Satanist* and *Satanism*, in fact, appeared much later (1559 and 1869 respectively) and have never meant anything but devil-worshipper/devil-worship. So-called theistic satanists have a far more legitimate and logical claim to the terms than LaVeyan atheists.

Another recurring issue is the Church of Satan's insistence that it alone is the only legitimate Satanic church. All others are merely pretenders to the throne, *pseudo*-Satanists. This injunction, originating with LaVey, is all-encompassing: "Anyone who resists affiliation with the Church of Satan yet draws from it for any reason, personal or financial, is not independent, only parasitic."[39] This attempt to monopolize the ideology and doctrines of mod-ern Satanism may be an empty pose, but the Church of Satan maintains it resolutely. It is certainly the predominant organization within the subculture and draws a certain diabolical legitimacy from LaVey and his bible, but an ideology can hardly be copyrighted. Once popularized, it exists for anyone to adopt, adapt, and utilize. To claim that anyone who doesn't hold one of the Church of Satan's laminated red membership cards is not a Satanist is both impractical and illogical, something akin to Comrade Stalin insisting that Chairman Mao is not a *real* communist. Or, to use a religious analogy, a Catholic insisting that a Protestant is a *pseudo*-Christian. A Satanist, then, is anyone who self-identifies with the general concept enough to declare him-self a Satanist. Adherence to an ideology does not require membership in any given sect. The great irony of this internal bickering is that the general public would consider a Satanist who doesn't believe in Satan a *pseudo*-Satanist.

As is apparent from the organizations discussed in this chapter, many Satanic churches are extremely derivative. Accordingly, few individuals or groups other than LaVey have had any substantial or lasting influence. Even the Temple of Set's influence has been limited to its own members and the more underground currents of long-term adherents, as have the writings of Anton Long and Kerry Bolton. For many Satanists, the field begins and ends with *The Satanic Bible* and LaVey's other works. This fact is reflected in the enormous levels of plagiarism of his writings within smaller Satanic organizations, few of whom appear to realize that reproducing passages from LaVey's work without proper acknowledgement is copyright infringement. The Church of Satan polices its copyrighted material carefully and is unyielding in forcing the removal of offending content. Nonetheless, modern Satanism was born of plagiarism and intellectual expropriation, and the tradition continues apace.

To a large degree, modern Satanism has simply trodden water for 40 years, relying on empty denunciations of herdism and so-called sheeple to buttress its appeal, endlessly reformulating the same principles with which proceedings commenced in the 1960s. With the possible exception of the Temple of Set and a few rare examples, it is difficult to find a Satanic organization whose key doctrines differ from the Church of Satan in any substantive way. Though many groups claim to be non-LaVeyan, every Satanic organization invariably appeals to fallacious notions of natural law, the oppositional pedigree of the label "Satanist," pathological hostility to Christianity, and disdain for equality as their primary justifications. None of the various strands of modern Satanism represent any radical departure from original principles. Rather, there has been a process of synthesis with other traditions, a syncretistic augmentation of the core ideology with compatible principles and beliefs. As Gilmore notes, Satanism "is a system without frozen dogma, being inherently flexible."[40] As such, it is readily embellished, as the analysis of Satanism and the occult tradition will readily show. The National Socialism/paganism connection is the one area in which Satanism has moved beyond its origins, by divesting itself of the more theatrical elements and following the underlying ideology to its logical extremes. In doing so, fascist/neo-Nazi forms of Satanism generally downplay the staunch individualism of LaVeyan (libertarian) Satanism, instead stressing racial and/or national identity. Yet early-1970s neo-Nazi connections and splinter groups illustrate the ease with which Satanism and the politics of the extreme right are fused. Rather than a reforming of Satanism, this phenomenon is primarily an extension of preexisting themes.

From the central ideas popularized by LaVey in the 1960s, a widespread heterogeneous subculture has grown. The original organization still defines the field, though by heritage and possession of the principle brand name rather than innovation. Nonetheless, it is extremely unlikely that any group will ever supplant the Church of Satan. The Temple of Set continues its more low-key exploration of the occult and Egyptian mythology. In 1996, Aquino retired as head, ceding control to Don Webb, who was in turn succeeded by Magistra Patricia Hardy in 2004. Nicholas and Zeena Schreck departed the temple and America in 2002, moving to Europe and establishing The Storm, but have since faded from view. In America, Zeena's estranged son Stanton LaVey, born to the teenage Zeena in 1978, promotes himself as a dynastic Satanist, a member of the first family of Satanism. Thus far, he has done little more than trade on his grandfather's name and court celebrities (Marilyn Manson and Glenn Danzig were present at his 2006 wedding). If the family tradition holds, his teenage uncle Xerxes will one day try to claim his family heritage. Regardless, Satanic churches will form and splinter, threats and curses will be exchanged, and heartfelt paeans to egoism and individualism penned. Above all, an unspecifiable entity known as the herd will be vilified and pilloried, ad infinitum, in the sacred cause of convincing Satanists that they are unique.

The Left Hand Path: Satanism and the Occult Tradition

And he will separate the people one from another as a shepherd separates the sheep from the goats. He will put the sheep on his right and the goats on his left.

—Matthew 25:32–33

What constitutes the difference between a Satanic ceremony and a play presented by a theatre group? Often very little.

—Anton LaVey, *The Satanic Rituals*, p. 18

Occult Studies is a haven for the impractical and inept, just as other useless tradesmen find asylum in other arenas.

—Anton LaVey, *Satan Speaks!*, p. 9

"The driving force behind black magic is hunger for power." Thus Richard Cavendish began his notable study of the occult tradition's dark underbelly, *The Black Arts*. The magical practices Cavendish addresses are not the standard fare of anthropological studies, the naïve world of fertility rites, traditional superstitions, and folklore. Neither are they the love potions, charms, crystals, good luck, or healing spells of white magic. Rather, the aim of black magic is to tap into the secret, hidden, and frequently malevolent power of the cosmos to further one's own ends. In doing so it eschews the selfless goals of white magic in favor of personal empowerment. Black magic is the ultimate forbidden fruit, the attempt to gain knowledge that will place the practitioner on a par with the divine. "Carried to its furthest extreme,"

Cavendish writes, "the black magician's ambition is to wield supreme power over the entire universe, to make himself a god."[1] The relevance to modern Satanism hardly needs to be stated.

ORIGINS

The Western occult tradition can be traced back to its origins in early Neo-platonism, Gnosticism, and Hermeticism. One of its primary roots is Plato's assertion that the world we see, that of material objects, is merely illusion. To Plato, the world most people perceive is nothing more than transitory and imperfect replications of a hidden, almost divine realm of endless, unchangeable forms. His belief that ultimate truth lay somehow beyond the material world was pervasively influential. The religious philosophy of Neo-platonism developed from its namesake's philosophy to describe an all-encompassing metaphysical unity of reality in a vast, incomprehensible order described as the One. For the individual, unity with this order could only be reached through mystical experience, and only by the most dedicated. Gnosticism, with its focus on gnosis, knowledge, and a dualist description of the cosmos, was also heavily influenced by Platonic thought, although it stressed the corruption of the material plane and purity of the spiritual. In the pessimistic vision of Gnosticism, the aim was to release the soul from its fleshly prison through the acquisition of knowledge. These schools of thought were readily combined with the mystical doctrines of Hermeticism. The flexible spiritual pantheism of Hermeticism incorporated an optimistic outlook promising the primordial wisdom of the ancient world, particularly that of Egypt. The primary works of the *Corpus Hermeticum* are attributed to the mythic Hermes Trismegistus, a purported contemporary of Moses, thus giving the texts similar sanctity to the Bible—to their enthusiasts at least. It is from Trismegistus's alchemical text the *Emerald Tablet* that the occult dictum "As above, so below," the foundation of astrology, derives.

Together, these philosophies articulated a captivating vision of a hidden world and hidden powers behind the material plane. With the coming of the Renaissance, many of these long-neglected doctrines, particularly the Hermetic writings, were rediscovered. They were reconciled with Old and New Testaments by use of a Christianized version of Kabbalah, medieval Jewish mysticism. Kabbalah, in this interpretation, validated Christian belief; witness Pico della Mirandola's much cited refrain "no science can better convince us of the divinity of Jesus Christ than magic and the Kabbalah."[2] Scholar-magicians such as Cornelius Agrippa (1486–1535) and John Dee (1527–1608) were crucial to this development, promoting a blend of astrology, alchemy, magic, esoteric knowledge, and philosophy. Agrippa's encyclopedic *Three Books of Occult Philosophy* constituted a systematic account of occult (literally "hidden") knowledge. He emphasized the assertion of will as central to achieving magical results. "[H]e that works in Magick must be of a constant belief, be credulous, and not at all doubt of attaining the effect."[3] Agrippa's Welsh follower, Dee, was an eminent Elizabethan mathematician and astrologer, immortalized by Shakespeare as Prospero and King Lear. As pious Christian Kabbalists, Agrippa and Dee were practitioners of distinctly white magic, despite rumors that gave them reputations as the blackest of conjurers.

Dee is the first explicit intersection of the occult and Satanism, arising from LaVey's inclusion of Dee's Enochian Keys in *The Satanic Bible*. Dee, with the assistance of associate Edward Kelly, claimed to be able to summon angels through séances. The results of Dee and Kelly's endeavors were recorded in notebooks in the Enochian language, supposedly a proto-Hebrew script that God used to create the world. Both this claim and the integrity of his assistant, the seer Kelly, the only one to commune with the spirits, have been challenged repeatedly. In regard to Satanism, however, the means of composition is of little consequence. The Satan-exhorting interpretation of the Enochian Keys in *The Satanic Bible* is assuredly a complete contradiction of any spiritual revelation that Dee experienced or wished to experience. Although his studies made him acutely aware of the dangers of contacting the celestial realm of angels and divine figures, he had complete faith that the Kabbalah would protect him from demonic interference. LaVey regardless declared, on his own authority, that Dee's version was a whitewash. LaVey's translation alone exhibits the "true Enochian Calls, as received from an unknown hand." Hitherto, their meaning had remained hidden, "because occultists to this day have lain ill with metaphysical constipation." Despite the transparency and sheer outrageousness of these claims, diabolical versions of "the Satanic paeans of faith" have become standard occult texts of any Satanic group, and remain widespread, presumably from overuse of metaphysical laxatives.[4]

THE OCCULT IN THE MODERN ERA

Following the work of the Christian Kabbalists, the occult became, to a large extent, the domain of Rosicrucian philosophy. This seventeenth-century development was supposedly based on the rediscovered writings of the mythic Christian Rosencreutz. In the immediate post-Renaissance era, this chimerical movement was the dominant magical school throughout Europe, particularly in the rapidly spreading Masonic orders. Though falling out of favor in the time of the Enlightenment, increasing secularization in the mid-to-late nineteenth century saw a widespread revival of alternative spirituality and occult interests. At the forefront of this revival was Madame Blavatsky's Theosophical Society in America and Europe, the French occult revival, and the birth of the Hermetic Order of the Golden Dawn in England. These three interrelated developments contain the seeds of most forms of modern occultism, and are undoubtedly modern Satanism's key magical predecessors.

The key figure of the French occult revival was Éliphas Lévi (Alphonse Louis Constant, 1810–1875), an influential, if occasionally fanciful, popularizer of magic. Expelled from a Catholic seminary for heresy, he turned to private research of the occult. Lévi's attempt to systematize the occult tradition resulted in three central ideas: that there is a correspondence between man and the universe, of microcosm to macrocosm; that human will, properly controlled, is capable of anything; and that the material world was only one level of reality, and all of nature was permeated by Astral Light, a cosmic fluid that could be molded according to will. Though his works were outrageously Romantic and full of overblown prose, his insights stirred the following generation of magicians.

Most importantly for Satanism, Lévi established the Baphomet and its web of dubious historical associations. Represented as the Sabbath he-goat, the Baphomet is related to numerous occult and religious precedents. Legend—more accurately, slander—holds that the Baphomet played a central role in the corruptions of the Knights Templar, where its origin as the medieval name for the false idol Mohammed was critical. (LaVey repeated this myth even more blatantly in his bible, writing "The symbol of Baphomet was used by the Knights Templar to represent Satan."[5]) It had also, according to Lévi, been worshipped in ancient Egypt as the goat of Mendes. He further linked it to the Jewish scapegoat ritual, as the symbolic bearer of people's sins, and to the pagan rites of the Witches' Sabbath. Lévi's Baphomet was, when these disparate strands were opportunistically drawn together, the multifaceted emblem of occult knowledge. For his coup de grâce he combined it with the pentagram, again with no historical precedent, and placed it on the cover of his seminal *Doctrine and Ritual of High Magic* in 1854. The text's description of its complex symbolism gives an indication of Lévi's approach:

> The goat which is represented in our frontispiece bears upon its forehead the Sign of the Pentagram with one point in the ascendant, which is sufficient to distinguish it as a symbol of the light. Moreover, the sign of occultism is made with both hands, pointing upward to the white moon of Chesed, and downward to the black moon of Geburah. This sign expresses the perfect concord between mercy and justice. One of the arms is feminine and the other masculine, as in the androgyne of Khunrath, those attributes we have combined with those of our goat, since they are one and the same symbol. The torch of intelligence burning between the horns is the magical light of universal equilibrium; it is also the type of the soul, exalted above matter, even while cleaving to matter, as the flame cleaves to the torch. The monstrous head of the animal expresses horror of sin, for which the material agent, alone responsible, must alone and for ever

bear the penalty, because the soul is impassible in its nature and can suffer only by materializing. The caduceus, which, replaces the generative organ, represents eternal life; the scale-covered belly typifies water; the circle above it is the atmosphere, the feathers still higher up signify the volatile; lastly, humanity is depicted by the two breasts and the androgyne arms of this sphinx of the occult sciences.[6]

Though Lévi's composition was controversial, both in the visual elements it combined and the different sources it drew from, his influence and authority saw it become an iconic image. The Baphomet/pentagram combination is now commonly regarded as an ancient representation of Satan, and serves as the primary symbol of modern Satanism. Prior to Lévi, there is only a collection of unrelated legends.

Spurred on by Lévi's repopularization and clarification of the occult, the famous Hermetic Order of the Golden Dawn was founded in England in 1888. The order was highly influential during its existence until the mid 1920s, its legacy continuing through the various splinter groups that both caused and arose out of its eventual collapse. The Golden Dawn drew from all preceding occult traditions, promoting an eclectic blend of ceremonial magic, ancient Egyptian religion, theurgy, Kabbalah, Theosophy and Enochian Magic. Its ranks included some of the most instrumental occult practitioners of modern times: the eccentric S. L. MacGregor Mathers, the pioneering Buddhist Allan Bennett, the prolific A. E. Waite (translator of the preceding Lévi quote), and the even more prolific Aleister Crowley. Through its offshoots and the students of its iconic members—Isralie Regardie, Kenneth Grant, Gerald Gardner, Austin Osman Spare—the Golden Dawn can be linked to virtually every magic or occult movement of the twentieth century.

Crowley, the Great Beast, is without doubt the nexus point in Satanism's relationship to the occult. Crowley's biography and oeuvre mesh extraordinarily well with the doctrines of Satanism: his legendary nomadic lifestyle, contempt for ordinary people and dominant moral codes, and the elitist Nietzschean overtones of his philosophizing, particularly the brutal antihumanitarianism of the social Darwinism–tinged *The Book of the Law* and *The Law Is for All*. Magically, his focus on humanity's sexual nature, central to his practice of sex-magick, blends seamlessly with the Satanic notion of man as a carnal animal—the extra "k" in *magick* represents *kteis*, the Greek term for the female genitals. Crowley, like LaVey after him, championed a philosophy of self-development and romantic individualism, as evinced by his famous dictum "Every man and every woman is a star." He refigured the occult for the post-Freud era by adopting a psychological point of view, promising the attainment of higher levels of consciousness through ritual practice, and placing the onus for advancement on the individual. "Man is ignorant of the nature of his own being and powers...Man is capable of being, and using, anything which he perceives, for everything that he perceives is in a certain sense part of his being."[7] Like Lévi before him, Crowley made a concerted attempt to clarify and articulate the central doctrines of magical practice, thus making the field more accessible—another factor in his continued popularity.

Crowley is also influential by having proclaimed himself to be a brother of the left hand path. The first to claim this tradition, he was presumably embracing Madame Blavatsky's pejorative use of the phrase "left hand path" to describe immoral religions. Blavatsky had encountered the term in relation to Tantra's left hand path, *Vamachara*, which involves heterodox practices such as animal sacrifice and the use of intoxicants. The label was new, but the taint was not. The left has a long pedigree of associations with evil. Babylonian omens held the left side to be bad and the right side good. Homer recorded similar omens in the direction birds flew—to the right was favorable, to the left unfavorable. Left-handedness too has long been stigmatized, as well as linked to homosexuality and sexual perversions, and is in many non-European cultures connected with toilet practices. In a contemporary context, use of the phrase Left Hand Path is a strong statement of self-identification by those adopting it. To its champions, it represents the exercise of free thought, individualism, and intelligence for self-empowerment, while denoting a departure from what is referred to as the Right Hand Path, those traditional religions that focus on altruism and submission to divine authority. As such, it mirrors the split between black and white magic. Followers of more traditional faiths deny that the dichotomy exists altogether, as it is a recently adopted judgment with no genuine pedigree and is only recognized by partisans.

SATANISM AND MAGIC

LaVey is explicit in regard to where his religion fits into the occult tradition: "Satanism is not a white light religion; it is a religion of the flesh, the mundane, the carnal—all of which are ruled by Satan, the personification of the Left Hand Path."[8] With the combined influence of LaVey and Crowley, use of the term has become widespread. Elements of LaVey's understanding of magic are, however, different. He states that there is no difference between white and black forms, as the former's selfless goals are based on the fallacy of altruism. "White magic is supposedly utilized only for good or unselfish purposes, and black magic, we are told, is used only for selfish or 'evil' reasons. Satanism draws no such dividing line. Magic is magic, be it used to help or hinder."[9] The target of this doctrine is most likely the rapid growth of the neo-pagan movement (Wicca) at the time of modern Satanism's establishment. Based on the work of Gerald Gardner, particularly his 1954 work *Witchcraft Today*, Wicca shares Satanism's origins in the Golden Dawn, the theorizing of Crowley, and *grimoires* such as *The Greater Key of Solomon*. Beyond this common heritage, the two diverge completely, with Wiccans regarded by Satanists as travelers of the so-called Right Hand Path. Satanists, Wiccans counter, drag magical practices into disrepute with their unprincipled egoism. Christians, generally, consider them both agents of Satan.

Despite some doctrinal changes, LaVey's definition of magic echoes Crowley's closely. Magic, *The Satanic Bible* states, is "The change in situations or events in accordance with one's will, which would, using normally accepted methods, be unchangeable."[10] Likewise, all forms of Satanism also maintain the traditional distinction between lesser and greater magic. Lesser magic is the most commonly employed form. As Temple of Set literature describes it, "Lesser black magic is the influencing of beings, processes, or objects in the objective universe by the application of obscure physical or behavioral laws." It is a manipulative activity, whereby one achieves one's will by surreptitious means. "Lesser black magic is an impelling (encouraging, convincing, increasing of probability) measure, not a compelling (forcing, making inevitable) one. The object is to make something happen without expending the time and energy to make it happen through direct cause-and-effect."[11] Influencing someone to do one's bidding, for example, is viewed as an example of lesser black magic. Far less common, greater black magic is the act of actually causing change by willpower alone. As it is harder to predict and control, and the physical and mental demands are much more pronounced, it is used only in the most important circumstances. Satanists are, in general, far less likely to claim any substantial ability in greater black magic.

Magic is primarily used through ritual application. *The Satanic Bible* outlines three ritual practices: lust, compassion, and destruction. In keeping with the modern occult renaissance, the emphasis is strongly focused on the psychological aspect of ritual practice. The setting for ritual practice is significantly detailed, with careful attention paid to aesthetics: the atmosphere and decoration of the room, the use of appropriate ritual apparatus, and clothing of the participants are all important. The location of Satanic ritual practice is described as a "intellectual decompression chamber,"[12] which can be interpreted as a purely psychological endeavor, with no supernatural factors. In LaVeyan Satanism, the ritual is simply a form of catharsis, with all significance purely subjective. LaVey's magical theory is uniformly focused on the emotional experience of the practitioner. Rituals can be public or private, but the main criteria for success is intensity of the magician's experience.

Despite remaining broadly in line with the occult tradition, Satanism makes some changes in specific areas. *The Satanic Bible* is explicitly opposed to drug use and animal sacrifice, injunctions that directly contradict the established occult tradition. Crowley, for example, indulged at times in animal sacrifice and almost continually in drug use—one widely repeated quote from

The Book of the Law is particularly unambiguous: "To worship me take wine and strange drugs...they shall not harm ye at all."[13] The medieval *grimoires* (magical texts, literally "grammars") often contain rites that involve the ritual slaughter of a goat or chicken, with occasional ambiguous references to human sacrifice. Blood was commonly believed to hold the animal's life energy and was therefore an important part of the ritual. The use of stimulants was also seen as a valid way to achieve higher spiritual consciousness and escape from material forms. Prohibiting these practices was no doubt necessary to launch an openly Satanic movement, but they are nonetheless indicative of the way LaVey diluted traditional occult doctrines. Though the use of alcohol was accepted, and is in fact a component of a number of rituals, the drug prohibition became official policy—of his church at least—justified as the need to be clear-headed. Outside the Church of Satan, these prohibitions are not necessarily followed.

When LaVey does discuss ritual human sacrifice he stresses that it is a symbolic act in the form of a curse or hex. To this end, the most important and commonly used Satanic ritual is *The Satanic Bible*'s destruction ritual, although its symbolic nature tends to become obscured in the hot winds of its author's prose. The destruction ritual is performed by the focusing of one's will and hatred on an effigy of the subject. The effigy can be a physical representation or simply their name written on paper. The target is selected with predictable Satanic arbitrariness. "The question arises, 'Who, then, would be considered a fit and proper human sacrifice, and how is one qualified to pass judgment on such a person?' The answer is brutally simple. Anyone who has unjustly wronged you."[14] For the typical Satanist, the ritual provides a satisfying illusion of empowerment and control:

> The main thing that I got from [LaVey's] philosophy was that it provided a healthy way for an individual to deal with and channel his hatred. Since I read this text, I have a very fun way to deal with all of these people who *irk* me. What I do is, I make effigies of them, and destroy them. And I think it's a really healthy thing to do with your hate, [to] destroy the effigies of your enemies, and hopefully the same thing will happen to them.[15]

Most non-Satanists would argue that the continual focus on vengeance and hatred can hardly be healthy. Remorse, obviously, is not a Satanic option: "If your curse provokes their actual annihilation, rejoice that you have been instrumental in ridding the world of a pest!"[16] LaVey's only proviso was the prohibition of the ritual sacrifice of animals and children.

The most dramatic and notorious Satanic ritual is the Black Mass. The traditional Christian Mass is a highly ritualized affair that can be regarded as a form of ceremonial magic. In the medieval era, it was often performed with the purpose of affecting the weather, crops, livestock, or health of the community. On occasion, wayward priests inserted the name of a living man into the Mass for the dead, transforming it into a curse and prefiguring its occult use. The inversion of the Christian Mass, the Black Mass, is both a mockery and a transformation of the Christian custom. Christian symbols are inverted, the Mass is recited backwards, and the practitioners' deity displaces God as the locus. The use of naked women as altars and the highly sexualized proceedings mock traditional religious conservatism while promoting opposing values. Though its adoption by modern Satanism creates a link to the Hellfire clubs and the slanders blighting the Cathars and Templars, LaVey's reinterpretation denies that the Black Mass is a vehicle for mere blasphemy. Rather it is a psychodrama whose "prime purpose is to reduce or negate stigma acquired through past indoctrination. It is also a vehicle for retaliation against unjust acts perpetrated in the name of Christianity."[17] Once former followers have seen the ceremony so comprehensively disparaged, this rationale claims, they will no longer be affected by its traditional enactment.

The performance recorded for the documentary *Satanis: The Devil's Mass* in 1970 now probably exceeds even the famed debauchery in Huysmans' *La Bas* as the most famous exemplar of the Black Mass. Despite its age, excerpts from the Church of Satan performance feature in almost every documentary on Satanism, the devil, or the occult. In his expansive work *Church of Satan*, Aquino describes LaVey-led Black Masses from the same era ending in the traditional manner, with the insertion of the Eucharist into the vagina of the woman serving as a living altar—a detail inexplicably not included in *Satanis*. Church of Satan performances became less regular after LaVey stopped using the Black House for church purposes in the early 1970s, and the Temple of Set does not afford the Black Mass the same importance. The largest recent performance was a High Mass at the Church of Satan's 40th anniversary celebration in 2006. In keeping with the church's current direction, it was presented more as a theatrical event, including the media-friendly "all religion is showbiz and we're the only religion that admits that" disclaimer from Magus Gilmore.[18]

With the focus on the subjective and psychological experience of ritual practice, aesthetics and symbolism are as important to Satanism as the rites themselves. Aesthetics are considered a form of lesser magic, a means of manipulating other's opinions, important enough that "Lack of Aesthetics" is listed as one of the Nine Satanic Sins.[19] Accordingly, a considerable array of iconography has been developed and appropriated, including pagan, occult, and Nazi symbols. The most recognizable is unquestionably the pentagram. Though historically used by ancient Sumerians, Judaism, the Pythagoreans, Christianity, occultists, and Freemasons with no demonic connotations, the five-pointed star has undergone a radical shift in meaning. Its association with the devil is a twentieth-century development, following its adoption by Lévi and Crowley. Yet even they used the more historically common pentagram, with one point at the top. The devil-worship notion is more a matter of bad reputation than practice.

Satanism has adopted the Baphomet with the inverted pentagram, a combination that first appeared in early twentieth-century Europe. The three points, now on the bottom, are said to symbolize the inversion of the holy trinity, a visual representation of the renunciation of Christian values. From an occult perspective, the inversion attracts evil forces and the two points at the top represent the horns of the Sabbat goat. The Sabbat goat inside the inverted pentagram—called the Sigil of Baphomet—is the primary symbol of the Church of Satan. The writing of the outer circle reads "Leviathan" in Hebrew, drawing a further association with Satan via the beast of Revelation. The pentagram's appropriation by the Church of Satan in the 1960s cemented its change in meaning. With a legion of heavy metal bands following suit, the symbol is now widely regarded as an ancient symbol for evil. The inverted pentagram is, however, not unprecedented, and not necessarily Satanic, though any chance for rehabilitation has assuredly long passed.

NAZI OCCULTISM AND NEO-PAGANISM

An equally important aspect of Satanic iconography comes from the more recent adoption of various pagan runes. The term *rune* means "secret," and they have long been believed to harbor magical properties. Runes associated with pagan practices were repressed by medieval Christianity as devilish symbols. The most widely appropriated is the Wolfsangle, particularly popular within the Church of Satan. Represented by a single line with a sharp hook at each end, the Wolfsangle (or Wolf's Hook) has origins in Germanic folk legends and is still used, usually in a vertical form, in various civic coats of arms in Germany. Though there are many different permutations of the design, the horizontal form the Church of Satan employs—with an extra vertical bar in the centre—is identical to that used by the Hitler Youth and a number of SS divisions. It is now widely adopted by neo-Nazi and white supremacist organizations. Although it is presented as a traditional Germanic rune, it is often used by Satanists in combination with the Totenkopf, or Death's Head, another notorious symbol of the SS.

The adoption of SS symbols is unsurprising given Satanism's sustained courtship with all aspects of Nazism. One recent work on modern Satanism, Gavin Baddeley's *Lucifer Rising*, devotes an entire chapter to Nazi occultism and the origins of *völkisch* racism (populist/folk racism), though with little explanation of the relevance of either to the topic at hand. Baddeley makes the redundant observation that Nazism wasn't Satanic, but he fails to address the issue of why Satanists are recurrently drawn to Nazism.[20] LaVey claimed to have gone to Germany with his uncle in 1945 and come into contact with remnants of the Nazi occult mindset. There he watched Nazi *Schauerfilmen* (horror films) at a Berlin command post. As no evidence exists in support of this story, and there is more than a little in opposition,[21] it is best regarded as another questionable addition to the legend of the Black Pope. The Das Tier-drama ritual in *The Satanic Rituals* is supposedly an artifact of Nazi occultism based on this visit, though its error-strewn German indicates otherwise.

Nazi occultism has been an area of intense interest and research in the postwar era, although not just by historians, but by occultists and conspiracy theorists. Many theorists feel that occult forces can help account for the Nazi's rapid rise to power and dramatic early war successes. The highly ceremonial nature of Nazi rallies gave them a quasi-religious aura, and the roots of their racialist doctrines can be traced, in part, to the various *völkisch* movements (populist folklore/nationalist groups) that preceded the Nazi party. Hitler himself had great faith in astrology, and his mesmerizing public performances gave rise to whispers of secret occult influences. Key Nazi figures Rudolf Hess, Heinrich Himmler, and Alfred Rosenberg all shared a deep interest in the occult. Heavily contested rumors detail legends about the Holy Grail, the Spear of Destiny, the Tibetan roots of the Aryan race, and the lost city of Atlantis. Various highly speculative commentaries have been written on these topics, and the influence and importance of the occult on Nazism is easily, and frequently, overstated.[22] As a result, "Nazi occult beliefs" more often denotes occult beliefs *about* the Nazis than occult beliefs *of* the Nazis.

Aquino's 1982 pilgrimage to the heart of Nazi Aryan spirituality at Himmler's Wewelsburg Castle is another facet of Satanism's fascination with the topic. Himmler was a devoted occultist who thought he was the reincarnation of medieval Ottonian King Henry I. He envisaged his Bavarian SS city as the center of the thousand-year Reich. The castle's north tower, containing the ritual chamber and crypt, was to be the very center of the world. The Black Sun (Schwarze Sonne—a large sun wheel with twelve jagged spokes) symbol that adorned the marble floor in the north tower's Gruppenführer hall has become the primary symbol of neo-Nazi esotericism. Its relative obscurity, to those unfamiliar with SS exotica, means it can be displayed without fear of its Nazi heritage being recognized, particularly in countries where the Swastika is outlawed. It is widely adopted by Satanists, presumably for similar reasons.

Nazi race theory, such as in the works included in the Temple of Set reading list, were also an important part of the regime's occult beliefs. Rosenberg's racial theories, drawing from Madison Grant's but more philosophical in nature (to compensate for his lack of scientific expertise), were central in the program to justify Nazi myths of racial purity and genealogy. These myths can ultimately be traced, via the *völkisch* Ariosophists, to the writings of legendary occult fraud Madame Blavatsky. Her work *The Secret Doctrine* (1888), based on her purported discovery of a monastery hidden under a mountain in Tibet, established the idea of a race called the Aryans, the fifth of seven purported root-races. Blavatsky claimed that the Aryan race was over a million years old. It had descended from the Atlanteans, the fourth root-race, who had perished on their mid-Atlantic continent in a great flood. She associated the Aryans with the Swastika, an ancient symbol of the sun and good fortune. The Nazi interpretation of Blavatsky's mystical racism established the Aryans at the pinnacle of the world's racial hierarchy, and forever dragged the Swastika into disrepute.

Closely related to the Satanists' interest in Nazi occultism and racialism is the increasing engagement with the modern revival of Norse paganism. Germanic and Nordic beliefs were central to the nineteenth-century *völkisch* movement. They have resurged in America and Europe in the post–World War II era through the Ásatrú, Odinist, and Wotansvolk movements. While some of the numerous pagan cults are more concerned with explorations of spirituality and cultural identity, others are simply fronts for virulent racism, deeply entwined with extreme nationalism, neo-Nazism, and white supremacy. Historian of Nazi esotericism Nicholas Goodrick-Clarke characterizes the Odinist movement as a wholesale rejection of the Christian heritage of the West. "Regarding Christianity itself as a Jewish cultural product with its origins in the Middle East, the Odinist movement articulates an unabashed racial paganism, invoking the gods of the Norse and Teutonic pantheons."[23] Wotansvolk, for example, is also an explicitly racist religion propounded (or reestablished from older forms) by prominent American nationalists David and Katja Lane and Ron McVan. Wotan, an acronym for "Will of the Aryan Nation," is adopted as an ancient archetype that represents the principal pre-Christian Germanic deity (known as Odin in Scandinavia). It is regarded as a link to the collective unconscious of the Aryan race and tied directly to ideals of genetic superiority and purity. As David Lane writes, "Wotan awakens the racial soul and genetic memory. He stirs our blood."[24]

The racialist theories of contemporary paganism are influenced by the thought of psychologist Carl Jung, especially his complementary notions of collective unconscious and archetypes. Jung theorized that people have pre-conscious psychic dispositions, a collective unconscious passed on from generation to generation. "In addition to our immediate consciousness, which is of a thoroughly personal nature and which we believe to be the only empirical psyche…there exists a second psychic system of a collective, universal, and impersonal nature which is identical in all individuals."[25] One facet of this universal unconscious are the archetypes, impersonal and universal patterns that structure our behavior and thoughts. "The concept of the archetype, which is an indispensable correlate of the idea of the collective unconscious, indicates the existence of definite forms in the psyche which seem to be present always and everywhere."[26] Jung claimed that many gods and mythic figures were embodiments of archetypes, a list that included Christ, Dionysus, Apollo, Nietzsche's Zarathustra, and Orpheus.

Contemporary pagan thought draws from Jung's 1936 article "Wotan." This piece directly linked the power of Adolf Hitler and National Socialism with the archetypical figure of Wotan, using the latter to explain Hitler's success and the reawakening of ancient tribalism. "The Hitler movement literally brought the whole of Germany to its feet, from five-year-olds to veterans, and produced the spectacle of a nation migrating from one place to another. Wotan the wanderer was on the move."[27] Though Jung was wary of Hitlerism, and in fact warned of the dangers of resurgent Wotanism, his theories have been adopted as an intellectual legitimization of National Socialism as a form of ancestral wisdom and culture based on a pre-Christian racial subconscious.

The incorporation of Jungian archetypes has seen the introduction of various pagan figures into the Satanic lexicon, including Loki, Fenris, Wotan, Odin, and Pan. In addition, any of the dozens of names that appear in *The Satanic Bible*'s list of Infernal Names can be invoked as representing a specific archetype. These range from the Indian goddess Kali to Zoroastrianism's Ahriman, the Babylonian Nergal to the Russian Tchort (devil)—even Dracula is included. The dramatis personae of these archetypal figures align well with the general themes of Satanism, as invoking ancient or pagan gods also invokes their long tradition of resistance to Christianity. The European pantheon represents a particularly direct challenge to Christian cultural hegemony. Early Christians regarded the northern gods as masks worn by Satan, which they thought accounted for the determined resistance to the spread of the Roman church in the Middle Ages. In one legendary incident in 782 C.E., Charlemagne beheaded 4,000 Saxons for their refusal to recant German polytheism in favor of Christianity. In a contemporary context, Satan becomes merely another archetype, one that specifically represents the laws of nature, an interpretation entirely in keeping with early Christian and Gnostic thought.

Neo-pagan influences are widely seen in smaller Satanic groups, as well as the Temple of Set's Order of the Trapezoid. In the Church of Satan, Gilmore's *The Satanic Scriptures* (2007) contains a ritual named the Rite of Ragnarök, based on the apocalyptic end of the world battle in Norse mythology—a central theme in neo-paganism. The text notes that the rite is not to be construed as "in any way representative of ancient or neo-pagan beliefs or practices."[28] It is, nonetheless, presented among a medley of pagan runes (including a circular Swastika), references National Socialist doctrines with the phrase "We glory in discipline and strength through joy,"[29] and incorporates familiar neo-pagan themes:

Time to shatter the bonds of OUR Gods,
to loose the primal powers that bore our

ancestors. March forth to total war. Smite
the worshippers of the weak and frail! Fill
your hearts with berserker frenzy! Mind
and force shall reign supreme. The time
has come, to cleanse and purify, a time for
birth, spilling an ocean of blood![30]

In "Apocalypse Now," another essay in the same collection, Gilmore contradicts his own disclaimer, writing "we are truly in the 'end times'...The
best is awakening, throwing off two thousand years of slumber to once again
clear the dross and re-establish the rule of fang and claw. Fenris' chains have
been shattered and his Jaws shall crush the feeble crucifix to splinters."[31] The
implications of neo-paganism are fully acknowledged, and unequivocally supported: "We have exposed the 'prince of peace' as the agent of decay, through
his championing of the weak at the expense of the strong. The pendulum is
now swinging in the opposite direction. Ragnarök is witnessing an influx of
extremism to work towards the re-establishment of meritocracy."[32]

The influence of the Satanism/neo-paganism association has also affected
the aesthetic sensibilities of the former, with the widespread incorporation of
a number of pagan or quasi-pagan symbols into Satanic iconography. Though
some of these symbols have established pagan ancestries, the majority adopted
by Satanists are those with explicit Nazi—specifically, SS—connections: the
Black Sun motif from Wewelsburg Castle, the Wolfsangle, and the Totenkopf. In the Church of Satan for instance, all three have become semi-
official church symbols and figure extensively in church iconography; only
the Baphomet and LaVey's personal magical symbol, a sig rune lightning bolt
through an inverted pentagram, are more widely used.

Pagan archetypes and runes represent pre-Christian values and an explicitly European cultural identity, easily given an explicitly racist focus. Although
Jung regarded them as universal types, neo-pagans commonly see them as part
of a specific tribal consciousness, an intellectual crutch on which to rest racialist
bigotry. Modern Satanism, though careful not to be doctrinally racist itself (in
its larger churches at least), is easily blended with the tenets of extreme right
and neo-pagan movements. All exhibit a similar appraisal of human nature, a
repudiation of contemporary ethical norms in favor of natural law, and twisted
perceptions of evolutionary progress and genetic purity. The attraction of supposed Nazi occult secrets merely amplifies the existing parallels. In practice,
the largest problem in combining Satanism with Nationalist Socialist or neo-
pagan thought lies not in integrating their beliefs—for they are based on remarkably similar anthropological and sociological presuppositions—but in
white supremacists who react adversely to the Jewish origins of Satan, as
opposed to the Eurocentric purity of Wotan, Odin, or Fenris.

CTHULHU, CHAOS, AND SHAITAN

Another, less controversial, aspect of Satanic occultism is the popularity of the Cthulhu Mythos, product of the tormented mind of revered horror writer (and serial abuser of adjectives) H. P. Lovecraft (1890–1937). The Cthulhu Mythos, created by Lovecraft with the assistance of a circle of science fiction/ horror writers, is a loose collection of fictional works, a pseudomythology, about a pantheon of ancient gods. Key works are Lovecraft's "The Call of Cthulhu" and his fabled grimoire, the *Necronomicon*. With the help of numerous subsequent writers, the mythos eventually developed far beyond its status as narrative background detail. The *Necronomicon* has become particularly influential, despite the fact it never existed beyond the imagination of the Lovecraft Circle, who frequently referenced each other's forbidden (i.e., apocryphal) texts in order to create an air of legitimacy. Since Lovecraft's death a number of versions have been authored, and it has come be recognized as a genuine medieval grimoire.

One of the stranger and less predictable outcomes of the Cthulhu Mythos has been its adoption by occultists and the development of Lovecraftian magic. Lovecraft's fiction is popular to occultists because it provides a powerful articulation of forbidden knowledge, the fragility of civilization, and hints of a deeper, darker reality hiding behind a world—our world—of illusion. It is, effectively, Platonism for ghouls. British Thelemite Kenneth Grant's *The Magical Revival* (1972) boosted this appropriation by setting out a number of purported correspondences between the New England horror master's fictions and the ideas of Crowley's magical system.[33] LaVey played a part in engendering the shift from Lovecraft-the-writer to Lovecraft-the-occultist by identifying Lovecraft's Goat of One Thousand Young (Shub Niggurath) as one of the readings of the Baphomet in *The Satanic Bible*, and including the Aquino-penned "Ceremony of the Nine Angles" and "Call to Cthulhu" in *The Satanic Rituals*. Many occultists claim that Lovecraft, an atheist and self-defined mechanistic materialist, was either unconsciously influenced by the deeper truths of cosmic reality despite himself, or a visionary who disguised his genuine occult insights as fiction. As such, Lovecraft's so-called magick realism has been adopted by Satanists, followers of Crowley's Thelema, Grant's Typhonian Ordo Templi Orientis, and practitioners of chaos magick, with considerable overlapping of interests between these groups.[34]

The rise of chaos magick has occurred alongside, and complementary to, the Lovecraft tangent of occultism. This flexible and nondiscriminatory non-system draws from all occult traditions, with special regard for the theories of Austin Osman Spare (1886–1956). A talented painter and one-time Crowley disciple, the Englishman was influential for his free-form, psychically oriented magic focused on the individual subconscious. Chaos magick has developed from its roots in Spare's thought into a highly eclectic and individualistic form of magical practice. It is popular amongst Satanists because of its extreme subjectivity and nondoctrinaire nature. Its loose central credo is the Nietzsche-derived "Nothing is true, everything is permitted."[35] Importantly, it allows fictional characters to be employed in magical rites, greatly broadening its conceptual possibilities. One of its primary nonformulators, Ray Sherwin, describes it as "beyond dogma and rules, relying on intuition and information uprooted from the depths of self." With these loosely prescribed parameters, chaos magick reflects "the randomness of the universe and the individual's relationship with it,"[36] allows the practitioner to define his own magical method, ethics, and goals, and confines his powers only to the limits of his imagination. Basically, anything goes.

Satanism's loose incorporation of the Cthulhu Mythos into its occult canon is an indication of both its doctrinal promiscuity and the continual blurring of lines between fact and fiction, legend and history. Another example is the incorporation of the *Al-Jilwah (The Revelation)* in *The Satanic Rituals* as the Statement of Shaitan. The *Al-Jilwah* is a work of medieval mysticism from the syncretistic Middle Eastern Yedizi faith (in what is now Iraq). The Yedizis worship a God that is assisted by seven archangels, of whom the primary is Melek Taus, represented by a peacock. Confusion arises from Melek Taus's second name, Shaytan, as it is similar to the Islamic name for Satan, Shaitan. Combined with suspicion of the secretive ethnic minority (Kurdish) sect and the poor regard of Muslims for Yedizism, the false charge of devil-worship was frequently repeated throughout history. Like the Cathars and Knights Templar, the Yedizis were victims of their opponent's slander, with even Lovecraft referring to them as devil-worshippers in the short story "The Horror at Red Hook."

LaVey, predictably, joined the chorus. Both *The Satanic Bible* and *The Satanic Rituals* stated that the Yedizis were undoubtedly devil-worshippers. Equally predictably, he corrupted the text in the latter. Though the original text states explicitly "Do not mention my name or my attributes," LaVey added a footnote, "No longer mandatory," before inserting "So saith Shaitan" at its culmination. These interpolations are crucial, as the passage is ambiguous in regard to the identity of the deity being discussed, and contains no hint of being in any way Satanic (or Shaitanic). LaVey also excised passages that conflict with his Satanic interpretation, including the introductory statement "Peace Be Unto Him" and the final few lines:

> And the garden on high is for those who do my pleasure
> I sought the truth and became a confirming truth
> And by the like truth shall they, like myself, possess the highest place.[37]

The mythology of Satan may be rich and varied, but the great deceiver has seldom been said to represent the truth, reside in a "garden on high," or "possess the highest place."

SCIENCE AND SATANISM

The corruption of texts is just one of the problematic issues of Satanic occultism. There is a substantial degree of tension in the propensity to draw on the authority of both scientific and occult traditions simultaneously. Quasi-scientific Satanic claims to represent the reality of the natural world sit very unevenly with any mention of magical, supernatural forces. Scientific knowledge rests most fundamentally on the fact that reality is both objective and consistent. It is underpinned by the metaphysical concept of naturalism, the view that all phenomena can be explained mechanistically by reference to natural causes and laws, rather than by supernatural or mystical explanations. Any employment of the occult alongside theories derived (supposedly) from scientific premises is therefore inconsistent. Scientific knowledge must be objectively testable and independently verifiable. The nature of magic is the opposite: subjective, personal, and unverifiable. At a fundamental level, the claims of magic are irreconcilable with the core presuppositions of *The Satanic Bible*. The extreme subjectivity and epistemological nihilism (belief that truth ultimately cannot be known) of chaos magick in particular is completely incompatible with scientific naturalism.

Of course, the occult and naturalism were not always at odds. Occult practices such as astrology and alchemy were regarded as legitimate branches of science in medieval times. In Sir James Frazer's classic *The Golden Bough* (1890) magic is portrayed as pursuing goals almost identical to those of science. Similarly, modern occultists often stress that magic is complementary to scientific inquiry, merely another way to achieve the same goal: knowledge. This détente became harder to maintain as scientific knowledge advanced and magic shifted away from the physical sciences in the late nineteenth century into a subjective/psychological paradigm.

An exemplar case of the quasi-scientific illustration of magical concepts is Crowley's highly influential *Magick in Theory and Practice*. The fruits of Crowley's attempt to naturalize his magical theory are questionable, despite—or perhaps because of—his clarity. His central definition is unambiguous, "MAGICK is the Science and Art of causing Change to occur in conformity with Will." In addition, "Every intentional act is a Magical Act." Unfortunately for Crowley, clarity is accompanied in this case with the collapse of illusion, for by these criteria making a coffee or petting a cat can be considered magical acts. They are *intentional*, done according to *will*, and *cause change* (i.e., resulting in delicious coffee or a happy cat). Crowley has, in effect, defined magic so broadly as to deny it any unique meaning. He acknowledges that by the use of "magical weapons" such as "pen, ink, and paper...[t]he composition and distribution of this book [*Magick in Theory and Practice*] is thus an act of MAGICK by which I cause changes to take place in conformity with my Will."[38] He later uses the same argument to define banking and potato-growing as magical acts. However, when any act—no matter how mundane—is determined magical, the term has become too vague to have any real meaning, especially when the act can be adequately explained by other means (i.e., pure physical science). All that is left is an unpersuasive word game. When everything is magic, nothing is.

LaVeyan Satanism, at heart atheistic and materialist, tries to escape these entanglements by placing even greater emphasis on the subjective, psychological nature of magic and ritual practice. Yet its progenitor was more than willing to claim supernatural powers when it suited him—consider the absurd invocation to Brother Satan (for the benefit of Jayne Mansfield's sick son) recounted in *The Secret Life of a Satanist.*[39] The same work contains an entire chapter of "Curses and Coincidences" that arose from his magical acts: a hex on a motorcycle cop that results in a "gruesome collision"; apes attacking the zoo director who took away LaVey's beloved Togare; a curse against a mocking television interviewer that results in a city-wide power blackout and, a year later, the death of the host; a magical working, born of frustration at the dissolution of Anton and Diane's relationship, that inspires James Huberty's 1984 massacre of 21 people in a McDonalds restaurant in San Ysidro, California; and, of course, the fabled Sam Brody destruction ritual, car crash, and Jayne Mansfield "decapitation."[40] With LaVey, these fables can reasonably be attributed to his willingness to tell people what they want to hear, to profess powers he himself was dubious of.

Though he draws from established tradition, a number of LaVey's occult doctrines are largely unprecedented and rest entirely on his own authority: the claim that a sacrificed animal's death throes and not its life-force (i.e., blood) are the source of magical power; the claim that blasphemy is not the focus of the Black Mass; the claim that there is no difference between white and black magic; the claim that curses are more effective if the victim is skeptical of their merit (the opposite is traditionally held); and the presentation of the Enochian Keys and the Al-Jilwah as Satanic works. LaVey clearly had very little respect for the traditions or texts he was dealing with, or the people reading his books, and liberally edited, altered, and fabricated both documents and doctrines to his pleasing. Similarly, he was prepared to repeat long-discounted slurs on the Templars and Yedizi as fact. Nonetheless, LaVey's authority is generally accepted as sufficient basis for acceptance within Satanism. Both the Enochian Keys and the Al-Jilwah are regarded as legitimate Satanic works and constitute the primary texts of many theistic Satanists. For practitioners of chaos magick, legitimacy is not even an issue.

Modern Satanism undoubtedly tries to have the best of both worlds. It claims the legitimacy of science to bolster its authority but desires the sense of mystery and personal empowerment provided by the occult. Any interest in the occult or any form of supernaturalism also directly contradicts the claim that Satanism is atheistic, though this fact is seldom recognized. For anyone able to ignore the tension between *The Satanic Bible*'s denial of supernaturalism and its promotion of magic, almost any occult belief or practice is compatible with modern Satanism. Accordingly, Satanic occult interests are promiscuous, opportunistic and indiscriminate, although LaVey's texts and Crowley or one of his myriad disciples are frequently the first points of reference. While numerous Satanic churches take the occult very seriously, most allow the individual to determine his own level of interest. There is no standard approach to magic beyond the general guidelines of *The Satanic Bible* and *The Satanic Rituals*, and attitudes toward the occult among Satanists accordingly range from scornful to deeply fascinated. Under Gilmore, the Church of Satan is, doctrinally at least, divorced from serious occult interests, despite his authoring of rituals for the purpose of so-called cataclysmic dramatics (Gilmore has even written an essay pointing out that the *Necronomicon* is a work of fiction). Yet, as one Church of Satan member notes, "Anyone who finds their way to Satanism has a passing, to avid, interest in magic."[41] Within an organization such as the Temple of Set, deep occult interests are a prerequisite. The foundational text, Aquino's *The Book of Coming Forth by Night*, explicitly places the Temple of Set in the tradition of Crowley's *The Book of the Law* (and also, controversially, establishes Aquino as Crowley's successor). Other temple members, notably Stephen Flowers (aka Edred Thorsson) and Don Webb, have also conducted extensive research and writing on the occult.

One characteristic of modern Satanism's occult practices is that it openly embraces that which almost everybody else shies away from. The use of magic for destructive means has long been taboo, even with the most dedicated practitioners. Accordingly, more traditional occultists hold Satanists in extremely poor regard. Virtually none of the historical figures mentioned here were actually adepts of black magic, or at least they didn't consider themselves as such. Their unifying characteristic is wariness of the topic. Even Crowley, awash in the blood and sexual fluids of his rituals, to many the very emblem of evil, eschewed black magic. Cavendish, who published *The Black Arts* in 1967, just as modern Satanism was emerging, concluded, "[Traditional] Satanism is as harshly rejected by most magicians as it is by Christians." The occult's deep philosophical roots in Neo-platonism, Gnosticism, Hermeticism, and Christian Kabbalah prevented such a purely Satanic application. "According to occult theory, there are forces and intelligences, whether inside or outside the magician, which are conventionally condemned as evil, but a god who is entirely evil is as inconceivable as a god who is entirely good. The true God, the One, is the totality of everything, containing all good and all evil, and reconciling all opposites."[42] In regard to the chaotic antinomian occult fringe that has developed since Cavendish's study, such rebuttals of purely selfish magical practices are far more difficult to make.

In the Company of Killers: Satanic Ritual Abuse and Satanic Social Politics

> If you're thinking dark thoughts, and your thoughts involve rape, and brutality, and murder, you're going to start thinking Satan's the god for you, not Jesus Christ.
>
> —Philip Carlo, biographer of
> "Night Stalker" Richard Ramirez

In 1980, Canadian Michelle Smith released *Michelle Remembers*,[1] a book she had coauthored with her psychiatrist, Lawrence Pazder. The work detailed a terrifying history of abuse that Smith said she had experienced more than two decades earlier. As a five-year-old, Smith had been forced by her mother to participate in the rites of a satanic cult. She had, she claimed, been sexually abused by men and women, forced to eat worms, imprisoned in a cage with live snakes, witnessed kittens torn apart in the mouths of cultists, and seen babies slaughtered and eaten. The abuse, long unknown to her, had been uncovered in therapy sessions with Pazder. The claims were strenuously denied by Smith's father, family friends, and her ex-husband (whom she left for Pazder), and the book ultimately stood up to scrutiny so poorly that it is now widely regarded as fiction. But, with no shortage of shocking details, the book was a bestseller, garnering international attention and helping to introduce the phrase "satanic ritual abuse" into the everyday vernacular.

Michelle Remembers was merely the first in a number of high profile satanic ritual abuse (SRA) cases. In 1983, the mother of a two-year-old boy at Mc-Martin Preschool in California complained to police that her child had been molested. The mother, later diagnosed a paranoid schizophrenic, related details of bizarre and often fantastical abuse. In the ensuing investigation the claims proliferated dramatically. It was alleged that the crimes had been masterminded by a shadowy satanic church and had involved hundreds of children stretching over two decades. With nationwide attention, the resulting trial lasted six years and was the most expensive in history, costing over 13 million dollars. Though nine preschools were closed and dozens of lives destroyed, no one was ever convicted. Once again, the lack of conclusive findings was of far less significance than the enormous attention given to the case. It, and numerous similar cases, became seen as part of a large-scale outbreak of satanic activity. By the time of the McMartin Preschool trial's anticlimactic conclusion, the SRA scare was in full flight.

Though at first focused largely on individual cases in North America, the SRA scare grew into a worldwide phenomenon. By the end of the 1980s, the belief in the existence of a highly organized international society of traditional satanic cultists was widespread. America alone had a reported 1 million cultists active in a shadowy underground network, engaged in a smorgasbord of criminal activities including kidnapping, animal sacrifice, sexual abuse, incest, infanticide, child pornography, snuff films, ritual murder, mutilation, dismemberment and cannibalism. Proponents cited terrifying studies, estimating that "between forty and sixty thousand human beings are killed through ritual homicides in the United States each year...in the Las Vegas metropolitan area alone six hundred people meet their deaths during satanic ceremonies each year."[2] America's unreported satanic murder figure was higher, it seems, than even its official, reported (non-satanic) murder rate. A Pandora's box of society's greatest fears had supposedly been revealed, all unified under the umbrella of the devil's pervasive and perfidious influence. Heavy metal music, most nontraditional religious practices, and even the role-playing game Dungeons and Dragons were held to be portals to satanic activity.

CAUSES OF THE SRA SCARE

The forces driving the SRA scare can be divided into five areas: the claims of victims and survivors, new psychotherapy techniques, media attention, the advocacy of anticult and religious organizations, and its validation by police experts known as cult cops. The first of these—the survivor/victim claims—was the original source of the phenomenon. Eventually, the claims became self-perpetuating. The publicity surrounding *Michelle Remembers* and the McMartin Preschool affair prompted numerous other victims of SRA to step forward with their stories. The most notorious received significant publicity, such as Lauren Stratford's 1988 work *Satan's Underground*.[3] Stratford's claims largely followed the template established by Smith's, if exceeding them in gruesome detail. Stratford recounted being raped as a six-year-old, being forced to engage in bestiality and pornography at eight, and joining a blood-drinking satanic cult as an adult, where she claimed three of her own children were sacrificed. This final allegation was the most prominent of the satanic breeder stories—the claim that women were bearing children specifically for the purpose of ritual sacrifice. Stratford's story was challenged by her sister and discredited as a hoax by an evangelical Christian publication, and the book was withdrawn from publication. There was, nonetheless, a market for the work. Another publisher quickly picked it up and Stratford continued to appear on talk shows detailing her story.

The victims' allegations, generally similar to those of Smith and Stratford, gained an important boost from the pioneering of a psychotherapy technique known as repressed memory therapy. This theory, central to the claims of *Michelle Remembers, Satan's Underground,* and most other survivor cases, held that memories of childhood sexual abuse were frequently unconsciously repressed by victims, resulting in later psychological disorders. These memories, specialists claimed, could be recovered during therapy sessions, frequently under hypnosis. The recovered memories were then used as the basis of criminal trials against the alleged perpetrators. Later studies cast doubt on these claims, arguing that the fluid, malleable nature of memories means that they are easily influenced by suggestion. When combined with the influence of overzealous prosecutors, priests, and social workers, it becomes impossible to tell true memories from false ones. Yet in numerous cases, highly unreliable evidence was given considerable authority. Repressed memory therapy eventually lost any semblance of scientific respectability, and is now generally referred to by its more appropriate title—false memory syndrome.

Boosted by its supposed scientific validation, the scare quickly became an industry of its own, with book deals, public appearances, and television interviews for victims and experts alike. Media outlets were a prime means for disseminating the claims. Though the major evening news programs of the major networks and the more prestigious press dailies were generally wary of the more sensationalist stories, other mass media outlets were not so discerning. Cable television and tabloid news magazines embraced the topic to improve viewer numbers and circulation. Ultimately, the larger networks joined the fray. The TV show *20/20* devoted an episode to the issue in 1985, and *Donahue, The Oprah Winfrey Show,* and *Sally Jesse Raphael* all eventually covered SRA and repressed memory therapy. Yet one show, aired on October 25, 1988, was by far the most influential—Geraldo Rivera's "Devil Worship: Exposing Satan's Underground." The two-hour special was the highest-rating show in history and, in combination with its follow-up specials, introduced the topic to an enormous audience, greatly influencing public opinion and belief in the scare.

The two-hour *Geraldo* special was a sensational affair. It began with stills of *The Satanic Bible* and excerpts from the documentary *Satanis: The Devil's Mass*. Footage of Charles Manson presented the lifelong detainee as a devious satanic killer rather than a race-baiting, drug-addled sociopath. With Zeena LaVey, seated in the studio alongside Michael Aquino, representing the Church of Satan and her father, the show gradually incriminated everyone from LaVey to theatrical heavy metal bands in a terrifying plague of demonic activity. Rivera's approach was simple. Rather than providing proof of widespread satanic abuse, he argued that SRA was real but underreported and underinvestigated. Skepticism, not lack of corroboration, was the problem, as the topic was "impossible to measure, easy to ridicule."[4] Extrapolating from anecdotal evidence, survivor claims, and examples of allegedly sloppy police work the show posited a nationwide network connecting a vast satanic underground. The special was enormously influential, and the period following the *Devil Worship* special was the pinnacle of the scare.

The heightened publicity brought to the issue occurred against a backdrop of growing unease regarding alternative religions and cults. In societies that had just, in the 1960s and 1970s, come to terms with the fact that sexual abuse was both real and pervasive, the new threat of secretive cabals of devil-worshippers practicing ritual abuse was also a more viable proposition. The proliferation of alternative religions in the 1960s counterculture and establishment of large scale religious cults in the 1970s had already produced a backlash, giving rise to the influential anticult movement. The organization fed off the growing unease regarding the blossoming alternative religious practices, particularly in the wake of 1978's Jonestown mass murder-suicide. With the emergence of SRA survivor stories, the anticult movement quickly shifted focus and became a major center for the dissemination of antisatanist material. Its eagerness in promoting the issue was noted by critics, who accused it of "jumping on the satanist bandwagon, and even giving the wagon a big push."[5]

In addition to the growing power of the anticult movement, the SRA scare occurred soon after the rise of mainstream religious fundamentalists such as Jerry Falwell's powerful Moral Majority lobby. Evangelists and fundamentalist leaders, themselves convinced of Satan's influence in world affairs, were equally quick to champion the issue. Their first question was not *is* Satan trying to destroy society, but *how*. With the ability to reach and influence large audiences, fundamentalist support for the issue was a significant factor in popularizing the scare. Sensationalist talk-show host Bob Larson is an exemplar of how the issue was exploited. The evangelist publicly supported SRA victims such as Lauren Stratford and carved out a lucrative niche as an expert on the unholy trinity of Satanism, the occult, and heavy metal. Larson's 1989 book *Satanism: The Seduction of America's Youth* is a prime example of SRA advocacy. In one passage, Larson relates a conversation with a teenager who called his talk show and announced it was his birthday the following month.

> "Happy Birthday," I [Larson] congratulated him.
> "You wouldn't say that if you knew what's going to happen on my birthday. I just found out myself last Saturday. I'm going to be sacrificed to Satan."
> "You're what!" I exclaimed. "Who's going to do it?"
> "My parents. They've been into Satan worship all my life. I never thought much about it. It's just the way I was raised, you know, like some kids are raised Baptist. For me, my parents worship Lucifer."
> "Why didn't you know before that you were destined to be sacrificed?"
> "The subject never came up until I went to church. Several days ago, a girl I like asked me to go to her church. When I got home, my brother told my mother where I'd been. That's when she told me I'd have to be killed."
> "How old are you?"
> "Fifteen. I don't want to die. But it's all there in the black box."
> "What black box?" I inquired.
> "My parents have this black box they keep for the devil. It has several things in it—*The Satanic Bible*, a picture of my mother, black candles, goblets, daggers, and my birth certificate. Keeping my birth certificate in that box signifies a pact that I have to die some day. Now that I've been to a Christian church, my mother's guardian spirit has told her I have to die on my next birthday."[6]

Larson's use of this exchange is indicative of how the evangelists fueled the scare. The evangelist accepts the claims of his anonymous caller at face value, provides no corroborating evidence, and publishes them as evidence of widespread satanic cult activity. Though claiming to have organized counseling for the distressed young man, Larson makes no mention of any criminal proceedings being brought against the would-be child-sacrificing parents. An anonymous phone call, it seems, is evidence enough.

The final group propelling the SRA scare was the police experts known as cult cops. By the mid-1980s, these occult specialists had become prominent at police seminars and anticult conferences, delivering presentations that placed heavy emphasis on the connection between Satanism and crime. As belief in claims of satanic abuse relied heavily on victim testimony and anecdotal evidence, the reinforcement by law enforcement officers was important in boosting the claims' credibility. Authorities like Ted Gunderson, former FBI chief of California, were prominent media commentators. For Gunderson, the word of victims was enough. "I've been told by a woman who was born into the movement, and was in it for more than fifteen years, that there are several hundred satanic groups across the nation, that practice human and animal sacrifice. [They come from] all walks of life—doctors, lawyers, airline pilots."[7] For the general public, the endorsement of an FBI expert was itself compelling evidence.

DEBUNKING THE SCARE

Given the extravagant nature of the claims being made and the extraordinary attention they were receiving, the public emergence of skeptics and debunkers was inevitable. The response to the seemingly authoritative acknowledgment of a widespread satanic conspiracy was led, appropriately enough, by an FBI agent who had formerly been accepting of many of the claims. Kenneth Lanning's 1989 study "Satanic, Occult, Ritualistic Crime: A Law Enforcement Perspective" analyzed how the SRA scare was being handled by police and other law enforcement agencies. In response to the partisanship he observed in other officers, particularly the strong Christian bias of many cult cops, Lanning remained religiously neutral. His focus was, primarily, the cult cops's seminars; his conclusions, damning:

> The information presented is a mixture of fact, theory, opinion, fantasy, and paranoia, and because some of it can be proven or corroborated (desecration of cemeteries, vandalism etc.) the implication is that all is true and documented. The distinctions among the different areas are blurred even if occasionally a presenter tries to make them. This is complicated by the fact that almost any discussion of satanism and witchcraft is interpreted in the light of the religious beliefs of those in the audience. Faith, not logic and reason controls the religious beliefs of most people. As a result, some normally skeptical law enforcement officers accept the information disseminated at these conferences without critically evaluating it or questioning the sources.[8]

Lanning noted that handouts at the seminars identified a wide variety of groups and pursuits as satanic, including Hinduism, Islam, Scientology, heavy metal music, paganism (Wicca), the KKK, Freemasonry, astrology, holistic medicine, transcendental meditation, Hare Krishna, Mormonism, Roman Catholicism, and even Buddhism. "Satanic" was evidently an entirely subjective term for the cult cops, used without distinction for whatever religion or movement they did not personally endorse. The Lanning report was far less partisan: "The fact is that far more crime and child abuse has been committed by zealots in the name of God, Jesus, and Mohammed than has ever been committed in the name of Satan. Many people don't like this statement, but few can argue with it."[9]

Lanning pointed out that most satanic criminals are already deeply disturbed individuals with an existing propensity for crime. "The important point for the criminal investigator is to realize that most ritualistic criminal behavior is not motivated simply by satanic or religious ceremonies." In addition, "the facts of so called 'satanic crimes' are often significantly different from what is described at law enforcement training conferences or in the media. The actual involvement of Satanism or the occult in these cases usually turns out to be secondary, insignificant, or nonexistent." Lanning concluded that there was "some connection" between satanism and vandalism, church desecration, animal mutilation, and teenage suicide. Links to child abuse, kidnapping, murder, and human sacrifice were "far more uncertain." Yet even identifiable links between satanism and crime were not a simple matter of cause and effect. "Blaming satanism for a teenagers' vandalism, theft, suicide or even act of murder is like blaming a criminal's offences on his tattoos: both are often signs of the same rebelliousness and lack of self-esteem that contribute to the commission of crimes."[10] Satanism, in this assessment, was more a symptom than a cause.

In 1992, Lanning released a second, lengthier version of his report, primarily to expand on the original report, but partly in response to the accusation he was a satanist who had infiltrated the FBI. To his accusers he responded that, far from being an apologist for satanists, he was concerned that because of the hysteria surrounding the SRA scare, "in some cases, individuals are getting away with molesting children because we can't prove they are satanic devil worshippers who engage in brainwashing, human sacrifice, and cannibalism as part of a large conspiracy."[11] By promoting unrealistic scenarios, Lanning countered, the scare was impeding police work and compromising the justice system.

Lanning's work was the beginning of a half-decade-long counter-wave of studies and books by government agencies, academics, and journalists. His analysis of the seminar police experts was echoed by Robert Hicks of the U.S. Justice Department. The author of *In Pursuit of Satan: The Police and the Occult*, Hicks described seminar presentations as "a pastiche of claims, suppositions, and speculations" that unrealistically linked "symbols, images, and unconventional behavior with incipient violent criminality."[12] Hicks also subjected the McMartin Preschool case to a conclusive critique, identifying critical problems in the lack of supporting proof and willingness to ignore contradictory evidence in pursuit of a conviction.

In 1994, journalist Lawrence Wright, author of the LaVey-mythos-puncturing *Rolling Stone* article, returned to the topic of Satanism. Wright's *Remembering Satan* detailed the case of Paul Ingram, a Washington State civil deputy and local chairman of the Republican Party.[13] While attending a religious retreat in 1988, Ingram's daughters began to recall a catalogue of abuse at his hands, including torture, incest, cannibalism, child sacrifice, and forced abortions. In police custody and under hypnosis, Ingram himself began to vaguely recollect repressed memories of these events. Dr. Richard Ofshe, an external cult expert, was called in and became convinced that the daughters were lying. Ofshe succeeded in manipulating Ingram into recalling false memories of forcing sex acts between his son and daughter, allegations the children never made. Ingram was never made aware of this fact and, encouraged by police and religious advisers, confessed to six uncorroborated counts of rape in order to spare his children a trial. Later, in prison, he reconsidered and withdrew his confession. The court refused to let him alter his plea, and he remained incarcerated until 2003.

Official studies continued to question the SRA phenomenon. In England, anthropologist Jean La Fontaine authored a government report titled *The Extent and Nature of Organised and Ritual Abuse*.[14] La Fontaine analyzed over 200 cases of group abuse and alleged SRA in Britain from 1987 to 1992. Though definite cases of abuse were involved, the report concluded that there was no proof of any satanic cult activity. The report criticized child services workers who interviewed the alleged victims for posing leading questions, and even interpreting silence as a sign of evil forces at work American SRA specialists were also blamed for accelerating the spread of the rumors and giving them undeserved credence. La Fontaine later added a book-length account of the report, *Speak of the Devil: Tales of Satanic Abuse in Contemporary England*, to the ever-growing pile of SRA-debunking literature.[15]

By then, however, the scare was over. In December of 1995, Geraldo Rivera issued an apology for his part in the SRA scare, acknowledging that repressed memory syndrome was fraudulent and that innocent people had been jailed. Rivera's apology came at a point when it was obvious the SRA scare had been a modern version of the Salem witch hunt. Following Lanning's report and La Fontaine's findings, a 1994 study funded by the U.S. federal government's National Center on Child Abuse and Neglect was released. The comprehensive investigation surveyed 6,900 psychiatrists, psychologists, and social workers, and over 12,000 suspected cases of suspected ritual abuse. Most clinicians (69%) reported no cases of suspected abuse, and the majority of the remainder reported one or two each. A very small minority of clinicians (1.4%) reported over 100 cases each, lending considerable credence to the claim that overzealous mental health professionals played a large role in fueling the hysteria. Of all the cases studied, there was no evidence of the existence of generational satanists, nor of a widespread satanic network (no satanically themed child pornography had ever been found in the United States). One case of the satanic ritual (sexual) abuse of a 16-year-old by his satanist parents was established.[16]

The SRA scare has been the most comprehensively covered area of any related to modern Satanism. It has been established beyond doubt that the episode was a vast catalogue of misinformation, hyperbole, paranoid fantasy, sensationalism, and self-interested opportunism. Its origins can be clearly traced to the compelling narrative of abuse constructed by a handful of individuals, whose stories became the template for later claims. The majority of accusations involved remarkably similar details, particularly after the publication of bestsellers like *Michelle Remembers* and the broadcast of shows such as Geraldo's *Devil Worship* (which was watched by Paul Ingram's family shortly before his daughter made her claims). The affair was augmented by the disproportional attention paid to a number of notorious serial killings and murders involving aspects of satanism. Although any criminal cases with elements of satanism continue to receive a large amount of media coverage, individual cases are no longer widely regarded as evidence of systematic satanic abuse or international cabals of devil-worshippers.

AFTERMATH

With the SRA scare buried, Satanism often receives more sardonic coverage from the media. A prime example is that of a British Royal Navy technician who was revealed in 2004 to be a (LaVeyan) Satanist. Though the revelation produced predictable gasps of shock from Tory parliamentarians and conservative broadsheets, the *Guardian* newspaper was concerned with more practical matters. Just how, the paper wished to know, would the seagoing Satanist, Leading Hand Chris Cranmer, perform his elaborate rituals in the tight confines of a naval vessel? Perusal of LaVey's texts uncovered a number of logistical issues: where he would source a naked altar, and where to stow his Baphomet, chalice, ritual robes, and paper-maché animal heads. Then there were the concerns arising from the performance itself. "Although the prancing, ringing, and gonging that accompanies these rituals is, no doubt, strictly harmless, sailors who overhear Cranmer shouting, 'I am rampant carnal joy!' in the next cabin may not feel totally at ease." The article also questioned how a military Satanist would overcome his aversion to herd conformity and still discharge his duties efficiently. And, though generally light-hearted, the piece ended with a more serious proviso: "The sanctioning of LaVey's smutty hocus pocus on board HMS Cumberland not only illustrates how unattractive a belief system may be while still earning official respect; it hints at the difficulties we may soon face in criticising anything that calls itself a religion."[17]

An even more effective piece was that posted by the online satire site *The Onion*, lampooning latent fears of satanic conspiracies. In an article titled "Harry Potter Books Spark Rise in Satanism among Children," the satirical news site announced that the enormously popular books were firing a tremendous interest in the occult. "Across America, Satanic temples are filling to the rafters with youngsters clamoring for instruction in summoning and conjuring." The numbers, according to the *Onion*, were staggering: "Today, more than 14 million children alone belong to the Church of Satan" (a number that exceeds even the church's inflated membership claims). The article ended with a quote, purportedly from the retiring Ms. Rowling herself, acknowledging that the books did indeed intend to lure children to Satan: "These books guide children to an understanding that the weak, idiotic Son Of God is a living hoax who will be humiliated when the rain of fire comes, and will suck the greasy cock of the Dark Lord while we, his faithful servants, laugh and cavort in victory."[18] Preposterous though the article may have been, the fervor that fueled the SRA scare was again displayed when the piece was spread widely by Christian youth counselors, who quoted it as a legitimate source.[19]

As could be expected, the comprehensive debunking of SRA has been welcomed by Satanists. The vindication has provided a sense of legitimacy to the movement, as critics of SRA have had to acknowledge and accept the presence of the Satanic churches that aren't part of a massive underground conspiracy. There are nonetheless a number of murder cases and serial killings with established links to modern Satanism, if not to underground satanic cults. Gauging the importance of Satanism to these crimes is difficult, as Lanning and others displayed, because of the strong tendency to overstate any Satanic or occult element. Even two decades past the height of the scare, the Satanism-as-conspiracy tendency still reappears intermittently. One recent work, William H. Kennedy's *Satanic Crime: A Threat in the New Millennium* (2006), attempts to breathe new life into the decidedly stale topic by linking Aleister Crowley, Anton LaVey, Charles Manson, Richard Ramirez, David Berkowitz, the Columbine killings, and the Belgium pedophile ring into one international devil-worshipping conspiratorial mélange.[20]

THE SATANIC PERSPECTIVE
ON SATANIC CRIME

An international criminal network of devil-worshippers undoubtedly doesn't exist. It is, however, illuminating to consider the doctrines of modern Satanism, their relationship to legal and social issues, and the attitude toward satanic crimes. LaVey's partner/biographer, rather than accept the exoneration provided by the very public defeat of SRA proponents, preferred to savor his influence. "Investigators, no matter how objective they may be, become disturbed by the increasing number of *Satanic Bibles* found at crime sites or in the personal effects of mass murderers. It may be that LaVey's Satanic thought can release forces within unstable people that they are not able to control."[21] Or it may be that his work's constant romanticizing and validation of strength, hatred, and vengeance is very easily used as a justification for violence. LaVey's reactions to documented satanic crimes are blunt:

> LaVey maintains that he isn't really concerned about accusations of people killing people in the name of Satan. He swears that each time he reads of a new killing spree, his only reaction is, "What, 22 people? Is that all?" [...]
>
> "I'd rather be in the company of killers than in the company of wimps. I don't think you'd find the pretentiousness in people like Ramirez, or Stanley Dean Baker, or Huburty, or Manson—I don't think you'd find the noise that all these puffed-up, empty barrel, supposed-Satanists make."[22]

The four killers of LaVey's preferred company were responsible, collectively, for more than 40 deaths. Baker was a cannibal who was found with half-eaten human fingers and a copy of *The Satanic Bible*. He was later judged insane. James Huberty machine-gunned down 40 people (killing 21) in a McDonald's restaurant after losing his job as a security guard. LaVey took credit for this crime in his list of "Curses and Coincidences" in *The Secret Life of a Satanist*,[23] an action even Aquino described as "vulgar."[24] The Night Stalker killer, Richard Ramirez, was one of the most notorious and high-profile satanic crimes ever. Ramirez committed a wave of brutal murders and rapes in California in 1984 and 1985. Appearing in court with a pentagram tattooed on his hand, convicted of 13 murders and 11 sexual assaults, Ramirez was given the death sentence. In a later addition to his personal mythology, LaVey claimed to have briefly met and brushed off the young killer in a chance street encounter. He commented, "When I met Richard Ramirez, he was the nicest, most polite young man you'd ever want to meet...a model of deportment."[25]

Given the evident approval of serial killers, it is pertinent to ask: What keeps a Satanist from breaking the law? In any case of illegal activities with a Satanic element, the established churches are quick to disavow knowledge of the person involved, and they generally deny the individual is a proper Satanist at all. This double standard is common. Despite its author's fondness for serial killers, *The Satanic Bible* emphasizes that Satanism is a law-abiding religion. One of its central doctrines is the tautological refrain "Responsibility to the responsible."[26] LaVey later elaborated, "in a Satanic society, everyone must experience the consequences of his own actions—for good or ill."[27] The meaning of this slippery doctrine was finally pinned down in the documentary *Speak of the Devil*:

> We believe in taking responsibility for our own actions, and not saying, of course, as a Christian would, that "The devil made me do it." And, if we do

something we have to answer for it. If it's an anti-social act, we have to weigh the decision to do it, whether or not, if we get caught, if we get punished, it's really worth it. And we don't depend so much upon conscience, as we do upon pragmatism.[28]

The Satanist, then, stays within the bounds of the law only out of fear of punishment, not out of respect for the principles of law or moral qualms concerning victims. Legal boundaries can be ignored at the individual's discretion—so long as the individual is ready to accept the consequences of being caught. The Satanic imperative to follow the law is entirely conditional. If the individual feels a particular act is justified, then she is entitled to commit it, regardless of any other considerations, be they legal, moral, or social. The suspicion that this is an open invitation to vigilantism is no misconception. LaVey, in addition to approving of Satanic killings, openly takes credit for them.

LaVey doesn't shirk responsibility for what his writings may catalyze. "If *The Satanic Bible* is spurring a changed perspective to unleash certain demons, certain elementals into the world, so be it...There will undoubtedly be more Satanically motivated murders and crimes in the sense that *The Satanic Bible* tells you "You don't have to take any more shit." But if Judeo-Christian society hadn't encouraged this immoral succoring of the weak, and made it laudable to buoy up the useless, then there wouldn't be this intensive need for a reaction against it. Of course, this extreme counter-swing of the pendulum, this vigilantism, will be interpreted as "mere anarchy loosed on the world," but in reality it will be, for the first time since cave days, justice.[29]

Through the prism of Satanic social Darwinism, mass killers such as Richard Ramirez, James Huberty, and Charles Manson represent justice. If a vicious sexual predator like Ramirez can be cast as a justified reaction to the presumed ills of society, then what exactly is justice, from a Satanic point of view? If existing moral standards and social policies are so deeply flawed, what do Satanists propose to replace them with?

SATANIC SOCIAL POLITICS

Though many Satanists comment on social issues, by far the most detailed set of Satanic social doctrines is that of the Church of Satan, which is closely echoed by smaller groups. Its social policy is formed by its endorsement of Lex Talionis, which it describes as the vengeance-based law of retribution. It was enshrined in one of its central propositions of LaVey's key 1980s essay "Pentagonal Revisionism": "*No tolerance for religious beliefs secularized and incorporated into law and order issues*—Re-establishing Lex Talionis will require a complete overturning of the present in-justice system based on Judeo-Christian ideals."[30] Though "Lex Talionis" is a Latin term and the concept is portrayed as an artifact of ancient Rome, its origins are far older. It in fact derives from the Babylonian King Hammurabi (c. 1792–1750 B.C.E.) and his concept of eye for an eye, tooth for a tooth, which later entered Hebrew thought and subsequently the Old Testament. In adopting this pre-Christian concept, Satanism adopts the Nietzschean dichotomy of Roman versus Judeo-Christian, master versus slave, morality. Predictably, the Roman model is chosen.

Lex Talionis is, in keeping with the general themes of Satanism, less focused on justice than on vengeance. It echoes the Fifth Satanic Statement, "Satan represents vengeance, instead of turning the other cheek!"[31] and the inflamed rhetoric of the Infernal Diatribe: "Give blow for blow, scorn for scorn, doom for doom—with compound interest liberally added thereunto! Eye for eye, tooth for tooth, aye four-fold, a hundred-fold!"[32] LaVey did not retreat from the militancy of these statements, and his later comments on retributive justice are extreme: "If a carefully tended shrub or plant is wantonly ripped up by the roots, the culprit's arm should be ripped out of its socket."[33] The advocacy of dismemberment as a fitting punishment for minor vandalism may be (charitably) attributed to rhetorical overstatement, but it is nevertheless indicative of the disproportionate nature of the policies being advocated. It is hardly an example of eye for an eye. Other Satanists support equally severe ideas, with Gilmore advocating forced labor and a Church of Satan magister calling for slavery, public executions, and the reintroduction of the Roman circus.[34] The establishment of a police state is also widely supported. These policies are unified by their repressiveness and reactionary, totalitarian character. "Eye for an eye" was, after all, in many ways a prototype for more appropriate forms of punishment. Most developed societies have discarded similar doctrines on the grounds that, rather than promoting stability, they represent disproportionate responses that merely encourage cycles of reciprocal violence. As Gandhi is reported to have said, "An eye for an eye, and soon the whole world is blind." Satanists, however, appear less concerned with establishing civil order and just principles than they are with vengeful destructiveness and entertaining fantasies of a carnival of brutality.

Another provocative aspect of Satanic social policy is its vocal support for eugenics. Due to its close association with the worst excesses of Nazism, the term "eugenics" often automatically provokes strong hostility. Immediate condemnation is nonetheless undeserved, as the term simply means "controlled selective breeding" (literally, "good life"), a definition under which numerous policies—some beneficial, some reprehensible—can be included.

Even abstention from alcohol during pregnancy is, technically, a eugenic practice. A helpful distinction, then, is that recently made between issues of *liberal eugenics* and *authoritarian eugenics*.[35] The label *liberal eugenics* encompasses noncoercive reproductive and genetic issues such as the termination of fetuses with debilitating or fatal genetic diseases. It also includes the bioethical issues of genetic modification and selection that are fast becoming technologically viable. The key issue to be recognized in these cases is that the interests of the individual whose life is in question are preeminent, and the decisions are the responsibility of those directly involved. *Authoritarian eugenics*, on the other hand, encompasses practices such as America's early twentieth-century sterilization program, or Nazi Germany's ideologically and racially motivated policies. In these cases, the interests and rights of the individual are entirely subordinate to state or group goals. In the Nazi quest for racial hygiene, it meant the forced sterilization of approximately 400,000 German people and gassing of 70,000 mental patients between 1933 and 1939, and the even greater crimes that followed.[36]

The issue then is: What form of eugenics do Satanists support? Both Church of Satan high priests have repeatedly used the term in reference to hopes of breeding a genetically superior Satanic elite. Gilmore has written a short essay on the topic, which attributes the decline of early twentieth-century eugenic policies to "the widespread growth of egalitarianism and collectivist thinking." Though he shies away from state-endorsed programs, he clearly does not support genetic technologies being available to all: "We wish the ranks of the 'superiorly abled' to increase in number, before time runs out and we all perish under the crush of mediocrity."[37] LaVey advocated a similar focus, if with more candor. He spoke in interviews of his desire to "enhance the growth of new, more intelligent generations, if I had the chance, by selective breeding. But this is so terrifyingly related to Hitlerism that usually I can't even talk about it." Indeed, many of his ideas closely mimic the group-oriented SS breeding policy: "Selective breeding, elitist stratification, advocacy of polygamous relationships for breeding purposes, and eventually building communities of like-minded individuals are Satanic programs antithetical to the cherished egalitarian ideal."[38]

Satanic eugenics is clearly focused on group, not individual, goals. These goals assume an undeniably authoritarian nature when LaVey, in his essay "Destructive Organisms," champions compulsory birth control, for which he provides the following justification: "A stupid, irresponsible woman should *not* have the right to 'decide' what she does with her own body." The reproductive abilities of men, too, should be controlled. "If he is stupid, insensitive and irresponsible, he should be sterilized. Irresponsible parents, male or female, should simply be kept from conceiving children."[39] Here, Satanism's open contempt for the interests and rights of others—what Gilmore refers to in his "Eugenics" essay as "the flaccid maxims of universal equality"—leads to draconian policies based upon staggeringly injudicious criteria.[40] By what standard are people deemed irresponsible or stupid, and who gets to make these judgments? The support for eugenic policies based on ideological grounds, accompanied by vaguely formulated ideals of genetic purity and disregard for individual rights, places the Church of Satan in line with historical authoritarian eugenics practices. By the standards of contemporary international law, specifically the injunction against forced sterilization in Article 7 of the Statute of the International Criminal Court, LaVey's enthusiasm for forced sterilization in "Destructive Organisms" advocates a crime against humanity.

Despite mimicking the social policies of the Nazis, LaVey attempts not to replicate their blatant racism. "Satanism is the first time in history where a master race can be built of genetically predisposed, like-minded people—not based on the genes that make them white, black, blue, brown or purple—but the genes that make them Satanists."[41] Ignoring the definitional contradiction of a nonracial master race, Satanic claims of genetic superiority are crippled by their ill-defined and unscientific nature. Merely agreeing with a particular ideology does not show that an individual has unique or superior genes. Much as any demagogue imagines that people who adopt his ideas do so because they are eminently discerning individuals, claiming that they are therefore biologically superior is clearly overreaching. The pretense that there is a specific Satanist gene is as fanciful as claiming that there is a gene for communists, environmentalists, or fans of Gothic fiction. Furthermore, modern genetics warn of the dangers embedded in this interbreeding policy—one of the key requirements of a healthy genetic population is the existence of genetic diversity, not uniformity. Close interbreeding only exacerbates the risk of genetic disorders. The desire to breed a genetic elite is, in a practical sense, little more than empty posturing, for no Satanic organization has resources to implement any such program, and none has ever tried.

ETHICS

Underlying many of these social policies are a set of ethical presumptions that are uniform across most Satanic organizations. The Temple of Set, though generally less interested in social policy than its chief rival, endorses almost identical ethical views. In an overview of the history of ethics and political theory prepared for initiates, Michael Aquino presents a standard Nietzschean assessment of morality. "Formula 'good/evil' values are merely appropriate for the profane masses, who can't—and don't want to—understand anything more precise."[42] Yet Aquino's ethical framework delivers no such precision,[43] and he concludes with an endorsement of extreme ethical subjectivism: the Setian's life is conducted "independently of morals codes, and customs imposed upon you by the politics and propaganda of society."[44] In rejecting both the objective basis for morality and the influence of normative morality (the dominant moral standards of one's culture and society), the Setian embraces the egocentric moral nihilism of Crowley's "Do what thou wilt shall be the whole of the Law." As with the Church of Satan and the majority of smaller Satanic organizations, all ethical issues are subordinated to the arbitrary will of the subject.

It is difficult to speak of Satanic morality when its moral codes devolve into empty, nihilistic slogans: Redbeard's "Might is right," Crowley's "Do what thou wilt," Nietzsche's "Nothing is true, everything is permitted," Aquino's encouragement to live "independently of moral codes," and LaVey's "Responsibility to the responsible." None of these principles provide any reason for the individual to consider anything beyond his own interests; none provide any basis for maintaining a stable, civilized society. None allow any criticism to be made of, for instance, a compulsive animal torturer. If such an individual is so disturbed that his actions feel appropriate to him, then by what basis can a Satanist judge him? Recall LaVey's injunction, "Good is what you like. Evil is what you don't like."[45] Once all moral standards are jettisoned—even the norms of one's society—there is no way to declare such actions wrong. A considerable contradiction lurks within these doctrines: the majority of Satanists are enormously moralistic and constantly make moral judgments of this type. Staunch opposition to animal mistreatment and child abuse are particularly prevalent themes. Yet, for anyone who genuinely accepts moral nihilism and the rule of the strong, such opposition is unjustifiable.

In addition to their self-negating ethics, most of the Satanists' critique of contemporary social values is directed at a straw man, as it is based on a straightforward misrepresentation of Western democratic justice and blinded by anti-Christian bias. LaVey's dismissal of the present legal system as "religious beliefs secularized and incorporated into law" is difficult to reconcile with America's decades-long reign of *Roe vs. Wade*. If traditional religious views were as all-pervasive as claimed, a country as religious as the United States would never have established the right to abortion. Similarly, the Satanist can't pretend that the dozens of countries moving toward (or implementing) the legalization of same-sex unions are doing so on the basis of traditional Judeo-Christian moral values. While our cultural heritage undoubtedly informs our moral judgments, the representation of Western justice systems as simply the secular consecration of Judeo-Christian values is a gross oversimplification. A brief study of the history of Western social policy will show that at numerous points Christian factions were strongly opposed to many of the liberal democratic reforms that are now standard, a trend that continues today.

The doctrines that Satanism offers in place of the current system suffer their own fundamental flaws, in particular in its principles of natural law and might is right. Whether one thinks that an eye for an eye is a practical system of justice or not, the acknowledgement of the need for *any* institutionalized justice system directly contradicts the central claim of Satanic ethics: that the bare facts of nature should determine our behavior. If the only normative ethics are those prescribed by natural law, what need is there for any formalized system of justice, even one as revisionary as Lex Talionis? If the only valid standards are those of nature, then whatever occurs naturally is completely acceptable. Implicit in the doctrines of Satanism is an admission that the extreme social Darwinism of might is right and survival of the fittest simply will not work—human society must be regulated in some way. Yet any form of regulation directly contradicts the claim that nature knows best, that the way of the world should be the way of the wild. Support for law and order, whatever the form, underscores the fact that human societies need structure other than that provided in a state of nature.

Modern Satanism's various positions on law, justice, and ethics are obviously extraordinarily problematic, and they ultimately sink into a morass of contradictions and totalitarian urges. Doctrines such as "Responsibility to the responsible" are both redundant and arbitrary. Rather than provide any reasons for obeying the law (other than out of fear of punishment), Satanists fall back on an egomaniacal insistence that they are the responsible and therefore are entitled to regulate their own behavior. When vigilantism, mass murder, serial killings, rape, dismemberment, forced sterilization, and slave labor are advanced as *just* practices, it is abundantly clear that being in support of law and order means little without identifying *whose* law and *whose* order is being supported. Any fascist, authoritarian, or dictatorial regime can be said to uphold law and order, but this does not make their laws just or equitable. Satanism all too often represents open contempt for democratic process and crucial concepts such as equality under the law and individual rights, substituting the arbitrary whims of a self-appointed elite as ethical and legal norms.

It is clear that the problematic aspects of modern Satanism's relationship to ordinary society have little to do with fears of organized ritual sacrifice and devil-worship. Rather, the greatest cause for concern lies in the values it popularizes. Of course, to argue that modern Satanism *causes* criminal activity is to overstate and oversimplify matters. The archetypical lone-wolf Satanic killer such as Ramirez no doubt is a profoundly disturbed individual, regardless of any contact with a Satanic church. Yet Satanism certainly attracts those predisposed to antisocial or criminal acts, and undoubtedly reinforces the belief that their acts are justified. No one will ever claim that *The Satanic Bible* provided them with the skills needed to assimilate as a constructive member of society, or provided them with the perspective needed to temper antisocial tendencies. Satanism instead encourages and exacerbates such inclinations. Iconic killers and criminals—in particular Charles Manson—have achieved a dubious celebrity with Satanists, and their actions have been interpreted as a real-world example of Satanic principles. Ultimately, the most concerning aspect of Satanism is its consistent support for values that can be described as crypto-fascist, in that a movement ostensibly focused on individualism frequently advances political doctrines in line with the worst instances of totalitarianism.

The Plague of Nazism: Satanism and the Extreme Right

If there is anything fundamentally diabolical about LaVey, it stems more from the echoes of Nazism in his theories than from the horror-comic trappings of his cult.
—*Newsweek*, August 16, 1971

With due respect to Mr. Hitler…
—Anton LaVey, "Introduction," *Might Is Right*, p. 7

Mein Kampf is a political *Satanic Bible*.
—Michael Aquino, *Church of Satan*, p. 367

One of the most consistent and recurrent themes of modern Satanism are its connections to fascism and neo-Nazism. At times these links are ambiguous, as with the occult interests of Satanists and the frequent adoption of fascist or quasi-fascist iconography. At other times they are more readily apparent, such as in ideological and political issues, areas in which the doctrines of Satanism are frequently appear only minimally removed from National Socialism, if at all. Frequently, the links have been more explicit, as is the case with numerous smaller groups since the movement's inception. Fringe Satanic organizations such as the Order of Nine Angels, the Order of the Black Ram, the Black Order and Satanic Skinheads represent a thorough synthesis of Satanism and neo-Nazism. In regard to the primary figures of Satanism, however, the issue is fraught with speculation and accusations, with the two main churches long maintaining that suspicions are based on misinterpretations and overreactions on the part of those scared of Satanism.

Public fears of Nazi affinities in the axioms of modern Satanism were present from the very beginning, as evident in the 1971 *Newsweek* comment at the beginning of this chapter. The previous year, another *Newsweek* article on the Church of Satan had noted the presence of Swastika and Confederate flags besides LaVey's desk. He referred to them as "symbols of aggression and power...that may be used in later rituals."[1] Pagan author Isaac Bonewits, who was briefly in the Church of Satan in the late 1960s and appeared in *Satanis: The Devil's Mass*, stated in 1971 that LaVey "plagiarized Nietzsche and Hitler to put together a philosophy that appealed to fascists countrywide."[2] He later wrote of witnessing Church of Satan members turning up to rituals dressed in authentic Ku Klux Klan robes and Nazi uniforms.[3] Bonewits was echoed by LaVey's friend Willy Werby, who admitted attending early Church of Satan Halloween parties until "a group of guys showed up in Nazi uniforms."[4] In 1972, a journalist referred to Hitler, Charles Manson, and Anton LaVey as an "unholy trinity," describing LaVey's focus on weeding out the weak as advocating "an essentially fascist state."[5]

The charges of profascism or pro-Nazism became stronger in the late 1980s, when a new generation of more publicly extreme Satanists became prominent. As a result, the larger Satanic organizations—particularly the Church of Satan—have often been forced onto the defensive, frequently downplaying associations with fascism, and actively denying any Nazi links. The responses are now well-rehearsed. Satanism is commonly described as apolitical, attracting people from all points on the political spectrum. Peter Gilmore presents the standard defense:

> The Church of Satan is not a NAZI organization. As has been said many times before, one's politics are up to each individual member, and most of our members are political pragmatists. They support political candidates and movements whose goals reflect their own practical needs and desires. Our members span an amazing political spectrum, which includes but is not limited to: Libertarians, Liberals, Conservatives, Republicans, Democrats, Reform Party members, Independents, Capitalists, Socialists, Communists, Stalinists, Leninists, Trotskyites, Maoists, Zionists, Monarchists, Fascists, Anarchists, and just about anything else you could possibly imagine. It is up to each member to apply Satanism and determine what political means will reach his/her ends, and they are each solely responsible for this decision. Freedom and responsibility—must be a novel concept for those who aren't Satanists.[6]

The majority of groups on this list can be removed with little discussion. The idea of a liberal Satanist is far from convincing, as the Satanic eschewal of compassion, contempt of democratic conventions and scorn for egalitarian values is diametrically opposed to the most basic liberal principles. Satanic ethical individualism is also completely incompatible with any form of socialist or communist collectivism. Satanists are typically politically conservative, tending towards the extremes of conservatism. Its natural political affinities are with the far right, and with the doctrines of fascism and Nazism in particular. As a senior Church of Satan member notes in an online discussion: "I will say that certain ideologies do seem more resonant with our philosophy, and these should be evident after a reading of our central texts by Anton Szandor LaVey."[7]

One of the problems with linking Satanism with fascism is that the latter has developed since World War II into an amorphous term of abuse that is easily rebutted. "Fascist" or "fascism" are commonly used as a slurs on one's enemies. In everyday speech, they represent a charge of authoritarianism, oppression, or any form of intolerance, be it political, religious, or ideological. In this form they are used indiscriminately to describe conservatives, liberals, bureaucrats, fundamentalist Christians or militant Islamicists; even LaVey lambasted "politically correct liberal fascism."[8] "Nazi" often functions the a similar way. Obviously, the reason that "Nazi" and "fascist" are so widely used as pejoratives is because of their association with the most infamous political regimes and notorious crimes of history. Mere name-calling, however, does not clarify matters.

A narrower definition of fascism, which is henceforth used here exclusively, focuses instead on its historical sociopolitical form. It is most famous for the Italian fascist government of Benito Mussolini (1922–1943) and Germany's Nazi regime under Adolf Hitler (1933–1945) but also includes Spanish, Portuguese, Hungarian, French, British, and Romanian political parties of the same period. The common denominators of these groups are their authoritarianism, ultranationalism, staunch anticommunism and antiliberalism, political and social elitism, militarism, and willingness to use violence as a political tool. Also typical are extensive use of propaganda and iconography, xenophobia, racism, victimization of minority groups, and entrenched lack of compassion for underprivileged members of the body politic.

A particularly good definition, one that captures the nature and character of fascism in practice rather than theory, is advanced, after due deliberation, by Robert Paxton in his excellent study *The Anatomy of Fascism:*

> Fascism may be defined as a form of political behavior marked by obsessive preoccupation with community decline, humiliation, or victimhood and by compensatory cults of unity, energy, and purity, in which a mass-based party of committed nationalist militants, working in uneasy but effective collaboration with traditional elites, abandons democratic liberties and pursues with redemptive violence and without ethical or legal restraints goals of internal cleansing and external expansion.[9]

Undoubtedly, the most extreme example is Germany's Nazi regime. Nazism combined all of the above characteristics with explicit and institutionalized racism and anti-Semitism. Nazi theories of racial superiority cast the Germanic people as the leader or master race with others, such as the Slavs of Eastern Europe, as slave races. These races were considered parasitic upon the master race, an impediment to its historical and cultural development. As such, they were expendable. Nazi propaganda systematically dehumanized enemies by using the term *Untermensch* (subhumans) to refer to Czechs, Gypsies, Poles, homosexuals, the handicapped, and especially the Jews. Their supposed inferiority was used as justification for their systematic mass extermination. The Holocaust took the lives of an estimated 6 million Jews and 2 million Poles. Another 7 to 11 million Slavs, Soviets and political prisoners were also killed (these are not considered part of a systematic genocide). The Nazis are the prime example of a fascist regime in action; implementing the policies of extreme social Darwinism and attempting to engender a superior race based on strength, might, and purity.

THE FERAL HOUSE/ABRAXAS CLIQUE

Within Satanism in the 1980s, the charges of fascist or pro-Nazi sympathies became stronger as a new generation of Satanists with links to the extremist fringe rose to prominence. A small group of individuals in particular befriended the reclusive LaVey in this period and became the most visible public proponents of Satanism: Adam Parfrey, Nikolas Schreck, Michael Moynihan, and Boyd Rice. In conjunction with LaVey's daughter, Zeena, these figures played an important role in further radicalizing Satanism with their shared obsessions: the idolization of Charles Manson, the notion of the decline of Western culture, collaboration with the far right, and an increasingly heavy emphasis on radical social Darwinism.

Parfrey was a writer and journalist who rose to fringe-culture fame in 1987 with his work on so-called extreme sociology, *Apocalypse Culture*, a compendium of works on topics such as eugenics, Oswald Spengler, necrophilia, and self-castration. The following year he complied *The Manson File*, an unabashedly pro-Manson collection of the killer's writing presented as the authentic voice of a counterculture icon. He eventually set up the independent publisher, Feral House, and specialized in works on serial killers, conspiracy theories, and Satanism—including all five of LaVey's books.

Parfrey was unwilling to publish *The Manson File* in his own name, and enlisted Manson advocate Nikolas Schreck to put his name to it as editor. Schreck was a member of the Gothic band Radio Werewolf with a deep interest in the occult and Nazism—"Radio Werewolf" was a Berlin-based Nazi propaganda unit in the closing days of World War II. He continued campaigning on Manson's behalf, portraying him as a misunderstood icon-oclast in the 1989 documentary *Charles Manson: Superstar.*[10] Involved with Zeena LaVey, whom he later married, Schreck later departed the Church of Satan with Zeena and eventually joined Aquino's Temple of Set.

Self-professed fascist Michael Moynihan, another member of this loose network of friends and social agitators, also bears well-documented radical right links. In 1992, Moynihan's Storm imprint published neo-Nazi James Ma-son's *Siege*, an anthology of violent National Socialist writings (Mason had also contributed to *The Manson File*). In addition to its predictable racism and anti-Semitism, *Siege* lauds Hitler as one of the greatest men in history, and exhorts Charles Manson and other mass murderers as supreme examples of defiance against the system. Mason also befriended LaVey, and was in return presented with a signed copy of *The Satanic Bible*. The volume bore a personal dedica-tion from LaVey praising its recipient as "a man of courage and reason."[11] Moynihan was a member of Mason's Universal Order, a shadowy militant collective outlined in *Siege*. He later wrote *Lords of Chaos*, published by Feral House, an analysis of Satanism and the murderous Norwegian black metal scene that trails off into lengthy, tenuously linked discussions of Moynihan's far right Odinist/Nordic occult agenda.

A most prominent member of this extremist clique was industrial musician Boyd Rice of the band NON. A self-described aesthetic fascist—frequently utilizing fascist imagery in live performances—with connections in the Na-tional Front, Rice's ideological affinities are in no way obscured. In 1984 he founded The Abraxas Foundation, a social Darwinist think tank, with revi-sionist historian and Holocaust denier Keith Stimely (who later worked for Parfrey). Abraxas members also included Schreck and Moynihan. Rice is blunt in the reasons for his support of the theory:

> Social Darwinism is simply the idea that the Darwinian concept of "survival of
> the fittest" applies to man. It's the idea that within a culture, superior individuals
> will rise to the top, and inferior individuals will sink to the bottom, as a part of
> natural selection. It isn't related to fascism, Nazism, or racism—it's just the way
> of the world.[12]

Rice's assessment of social Darwinism is a little misleading, as the creed does not simply advocate that supposedly superior individuals be allowed to rise to the top but rather that they be proactively assisted, at the expense of those who are forcibly repressed. Furthermore, many would disagree with the final sen-tence denying its connections to Nazism and fascism. Hitler himself wrote:

> A stronger race will drive out the weak, for the vital urge in its ultimate form
> will, time and again, burst all the absurd fetters of the so-called humanity of

individuals, in order to replace it with the humanity of Nature which destroys the weak to give his place to the strong.[13]

At this point it is apparent just how close the tenets of Satanism and Nazism are. The only difference between Rice's comments and the passage from *Mein Kampf* is that Hitler explicitly frames his theory in racial terms; ideologically, their claims are identical (as Rice, an enthusiastic supporter of *Might Is Right*, is no doubt aware). Nonetheless, Rice is open in his endorsement of the bankrupt claims of social Darwinism, and unperturbed by his reputation as a neo-Nazi:

> When all is said and done, I have no great quarrel with being labelled a "fascist." While it is not the whole story, it implies (to me) a sort of Marquis De Sade worldview that sees life in terms of master and slave, strong and weak, predator and prey. I know such views are highly unfashionable, but to me they seem fairly consistent with what I've seen to be true.[14]

A member of the Church of Satan from the early 1980s, Rice became a magister, the highest level below the high priest, and close friends with LaVey. As a member of the church's governing body, he was offered the chance to succeed as high priest upon LaVey's death in 1997, but declined. He appeared so often during this period as a senior representative of the Church of Satan he was erroneously recognized as its high priest on several occasions. In the early 1990s Rice developed a near symbiotic relationship with fundamentalist talk show host Bob Larson, with the ratings-and-revenue–motivated evangelist banking on Rice's willingness to shock listeners with naked anti-Christian prejudice. Rice in turn milked denunciations such as an infamous on-air "Boyd, you are Satan!" as little less than celebrity endorsement.

The new breed of Manson-revering, neo-Nazi-courting Satanists made their collective mark in San Francisco on August 8, 1988 with an unashamedly fascistic rally. The significance of the date comes from two sources: the eighth letter of the alphabet, representing Hitler ("88" is neo-Nazi code for "Heil Hitler"), and the anniversary of Manson's 1969 murder of Sharon Tate, symbolizing the death of the virtues of the 1960s, a so-called decade of corruption. Organized by Rice, and featuring Parfrey, Schreck, and Zeena LaVey, with Bob Heick, founder of the Californian skinhead gang American Front, also present, the event was an explicitly militaristic occasion for the new radicals of Satanism. As Rice introduced it, the event was a sacred day: "We mourn not its victims, we honor its victors…I would remind those here that murder is the predator's prerogative, and there is no birth without blood."[15] Rice later described the event as "a recapitulation of a destruction ritual that Anton LaVey performed on August 8, 1969."[16] The collaborations between these figures and their various publishing, musical, and activist activities set the tone for Satanism in the 1980s and 1990s.

DEFENSES: NAZISM SCARES PEOPLE, SATAN SCARES PEOPLE

The emergence of a publicly harder-edged Satanism did not go unnoticed. Either Satanism had lurched violently to the right, or the preexisting tendencies had simply become more obvious. LaVey was clearly aware of the danger that accusations of neo-Nazism posed to his organization's thin veneer of respectability as an alternative religion. In the early days of the church he had often referred to Satanism as "one part the most blatant outrage with nine parts of social respectability." As the scales tipped dramatically in favor of outrage, he no doubt recalled the fate of the Process Church and became actively involved in trying to insulate Satanism and protect his primary income source—the Church of Satan.

Satanists' denials of Nazi or fascist sympathies generally follow two lines: that Satanism is politically nonprescriptive (as already argued by Gilmore) and that the similarities are merely a matter of aesthetics. In the essay "A Plan," LaVey advanced a version of the second defense: "The aesthetic of Nazism is grounded in black. The medieval black magician, usually a Jew, practiced the 'Black Arts.' The new Satanic (conveniently described as 'neo-Nazi') aesthetic is spearheaded by young people who favor black clothing, many of whom have partially Jewish backgrounds."[17] For LaVey, the issue could be resolved by acknowledging commonalities in dress sense and a questionable reference to occult traditions (while medieval occultism drew heavily on Jewish mysticism, the most influential practitioners were almost exclusively *Christian* Kabbalists).

Unsurprisingly, such flimsy defenses achieved little. In the mid-1990s, Peggy Nadramia, wife of Peter Gilmore and future Church of Satan High Priestess, made a widely circulated defense of the Church on the online alt. satanism bulletin board. She began with an attempt to exculpate the reputation of Boyd Rice by drawing attention to his nonpolitical interests: "The last time I talked to Boyd, we discussed our Barbie collections. Some Nazi [he is]." Nadramia's main argument was simple: "Nazism scares people. Satan scares people. Some Satanists like to scare people, so they dress in Nazi fashion and have fun goosestepping down the strasse. B.F.D." Without addressing why Nazism scares people, she continues: "'The plague of Nazism' is being trumped-up by those who would choose to drive a wedge between us, disperse us and weaken us. Don't let them do it. Lighten up."[18]

Nadramia's response is notable for two points. Firstly, it makes no substantive arguments as to how the affinities between Satanism and Nazism are mistaken, instead arguing vaguely that "Satanists see nature as a dark force, a very fascist force."[19] Secondly, her cavalier dismissal fails to acknowledge that the Nazis did far more than scare people: the regime's warmongering was directly responsible for the deaths of tens of millions of people, and its social policies resulted in the industrialized extermination of millions in custom-built death factories. Yet, within the Church of Satan, the most infamous and inhumane crimes in history are *no big deal*. Spurious though they may be, Nadramia's disavowals of Nazi and fascist affinities have been widely accepted as convincing by those Satanists requiring reassurances that the accusations are unfounded.

The claim that the Satanism/Nazism issue is merely a matter of aesthetics is the most frequently recurring apologia. The following comments come from an interview with LaVey and his partner of later life, Blanche Barton, in Moynihan's *Lords of Chaos*. In response to the statement "Many fear a strong connection between Satanism and some forms of Fascism,"—itself a deeply ironic comment, in that it was made by a Satanist who belonged to a neo-Nazi organization—Barton and LaVey replied:

> Barton: It's an unholy alliance. Many different types of such people have made contact with us in the past. The anti-Christian strength of National Socialist Germany is part of the appeal to Satanists—the drama, the lighting, the choreography with which they moved millions of people [...]
>
> LaVey: Aesthetics more than anything are the common ground between Satanism and fascism. *The aesthetics of National Socialism and Satanism dovetail* [emphasis added] ... The aesthetics of Satanism are those of National Socialism. There's the power of romance and drama, coupled with the romance of overcoming such incredible odds.[20]

Typically, LaVey and Barton make very little attempt to distance Satanism from fascism, offer no criticisms of National Socialism, and attribute the similarities to aesthetics and "anti-Christian strength."

The "Satanic aesthetics equals fascist aesthetics" argument is extremely revealing. German cultural critic Walter Benjamin noted as early as 1936 that fascism represented a calculated substitution of sensory experience for reasoned debate. "The logical result of Fascism is the introduction of aesthetics into political life."[21] Nazi iconography in particular was designed to articulate a sense of power and elicit an emotional reaction from the German public. The massive rallies at Nuremberg were effectively enormous rituals, part of the vast Wagnerian drama at the heart of the National Socialist message, and a substitute for open debate. A prime example is the immortalization of the rallies in Leni Riefenstahl's 1935 propaganda documentary *Triumph des Willens* (*The Triumph of the Will*). A visually enthralling exercise in the pure aestheticization of political ideology, the work makes little effort to articulate Nazi doctrine, instead focusing on "the power of romance and drama" in the Nazi aesthetic. In this manner the aesthetics of National Socialism played a central part in supporting the Third Reich. As historian George L. Mosse notes, "Aesthetics shaped the fascist view of man, of his surroundings and of politics. It was the cement which held fascism together."[22]

The terms "aesthetic fascist" or "aesthetic fascism" are therefore tautological. To employ the aesthetics of fascism is to align yourself with fascism; to be an aesthetic fascist is to be a fascist. Rather than distancing Satanism from Nazism, the acknowledgement of the accord between their respective aesthetics only strengthens the underlying ideological similarities. Combined with the consistent downplaying of Nazi crimes—usually by omission—to acknowledge that the "aesthetics of National Socialism and Satanism dovetail" is to admit far more than LaVey and Barton realized. It is impossible to regard or employ the visual imagery of fascism in general, or Nazism in particular, without regard for the actions the nations under fascist control committed. Anyone who does so is either morally anaesthetized, implicitly supporting of those actions, or both. Either way, the argument creates no distance between Satanism and fascism or Nazism. Rather, it binds them together.

Attempts to decouple Satanism and fascism on the grounds of the apolitical nature of the former are equally superficial. As the previous chapter's discussion of social policies displayed, Satanism embodies a specific ideological and social agenda that can be clearly placed to the extreme right of the political spectrum. The fact that prominent Satanists are prepared to flirt with Nazism and fascism is instructive. Their indifference to the realities of Nazism and its crimes shows the natural affinities between the two ideologies, and gives an indication where the central tenets of Satanism—social Darwinism, elitism, group-oriented eugenics, contempt for equality, eschewal of pity and compassion—actually lead. In this context, it is surprising that *The Satanic Bible* contains only a single reference to Hitler or Nazism. It is unsurprising, however, that the reference is principally uncritical:

> From every set of principles (be it religious, political, or philosophical), some good can be extracted. Amidst the madness of the Hitlerian concept, one point stands out as a shining example of this—"strength through joy!". Hitler was no fool when he offered the German people happiness, *on a personal level*, to insure their loyalty to him, and peak efficiency from them.[23]

To interpret "strength through joy" as an example of the Führer's largesse towards the German populace is to rewrite history. The Strength Through Joy leisure-time organization was one of the Third Reich's primary instruments of control. By carefully manipulating group dynamics, the Nazis used peer pressure and majority influence to enforce conformity to Nazi ideals and minimize internal dissent.[24] The movement, like the party rallies and the aesthetics of Nazism, played an important part in the wholesale indoctrination and manipulation of the German populace. Strength through joy, for its part, has become a recurring slogan within Satanism, an outwardly innocent statement that bears a clear link, for those who recognize its origins, to Hitler and Nazism.

MEIN KAMPF AS A POLITICAL TEXTBOOK

Given the strong parallels between Nazi and Satanic doctrines, it seems implausible that serious, long-term Satanists are unaware of the commonality, despite repeated public denials. In *Church of Satan*, his account of his time within LaVey's organization, Michael Aquino provides a communication he sent to prominent members of the church, including LaVey, in 1974. In it Aquino discusses in detail the relationship between Nazism and Satanism. His appraisal of their affinities is revealing and worth quoting at length.

> According to Satanic criteria, the importance of Nazi Germany is that it succeeded in touching the very core of human behavioral motivation factors. In short, Adolf Hitler knew what really makes people tick, and he formed a political party designed to make those desires legitimate and respectable in German society. As you know from the *Satanic Bible*, people are motivated basically by crude and bestial emotions—greed, lust, hatred, envy of others' success, desire for power, desire for recognition, etc. Civilization has repressed such anarchic emotions in order that people may live together with a certain amount of peace. When one deliberately unleashes those emotions, consequently, there is going to be a bit of unpleasantness—war, domestic purges, or the like.
>
> The keys are there for those who can read them. They are spelled out in extraordinary detail in the most obvious place: *Mein Kampf*. It is in vogue today to say that *Mein Kampf* is boring, disorganized, illogical, and unreadable. This is true—for minds conditioned to the platitudes of egalitarianism. A first-grade reader wouldn't get very far with a textbook on atomic physics either.
>
> *Mein Kampf* is a political *Satanic Bible*. For control of mass movements of human beings, it is far more important than anything ever written by Jefferson, Locke, Marx, Lenin, or Kissinger...[w]hen you read *Mein Kampf* as a political textbook, however, you must mentally eliminate the dependence upon anti-Semitism which pops up now and then. This was a personal quirk of Hitler's, which later became a convenient scapegoat for German frustration. It is essentially unimportant to the main points of *Mein Kampf* [...]
>
> We are fortunate that the Auschwitz taboo prevents people from looking too closely at the rest of Nazi Germany, or from experimenting with any of its

regular governmental doctrines. Because they work. They are the essence of true political power. Anti-Semitism is irrelevant to them.[25]

Though he distances himself from Hitler's anti-Semitism and racism, there is little else that Aquino disapproves of: Nazi ideology is Satanic ideology politicized; the psychology and sociology of the two are identical; war and "domestic purges" are merely a "bit of unpleasantness"; and *Mein Kampf* is a work of profundity and importance, its bad reputation the result of the inability of lesser minds to understand it. The fascist state, according to Aquino, is the political embodiment of Satanic principles.

At the time of writing the memo, a year prior to founding the Temple of Set, Aquino was the second-highest member of the Church of Satan, editor of its official mouthpiece *The Cloven Hoof*, and the organization's most prolific writer, apart from its founder. This exchange took place at the time James Madole's neo-Nazi National Renaissance Party was trying to form an alliance with the Church of Satan. LaVey spent time with Madole and described him "a nice chap who is doing his thing," though he ultimately repelled the NRA's advances, mocking the intelligence of the skinheads. Fortunately, there is no need for speculation regarding LaVey's private opinion on the issue of Nazism and Satanism, for Aquino included the High Priest's reply: "Your analysis of the relative merits of National Socialism and the lack of understanding by some of the American neo-Nazi types is of course accurate."[26] LaVey, like Aquino, suffered no illusions regarding the commonality between the two ideologies.

THE JEWISH QUESTION

Though the key Satanists' approval of Nazism is straightforward, the issues of anti-Semitism and racism are more complex. It is, of course, far more difficult to separate Hitler's anti-Semitism from his political doctrines than Aquino acknowledges. Hitler saw the struggle against the Jews as a world-historical struggle, and this vision influenced every decision he made. As noted previously, the wellspring of Satanic ideology, *Might Is Right*, is also riddled with anti-Semitism. It also prefigures key elements of Nazism, to the extent that one study of social Darwinism labels it "proto-fascist."[27] This fact has not been unnoticed by white supremacists and neo-Nazis, for whom the work has become a popular text. LaVey was also well aware of the resonances, just as he was always privately aware of the deep concordance between Satanism and Nazism. As he noted in his mid-1990s foreword to Redbeard's work:

It has recently been claimed that *Might is Right* was the inspiration for the Nazi movement. With due respect to Mr. Hitler, Satan rest his soul, I don't think he ever set eyes on *Might is Right*, but had done his own share of homework and thinking out the premises for *Mein Kamf* [sic]. Again: diverse minds can think similar thoughts.[28]

Given the extent to which prominent Satanists publicly deny fascist/Nazi sympathies, it is surprising to hear LaVey acknowledge so candidly the doctrinal similarities of *Might Is Right*, the ideological ur-text of Satanism, and *Mein Kampf* (Aquino's letter regarding *Mein Kampf* was, until recently, a private affair). LaVey, however, could be confident that he was speaking to a select group: his foreword was originally published in a 1996 edition of *Might Is Right* edited by white nationalist Katja Lane. Katja Lane was the wife of David Lane, author of the infamous 14 Words: "We must secure the existence of our people and a future for white children."[29] David Lane, a prominent neo-pagan and convicted neo-Nazi terrorist, died in prison in 2007 while serving a 190-year sentence for racketeering, conspiracy, and civil rights violations stemming from his involvement in the 1984 assassination of Jewish talk show host Alan Berg. This edition of *Might Is Right* also contained an afterword by George Hawthorne, then a member of Canadian white supremacist band RaHoWa (an abbreviation of "racial holy war").

LaVey's readiness to be published alongside militant white supremacists is a clear indication of how far involved with the extreme right he had become. He was semipublicly expressing his admiration for Hitler and had joined his new generation of followers in openly collaborating with hate figures. This foreword was later reprinted in an edition of *Might Is Right* published by then Church of Satan member Shane Bugbee (effectively a Church of Satan special edition). In addition to LaVey's foreword, the Bugbee edition contains an afterword by Gilmore where he praises the work, now clearly associated with the racialist far right, as "an accurate depiction of how human societies function."[30] Again, LaVey and Gilmore could be confident their audience was select.

Despite being published alongside vicious anti-Semites, LaVey's relationship with Judaism and anti-Semitism is a confusing, often bizarre state of affairs. His published comments indicate he was simultaneously trying to achieve two seemingly incommensurate goals: to insulate the Church of Satan from charges of neo-Nazism whilst excusing his Jewish blood to his extremist associates (in a 2003 interview, *Siege* author James Mason admitted that he "liked and admired LaVey" but couldn't ignore that "LaVey was, of course, a Jew").[31] In "A Plan," LaVey made a spectacularly misguided attempt to defuse charges of anti-Semitism by reconciling Satanism and Judaism. "To be a Satanist is, by association, already to be aligned with the universal devil Jew. The Jews have always had the devil's name." In LaVey's mind, Jews are outsiders, Satanists are outsiders, therefore a pragmatic "Jewish/Satanic connection" is the obvious outcome.[32] This logically fallacious attempt to co-opt

Jews into Satanism concludes by collapsing into incoherence:[33] "The only place a rational amalgam of proud, admitted, Zionist Odinist Bolshevik Nazi Imperialist Socialist Fascism will be found—and championed—will be in the Church of Satan."[34] Whatever this statement is supposed to mean—if anything—LaVey fails to recognize that Jews, unlike Satanists, did not *choose* to adopt a pose as rebellious outsiders and social pariahs; they became so as the result of centuries of persecution and vilification that culminated in attempted genocide.

LaVey continued his campaign by calling attention to the Jews who collaborated with the Nazi regime. In the essay "The Jewish Question?" LaVey cites five Nazi collaborators, a few historical anti-Semites with Jewish origins such as composer Richard Wagner, declares that "[t]he list seems endless," and concludes that there is no longer any issue to be addressed in Jewish-Nazi history: "What's a little holocaust between friends? The Holocaust needs no revisionism."[35] Having belittled the deaths of millions, he then writes approvingly of the fraudulent *Protocols of the Elders of Zion*, declaring them a fine example of a master plan, ignoring their long history in the justification of anti-Semitism and central use in *Mein Kampf* and Nazi propaganda. These remarks are both offensive and imbecilic. The attempt to link Jews with Nazism and Satanism is crude and illogical, and the cavalier downplaying of the magnitude of the Holocaust is grossly insensitive. Combined with his evident respect for Hitler and collaboration with violent white supremacists, serious questions exist concerning LaVey and the issue of anti-Semitism. That he was—as his defenders point out—himself part Jewish is of little relevance; he never identified as being Jewish or was part of the wider Jewish community,[36] and in fact identified strongly with Jewish anti-Semites:

> Any person I've ever met who's accomplished something in his life has had a real disdain for his own people. [Not that they hate Jews or Germans or Irish or Italians per se—just that they hate stupidity and herd mentality.] Some people that come from Jewish backgrounds, where Judaic traditions were really emphasized in the home, are the most rabid anti-Semitic people I know. And I don't blame them.[37]

The strained relationship with this issues is continued by LaVey's successor. In his afterword to *Might Is Right*, Peter Gilmore makes no attempt to distance himself from Redbeard's anti-Semitism, instead praising him as "the type of individualist who would be LaVey's kin by nature in a rejection of the fetid Nazarene."[38] In a laudatory afterword to a consistently anti-Semitic text, he makes no attempt to distance himself from its contents, instead bemoaning the "continued assertion of these foul Nazarene doctrines on our civilization."[39] Though Gilmore has issued denials of racism within the Church of

Satan elsewhere, it is obvious that the most fitting place for them, if genuine, would be in the afterword to a text embraced by white supremacists. In truth, anyone genuinely opposed to racism and anti-Semitism would not wish to be associated with a work as nakedly prejudiced as *Might Is Right*.

ADMIT NOTHING, DENY EVERYTHING, MAKE COUNTER-ACCUSATIONS

In general, the main Satanic churches' relationship to racism and anti-Semitism is best characterized as systematically ambiguous. It is a pattern already seen in the Temple of Set's racialist reading list, LaVey and Gilmore's consistently mixed messages, and Gilmore's endorsement/nonendorsement of racial neo-pagan occultism. It is a tradition continued today by Church of Satan Magister James Sass (aka Magister Svengali), another former Charles Manson pen pal who flaunts his links to the incarcerated killer and promotes James Mason's *Siege* from his blogs. Like many Church of Satan members he maintains a neither-confirm-nor-deny stance toward controversial issues. In a blog post titled "Am I a Racist? Do I Care?" Sass declares: "I love ambiguity, especially because most people can't handle it":

> My pureblood peckerwood ancestors owned slaves in North America. What do I think about "reparations" for slavery? I demand "reparations"…I want my slaves back! […]
>
> A lot of so-called "racism" in the world is justified, because most people look, think, and act like caricatures of themselves drawn by their worst enemies.
>
> I'm also not someone to hide behind "misanthropy" saying "I hate all people equally", like some kind of half-assed politically correct loser trying to be "edgy". I do detest the human race as a whole, but some groups are more deserving than others, at different times and for various reasons, and I won't hesitate to "call a spade a spade" if the shoe fits. I don't care what color your mammy was, her offspring should suffer the swift consequences of their own idiocy.[40]

Sass's emphasis on ambiguity allows controversial claims to be addressed without clarification. The issue of slavery is addressed with a joke, racism is largely "justified," yet excused as part of his general prejudice and misanthropy, and any clear articulation of his views becomes ensnared in a bottleneck of clichés. Although controversial topics have been raised, the reader is left more baffled than informed: "some [racial] groups are more deserving than others," but just which ones is left unanswered. All of which fits well with the magister's personal motto: "Admit nothing. Deny everything. Make counter-accusations."[41] This refusal to state a clear position is evident throughout Satanism and is a common defense against charges of Nazi and fascist leanings, racism, and anti-Semitism. Rather than present a clear position on any of these issues, Satanists instead issue spurious, noncommittal denials that are inevitably followed by contradictory or mitigating comments.

A similar phenomenon is evident in the widespread appropriation of Nazi iconography such as the Wolfsangle, sig runes, Black Sun motif, and Totenkopf (Death's Head). In defending their use, Satanists draw attention to their historical origins, as most have origins that precede their Nazi application, some stretching centuries back into the past. The swastika is a prime example, as its different forms have a lengthy history and are still used extensively in Eastern faiths. What this defense fails to explain is why, of all the traditional runes and symbols available, Satanists almost exclusively adopt those with well-established Nazi associations. More specifically, they adopt the primary iconography of the SS, the Nazi's own elite order. With these symbols, many of the pre-Nazism connections are questionable. Of the numerous permutations of the Wolfsangle, Satanists adopt the form used by the SS and contemporary fascist organizations. Likewise, the Totenkopf used in the nineteenth century by the Prussian military was markedly more cartoonish than the SS's Death's Head version, which is the version Church of Satan members use. The Black Sun motif is even less ambiguous. Though based on medieval German symbols, the Wewelsburg mosaic is a unique design commissioned specifically for Himmler, and its primary contemporary association is Nazi occultism, for which Nazi Satanic groups and esoteric neo-Nazis adopt it. Furthermore, Nazi symbols are frequently used in combination with each other, such as the popular image of a Totenkopf superimposed over a Wolfsangle. When the Church of Satan Emporium (its online store), for example, advertises its Wolfsangle rings backgrounded by a Black Sun motif, there can be little doubt of the reference being made by two primary symbols of the SS. Despite the systematic exploitation of ambiguity, any denial that Nazi symbols are being used *as* Nazi symbols is both disingenuous and unconvincing.

The result of these evasions is that more moderate Satanists accept the denials at face value and are unable to assess them objectively. British Satanist Gavin Baddeley addressed the Church's far right involvement with apparent distaste in his book *Lucifer Rising*. Although obviously uncomfortable with individuals such as Schreck, Rice, and Moynihan, Baddeley however fails to address—or recognize—why Satanists find themselves drawn to fascist imagery and Nazi ideology. Baddeley's primary concern, evidently, is to protect the reputation of LaVey, which he continued in the short 2006 documentary *The Devil's Disciples*. "Even if you think that LaVey is a complete fraud, even if you think that he preached proto-fascism...the fact remains that he is a fascinating character who clearly had his finger on a particular pulse at a particular point in history." The fact that LaVey is an interesting character is evidently more important to Satanists like Baddeley than his popularizing of fascist doctrines. The fact that neo-Nazis have their fingers on the same pulse doesn't occur to Baddeley, who regards *The Satanic Bible* as "largely common sense with a good dose of blasphemous outrage,"[42] "a manual for *productive* misfits and *creative* outsiders."[43] Baddeley, it is worth noting, has few pretensions of objectivity—he acknowledges prominently that LaVey made him a priest of the Church of Satan *while* he was researching *Lucifer Rising*.

SATANISM AND NAZISM: THE COMMON GROUND

Baddeley's milquetoast assessment of Satanism can be juxtaposed with the more objective work of Norwegian researcher Roald Kristiansen. In the course of mid-1990s research of a PhD dissertation, Kristiansen was one of the few scholars to study the doctrines of modern Satanism in any depth, at a time when almost all academic attention was focused on debunking the SRA scare. Kristiansen closely analyzed the literature available at the Church of Satan and Temple of Set Web sites. One of the few commentators to recognize that the doctrinal presuppositions of Satanism were of far greater concern than the symbolic use of Satan, Kristiansen was particularly concerned by Michael Aquino's fascination with Nazism and the rumors surrounding the deep interest in Nazi occultism in the Temple of Set's Order of the Trapezoid. He also clearly identified the true parallels to Satanism's elitism and skewed interpretation of the natural world.

> The Satanists' anthropology is of an extremely hierarchical nature. Humans are divided into categories according to their physical, mental and emotional strength. Those with superior strength in these areas are more valuable than those with lesser strength, and the ultimate ideal is to get rid of the lesser individuals as they disturb the exercise of the will of stronger persons. It is in this sense that the charge of fascism still makes sense. The link to fascism and to Nazi ideology is found in their anthropology, which advocates the rights of the stronger because they are the superior beings. The practical result of this anthropology is identical with Nazi social and political ideologies, which sought to eradicate peoples considered to be of lesser value (Jews, gypsies, blacks, homosexuals, etc.).[44]

Kristiansen's analysis identifies the reasons for the recurring connections between Satanism and neo-Nazism that some moderate Satanists, and many other academics, fail to see. Satanic political principles, like those of the Nazis, are in direct opposition to many of the values taken for granted in Western sociopolitical culture: the rule of law (specifically laws created by democratic process), the rights of the individual, freedom of expression, and protection of civil liberties. Furthermore, it is clear that the senior members of the Church of Satan and the Temple of Set are *fully aware* of the ideological commonality of Satanist and Nazi doctrine. Claims that the similarities are purely aesthetic are sophistry, as are claims that the organizations are politically agnostic. An organization can determine or reflect the views of its followers, and if either the doctrines of the organization or the sympathies of large numbers of its members are shown to be widely pro-Nazi, then the organization can be deemed so too. Both major Satanic churches and their senior members are demonstrably sympathetic to fascism and, in particular, Nazism.

Notwithstanding these points, there are important differences between Satanism and fascism or Nazism. The first is obvious: Satanism is a religious movement, not a political one. Beyond this point, Satanism could never function politically as it would never be able to accrue the mass support or complicity of the conservative elite that enabled fascists to come to power in the early twentieth century. The use of Satan as a positive figurehead is simply too repellent for the majority of society, particularly in America. Satanism, by virtue of being *satanic*, effectively damns itself to the margins. It could never be a populist movement. Secondly, Satanism has too strong a stress on individuality to be a mirror image of Nazism or fascism. Fascism, in all its forms, was focused on the primacy of the group and the subordination of individual rights to the requirements of the group/state—a point that Gilmore uses as his primary defense against "The Fascism Question." (Gilmore nonetheless acknowledges that in a fascist state "the clever Satanist would either attempt to be the person who pulls the strings, or, more likely, his associate.")[45]

Despite these qualifications, there is still a large degree of commonality. Satanism (as represented by the larger Satanic churches) may not be politically active, in the sense of actively engaging in the political process, but a large number its central policies are political in nature, dealing as they do with social policy, law, justice, and rights. Some of the Church of Satan's policies substantially mitigate its own focus on extreme individualism; for instance, its longstanding desire to breed a genetic elite: individuals don't evolve, populations do. Given Satanism's extreme positions on these issues, it is entirely unsurprising that Satanism attracts people from the far right, for there is considerable overlap. Nazism and fascism are certainly "more resonant" with their beliefs than mainstream political positions. The influence of extreme social Darwinism is present in both, as is the rhetoric of strength and opposition. The Nazi's arbitrary raising of one social group (on racial grounds) has a direct analogue in the bogus elitism of Satanism, and Satanism's pseudo-scientific doctrines of genetic purity slide easily into racialist theories. Likewise, the Nazi dehumanization and denial of rights of non–group members is repeated in the antagonistic rhetoric of Satanism. As Aquino's successor in the Temple of Set, Don Webb, states in his essay "Become Evil and Rule the World,"

> Satanism shares some aspects with Nazism. Both contain the notion of an elite which energize and direct the masses. Both are frank about the power of Darkness and the stimulation of dark images. Both draw power from the distant past and the far future. Both are committed to the ideal of speeding individual emotion. Where the Nazis went wrong was turning their dynamism against the life forces of others.[46]

Of course, when your ideology consistently emphasizes the special privileges, insights, and worth of the "elite" as opposed to the worthlessness of the "masses," there is little to keep the former from "turning their dynamism against the life forces of others."

The aesthetics of National Socialism and Satanism dovetail precisely because the ideologies of National Socialism and Satanism dovetail. Their commonality lies in the conclusion, stemming from Nietzsche and reinforced by social Darwinism, that compassion, pity, and egalitarianism are misplaced pieties at odds with the cold realities of the world. In *Social Darwinism: Science and Myth in Anglo-American Social Thought*, Robert Bannister analyses *Might Is Right* as an explicitly Nietzschean text, labeling it "undoubtedly the most bizarre product of the American Nietzsche vogue...the most forthright statement of social Darwinism in the annals of American literature."[47] Similarly, in *Morality: A Moral History of the Twentieth Century*, Jonathan Glover explicitly identifies the "hardness...rooted both in their Nietzschean outlook and in their social Darwinism" that enabled ordinary Germans to be made complicit in systematic, mass genocide.[48] Glover's analysis of Nietzschean ideals is quite clear about the conclusions of Nietzsche's amorality and elitism: "Struggle, egoism, dominance, slavery, the majority having no right to existence, peoples that are failures, hardness, the festival of cruelty, the replacement of compassion for the weak by their destruction."[49] As Glover points out, the danger lies in the Nietzschean program of embracing strength and elitism while systematically eliminating compassion and empathy. Satanism clearly represents the very same values and a similar response (an entirely unsurprising phenomenon, given how much of Satanic thought is in fact Nietzsche filtered through Redbeard), and therein lies the attraction of Nazism to Satanists: the shared ideological core and basis in bogus scientism.

Satanism's connections with fascism and neo-Nazism are undeniable, pervasive, and predictable. It is unsurprising that LaVey had a swastika in his study in the 1960s, just as it is unsurprising he collaborated with white supremacists in the 1990s. It is equally predictable that many Satanic splinter groups would slide over into extreme forms of neo-Nazism. Satanism certainly has been plagued by Nazism, but it is equally clear that the host has been more than accepting of the contagion. When not denying that he heads a neo-Nazi organization, Gilmore engages in particularly strident rhetoric:

> The principle of the survival of the strong is advocated on all levels of society, from allowing an individual to stand or fall, to even letting those nations that cannot handle themselves take the consequences of this inability. Any assistance on all levels will be on a "quid pro quo" basis. There would be a concomitant reduction in the world's population as the weak are allowed to experience the consequences of social Darwinism. Thus has nature always acted to cleanse and strengthen her children. This is harsh, but that is the way of the world. We embrace reality and do not try to transform it into some utopia that is contrary to the very fabric of existence.[50]

It would be difficult to overstate what is being advocated in this passage. The barely euphemistic reference to "a concomitant reduction in the world's population" as vast numbers are "allowed to experience the consequences of social Darwinism" echoes some of the worst aspects of Nazi doctrine. It calmly acknowledges that the implementation of the Church of Satan's vision would result in death on a massive scale. In this context, the use of the phrase "cleanse and strengthen" is particularly disturbing. History has shown very clearly how people experience the consequences of social Darwinism, how quickly *being allowed to experience* would shift to *being made to experience*, and the enormous human cost of scientifically illiterate representations of reality made by extremist demagogues.

The question of whether or not organizations such as the Church of Satan and Temple of Set are institutionally racist becomes, at a certain point, a non-issue. The form of discrimination they practice is every bit as baseless and dangerous as any form of racism, and they systematically pander to racists. The euphemistic rhetoric of Nazism and Satanism allows a very quick shift from allowing the strong to survive to preventing the weak from existing. No wonder then that the legitimate scientific community has long since recognized both the deep flaws and terrible consequences of social Darwinism, and has assessed it accordingly:

> As applied to society, the "survival of the fittest" almost invariably means the survival of the thugs with the big sticks. Mental defectives and cripples were doomed in Nazi Germany, where the survival of the fittest meant the destruction of the weakest, where the definition of fitness was determined by the strong and the means of selection was the truncheon and the death camp. The final degradation of the human spirit was reached by Dr. Mengele standing at the head of a line of concentration camp inmates and, with a gesture of the hand, directing the fitter inmates to one side, to work, and the ill and old to the other side to die.[51]

Natural Born Satanists:
The Psychology of
Discriminating Iconoclasts

Such men alone are my readers, my right readers, my predestined
readers: what matter the rest? The rest—that is merely mankind. One
must be above mankind in strength, in loftiness of soul—in contempt.
                              —Friedrich Nietzsche, *The Antichrist*,
                                 in *The Portable Nietzsche*, p. 569

Though the principles that Satanism represents have been amply discussed, a few key questions remain: *how many* Satanists are there, *who*
are they, and *why* do they adopt the creed? The first question is undoubtedly
the most difficult to answer, as the numbers of those who adhere to its general
principles are unclear. In its four decades of existence, modern Satanism has
consistently managed to attract a statistically small but nonetheless dedicated
fringe following. Though no single sect has ever had large membership, their
numbers would—even if made public—only represent a small percentage of
those who call themselves Satanists. As can be expected from a creed that
places such heavy emphasis on individualism, the majority of Satanists are undoubtedly satisfied to live the left hand path in private without formal membership in a larger organization.

Reliable data on the number of Satanists is scarce. The key organizations
have little transparency, and the decentralized, nebulous nature of the subculture provides few indicators. The best source for figures is official census
data, but even there specific figures for Satanists are often incorporated in the
general "other religions" category, as is unfortunately the case with its modern homeland, the United States. Regardless, the few countries that provide

detailed recent census data on alternative religions are instructive. Australia has 2,247 Satanists,[1] New Zealand 1,167,[2] Scotland 53,[3] England and Wales 1,525,[4] Northern Ireland 12,[5] Canada 850,[6] and Russia estimated at 2,000 plus.[7] Viewed as number of Satanists per 100,000 people, these figures represent: Australia 11.3, New Zealand 29, the United Kingdom 2.7, and Canada 2.9. The numbers for Australia and New Zealand, while significantly higher than other countries, are not unexpected. Given their populations, the two countries host disproportionately active Satanic communities. Only Scandinavian figures—particularly those of Norway, where Satanic black metal is a primary cultural export—could be expected to equal or surpass this number. The available data, while useful, is limited. With no figures for continental Europe and the United States, 800 million people in the primary demographic zone for Satanists—Western democracies with Christian heritage—are excluded. A global figure can therefore only be broadly estimated at 30,000–100,000.[8]

The issue of *who* Satanists are is easier to settle. An interesting analysis of the demographics of Satanism is presented in a 2001 study by James Lewis, an academic defender of alternative religions. His so-called statistical caricature of a Satanist is, entirely unsurprisingly, a single white atheistic male in his 20s. This typical Satanist practices magic, is nontheistic (i.e., does not recognize the existence of a sentient being named Satan), and comes from a predominantly Christian upbringing. Satanism is often not the first alternative religion he has been involved in, with experiments with other occult or neo-pagan belief systems figuring prominently. Lewis's study reaffirms the importance of *The Satanic Bible* and LaVey's preeminent position within Satanism, especially as the survey participants appear to be predominantly nonaffiliated, independent Satanists (a predictable phenomenon, given the reclusive nature of Temple of Set members and the Church of Satan's institutional insularity). *The Satanic Bible* is a doctrinal touchstone for many, which Lewis partly attributes to "LaVeyan Satanism's ability to hold together a number of diverse meanings found in the ambivalent symbol of Satan." Although the sample cannot be considered authoritative,[9] the general findings are a fair representation of the adherents of Satanism, and they are born out by earlier studies and the observations in researching the current work.[10] The only point to note is that the higher level hierarchies of the established churches tend to be long-term adherents who are generally a decade or two older.

THE HERO AS OUTSIDER

To discover the *why* of Satanism we need to turn to the diverse meanings captured by "Satan," to return to the psychology of the Miltonian/Romantic reappraisal of the devil and the individualist philosophies synthesized into

Satanism. A major factor in the attraction of Satanism lies in the presuppositions of its doctrines: the insistence that the Satanist is an inherently unique individual, a principled rebel who transcends the banality of everyday society. There is a strong parallel here between the attraction of Satanism and the legend that draws so many to the iconoclastic writings of Nietzsche. The German theorist is an important touchstone for Satanists, and the romance of his vision, articulated here by Nietzsche scholar and translator R. J. Hollingdale, is central to his continued popularity:

> The Nietzsche legend is the legend of the isolated and embattled individual: the hero as outsider. He thinks more, knows more, and suffers more than other men do, and is as a consequence elevated above them. Whatever he has of value he has created out of himself, for apart from himself there is only "the compact majority", which is always wrong. When he speaks he is usually misunderstood, but he can in any case be understood only by isolated and embattled individuals such as himself. In the end he removes himself to a distance at which he and the compact majority become mutually invisible, but his image is preserved in his icon: the man who goes alone [...]
>
> It is certainly not going too far to say that thousands who claim to have been enlightened by Nietzsche, and believe what they claim, have in reality been seduced by the legend of the man who went alone, the high plains drifter of philosophy.[11]

Hollingdale clearly identifies a fallacy in the Nietzsche worship of many—a confusion of his emotional and psychological appeal with the value of the philosophy itself. In reading Nietzsche there is an ever-present danger of succumbing to an impassioned, inspired intellect. Nietzsche, admittedly a thinker and writer of great genius, is also a manipulative figure, possessing a seductive voice that systematically flatters readers. His vivid prose actively creates the illusion that by reading his works, the privileged few are being exposed to secrets that the vast (inconsequential) multitude will never avail themselves of. "*We aeronauts of the spirit!*—All those brave birds which fly out into the distance, into the fartherest distance."[12] Once Nietzsche has been read—more correctly, *experienced*—the reader is set apart from the majority, never to return. "*Horizon: infinity*—we have left the land and taken to our ship! We have burned our bridges—more, we have burned our land behind us!"[13] Unfortunately, the mystique of this vision fosters a personal, emotional attachment to the philosophy that often impedes critical reflection.

Just as Satanic ideology echoes Nietzschean social doctrines, so too does it imitate the Nietzschean psychological model and the myth of the hero as outsider. The Satanist is the individual placed apart from mainstream society, forever misunderstood by the tepid majority. In "Nonconformity: Satanism's Greatest Weapon," LaVey expresses the idea clearly:

> The very designation of Satanism is described by its semantic designation, *The Other*…A Satanist should not allow himself to be programmed by others. He should fight tooth and nail against it, for that is the greatest enemy to his freedom of spirit. It is the very denial of life itself, which was given to him for a wondrous, unique experience—not for imitation of the colorless existence of others.[14]

The rhetorical seductiveness of these principles is also clear in Gilmore's "Rebels without Cause":

> The Satanist, who naturally sees himself as his own God, does not generally care what other people think about him. His monumental sense of self worth leaves no possibility for him to be touched by critiques from the unworthy, but he does examine the reactions of the individuals whom he has come to cherish and respect. Thus the discriminating iconoclast and true rebel dissents out of reason and passion, and possible options, not knee-jerk reactivity.[15]

As with Nietzsche, a great divide is established between the privileged, enlightened few and the impoverished masses. The modern Satanist is a principled, spirited rebel in the Byronic tradition, set above and beyond the "colorless existence" of the "unworthy."

The attractiveness of this romantic vision is undeniable. A British Church of Satan member in his early 20s who employs the motto "Strength through Joy" describes his conversion to Satanism:

> I discovered that I was a Satanist after reading the *Satanic Bible* at the age of 13.
>
> I felt that Dr. Anton LaVey echoed and expanded upon my thoughts and opinions and had created a wonderful philosophy that finally championed man's natural animal instincts and shunned the hypocritical self-denial doctrines espoused by the masses.
>
> After eagerly reading more from and about Dr. LaVey and reading, watching and listening to interviews with Boyd Rice, Blanche Barton, Peter H. Gilmore and Diabolus Rex, my obvious natural connection to the Church of Satan became even more apparent and solid and I realised that I had always resonated with the archetype of Satan on so many levels […]
>
> Several years later, once I had reached full maturity I finally became a member and proud Citizen of the Infernal Empire.[16]

In Satanism, the individual has encountered a body of thought that resonates deeply with him. He admires—with a tinge of hero worship—the established figures within the movement, identifies strongly with the doctrines, is swayed by its intellectual validation of otherness, and accepts the authority of LaVey uncritically. The early age at which he encountered Satanism is also common—Rice, Gilmore, and many others describe first encountering the movement during early adolescence.

The comment "I discovered that I was a Satanist" is of central importance, for it is a reaffirmation of a central doctrine—the belief that a Satanist is *born*, not *made* (an uncanny echo of the "begotten not made" phrase in Christian liturgy). This doctrine affirms that Satanists are somehow intrinsically different from the rest of society: one does not become a Satanist, one simply recognizes that one has always been a Satanist, and accepts the designation in recognition of this fact. Adherence to the doctrines of Satanism is far more than a mere lifestyle choice, it is the recognition of one's true nature, that one is special, unique, a part of the alien elite. This rationalization serves a crucial psychological role: the individual's feelings of alienation and social awkwardness are not merely accounted for—they are validated as reflecting a deeper truth.

In his 1988 work *Satan Wants You*, Arthur Lyons identified the psychological and sociological effect of this process. In identifying with an elite segment of society, the individual is given a sense of power and importance. Formerly out of sync with the majority of society, in Satanism the new convert recognizes that these feelings of alienation stem not from himself—the problem is with society in general, those who fail to see the world as it really is. Satanism, in preaching the *correct* view of society, validates the otherness of the convert. As Lyons notes, "an inferiority complex becomes a superiority complex."[17] The solution that Satanism represents provides an explanation for and justification of the feelings of alienation, inverting the prior situation: "When a person is economically, socially, or psychologically shut out of the mainstream of society, he will seek solace in extreme solutions."[18] In this interpretation of the world, it is the herd that is wrong; the Satanist stands alone with the privilege of his new insights. Furthermore, it is in no way a contingent development—discovering the truth of Satanism is presented as an aspect of the individual's nature; it is predestined.

Anthony Moriarty, a clinical psychologist with extensive experience dealing with young Satanists, reinforces this interpretation. "LaVey argues that embracing Satanism is an affirmation that you are not as disturbed as you or others might think."[19] Moriarty's attention is focused on the issue of adolescent Satanism, and the preexisting emotional problems that Satanism preys on and, frequently, exacerbates. In his assessment, young people "find Satanism to be an effective vehicle by which they can vent the anger and frustration caused by these underlying emotional problems. The process of accepting Satanism is a simple but powerful solution to a variety of emotional problems."[20] Moriarty highlights that most of the adolescents he has dealt with have been dabblers, those at an early stage of engagement with the ideology, and divides them into four self-explanatory categories: psychopathic delinquent, angry misfit, pseudo-intellectual, and suicidal impulsive. For them, the key to the attraction of the creed is its relentless individual egoism, heavy focus on personal empowerment, and its systematic predation on feelings of alienation, low self-esteem, and desire for uniqueness.

Moriarty's analysis is particularly concerned with the superficiality of Satanism and its promotion of false dichotomies that make it appear a logical necessity. One of the examples he cites is *The Satanic Bible*'s claim that Satanism is the only rational religion that properly acknowledges human nature and sexuality. This claim is combined with the representation of all other religions as incompatible with a healthy sexual life, thus making Satanism more enticing. Satanism also advances an us-versus-them dichotomy that exacerbates preexisting estrangement from mainstream society, simultaneously making Satanism a more attractive option while hardening passing tensions (for instance, adolescent angst) into long-term prejudices. The subject's world becomes divided into rigid categories of Satanists and non-Satanists, bolstered by shallow arguments and assurances of strength. These dichotomies, though false, are powerful and effective rhetorical tools.

STRENGTH, MASCULINITY, AND AUTHORITY

The strength provided by Satanism is another of its primary attractions. To individuals who feel disempowered and marginalized, Satanism provides an important boost to their sense of self-worth and empowerment. This empowerment comes in many forms: the description of violence as natural and therefore both acceptable and inevitable, the championing of revenge and concomitant need for enemies, the superiority complex entailed by its doctrines, and the confidence fostered by the belief that one has acquired knowledge and insights denied of the vast majority. From *The Satanic Bible*'s cry of "Death to the weakling, wealth to the strong!"[21] to the social Darwinian interpretation of the maxim "survival of the fittest," Satanic discourse constantly reaffirms the polarity of the strength derived from Satanism and the weakness of those who remain entrapped in herdlike passivity.

The Satanic focus on strength is extremely masculine, as are many other aspects of the creed. The virtues it champions are frequently very male-oriented, both in their content and presentation: aggression, vengeance, hostility, primal sexuality, and LaVey's conception of "man the animal." This emphasis is represented in the gender of Satanists, of whom the majority are male. Satanic rituals also have a persistent focus on male sexuality, which has often seen females reduced to little more than fleshly altar ornamentation (although later developments in sex-magick are more even-handed). Even LaVey's *The Satanic Witch*, often viewed as a work of feminine empowerment, largely reinforces chauvinistic conceptions of the abilities of women. The work features an explicit reaffirmation of traditional gender roles, detailing LaVey's views on what constitutes a "real man" or "real woman." Though written for a female audience, *The Satanic Witch* is in many ways a demeaning work, reducing females to their ability to physically attract and manipulate a man, which is presented as an occult power. Feminine empowerment, in LaVey's assessment, largely concerns dressing in a sexually provocative manner.

At times the Satanic ideal of masculinity manifests itself in a surprising fashion, such as with Church of Satan Reverend Jack Malebranche's prohomosexual/antigay *Androphilia: A Manifesto Rejecting the Gay Identity, Reclaiming Masculinity* (2007).[22] The work is a sustained assault on the gay community for promoting victimhood, effeminacy, and an unnatural approach to life through its endorsement of a separate gay identity for homosexuals. In contrast, Malebranche advances a view of homosexuality that celebrates "'manhood," arguing that an individual's sexual identity shouldn't determine his interests, views, and aesthetics. Arguing that the dominant gay identity has emasculated men, Malebranche consistently reasserts strength (not just physical, but of character) as a macho ideal and central ingredient to his conception of true masculinity.

The Satanic focus on strength and masculinity is undoubtedly a major factor in its attraction to many adherents. It provides a means to adhere to traditional conceptions of maleness in a feminist/postfeminist world, while the emphasis on primal sexuality maintains the feeling of transgressing mainstream moral conventions. It also provides active reinforcement to the dominant personalities of most Satanists and legitimizes their championing of strong, masculine ideals in a world where traditional conceptions of maleness are increasingly restrained.

Satanism's embrace of occult practices is another factor in this empowerment. Religions are generally an expression of human impotence in the face of the unknown, requiring supplication and praise to a superior force or entity. The realm of the occult, on the other hand, is focused on the acquisition of power and achieving control over one's surroundings. This is particularly true of the Left Hand Path / black magic occult forms attractive to Satanists (as opposed to the more benign white magic forms practiced in Wicca or other modern pagan beliefs). The occult is doubly attractive. Firstly because of its secret ("occult" = hidden) nature, and secondly because of its promise of supernatural powers and knowledge made available only to the skilled practitioner. The inherent humility of acquiescence in the face of the unknown is replaced by pretensions of control over dark forces. Even the Church of Satan, which officially denies the efficacy of occult ritual, still affirms the subjective, psychological value of ritual practice to the practitioner. An ex–Temple of Set member similarly makes explicit reference to the psychological importance of acquiring power:

> Over and over again at meeting... I heard [Setians] describe their everyday frus-
> trations, which led them to want power—such as problems with jobs and rela-
> tionships. Then, once they joined the group, they often used the practices they
> learned to counter these problems or vent their frustrations and anger. These
> practices in turn provided them with a socially channelled form to express their
> feelings.[23]

Unsurprisingly, the leaders of Satanic organizations have invariably presented themselves as skilled magical practitioners (the sole exception is Gilmore, who relies more on presenting an air of intellectualism). Their authority
comes from their privileged insights into the occult, ability to provide revelations of deeper truths to their followers, and stature as individuals. LaVey's
personal magnetism has been commented on by virtually everyone who met
him, and all analyses of the longevity of Satanism and its primary organizations have noted the importance of its iconoclastic founder. The LaVey
legend and what Aquino calls "Anton's undeniable charisma" facilitated his
ability to inspire fierce loyalty in his followers,[24] even after his death. Open
hero worship of the movement's founder is widespread, and his reputation
and dubious biographical claims are defended vigorously. LaVey represents
the "lone seer" that Hollingdale spoke of in reference to Nietzsche; the Black
Pope's dramatic appearance, personal mystique, and legendary background
are as important as anything his ever wrote.

Sociologist Max Weber influentially described this type of leadership as
charismatic authority. Common in new religious movements, the term denotes a form of leadership that draws its legitimacy from the specific personal
attributes of the central figure—normally in the form of supernatural powers
or insights that set him apart from the ordinary person. These powers or
knowledge constitute the entitlement of the leader, and result in a highly authoritative form of leadership. The leader/guru is able to pronounce on every
area of life with few restrictions. LaVey legitimized his authority in part by
presenting himself as the modern heir to a centuries-old occult tradition, in
part by presenting himself as the source of a new human potentiality movement with radical new insights into human nature. The reverence afforded
to both LaVey and *The Satanic Bible*, even outside his organization, are testimony to the importance of his charisma. It is, for many Satanists, difficult if
not impossible to separate the religion from the founder.

In his time observing the early Church of Satan, Randall Alfred noted that
LaVey's charisma served another important function, as it carries the "scent
of sanctity," an inversion of the "odor of rejection." LaVey's charisma enabled

him to make the outrageous acceptable. "Much of LaVey's charisma is diabolical in nature, and he has been eminently successful in taking the stigma attached to the symbol of the Devil and, by dress, demeanor, and grooming, as well as by philosophy and ritual, turning it into a positive force for the attraction of publicity and followers."[25] Once again, accepted standards are inverted, and what is commonly regarded as negative is interpreted in a positive light. The fact that the masses regard Satan negatively only reinforces the power of his appeal.

NARCISSISM AND GROUPTHINK

At the individual level, the psychology of Satanism is characterized by its deep and pervasive narcissism. Many of the factors that make the creed attractive are characteristic of the narcissistic personality type, the inordinate self-love in individuals whose ambitions and self-image are disproportionately inflated in relation to their actual abilities. Narcissism is distinguished by a number of characteristics: exaggerated sense of self-importance, sense of entitlement, belief that one is special and should only associate with similar high-status individuals, arrogance that engenders contemptuous behavior toward others, lack of empathy, the requiring of excessive admiration, and preoccupation with fantasies of unlimited power and brilliance.[26] Satanism meets each of these criteria comprehensively. The Satanist's lack of empathy, misanthropy, strong antisocial tendencies, and delusions of superiority are typical of a narcissist personality type. The creed's foundational text is an open appeal to vanity and low self-esteem, systematically promoting an air of exaggerated self-worth and importance in its adherents while belittling any non–group members. Satanists' extraordinary sensitivity to criticism and aggravated hostility toward detractors are also indicative. As psychiatrist Erich Fromm observed in *The Anatomy of Human Destructiveness*, the narcissistic personality type

> needs to hold on to his narcissistic self-image, since his sense of worth as well as his sense of identity are based on it. If his narcissism is threatened, he is threatened in a vitally important area. When others wound his narcissism by slighting him, criticizing hem, showing him up when he has said something wrong, defeating him in a game or on numerous other occasions, a narcissistic person usually reacts with intense anger or rage, whether or not he shows it or is even aware of it.[27]

The narcissistic tendencies of Satanism are borne out by its focus on vengeance, frequent infighting, and the centrality of rites such as the destruction ritual.

Fromm also identified narcissism at the level of group interactions. Though Satanism is highly individualist, it nonetheless provides a community for the isolated individual to be a part of, the feeling that "there are others like me." LaVey, tellingly, repeatedly described his church as a group for nonjoiners. Fromm diagnosed group narcissism as an important factor in sustaining groups that appear, to the external observer, to be founded on unrealistic or grossly exaggerated claims. The central characteristic of such bodies is the assertion that the individual's group—be it a nation, religion, or political party and so forth—is the supreme iteration of its type. This claim "appears to be a realistic and rational value judgement because it is shared by many members of the same group." The fantasy upheld by the group's doctrines is transformed into social reality, but it is a reality "constituted by general consensus and not based on reason or critical examination." This phenomenon is particularly relevant to the larger Satanic organizations, which consciously set themselves apart from any outsider interference. Group narcissism

> is extremely important as an element giving satisfaction to the members of the group and particularly to those who have few other reasons to feel proud and worthwhile. Even if one is the most miserable, the poorest, the least respected member of a group, there is a compensation for one's miserable condition in feeling "I am a part of the most wonderful group in the world. I, who in reality am a worm, become a giant through belonging to the group." Consequently, the degree of group narcissism is commensurate with the lack of real satisfaction in life.[28]

Fromm's insights into group narcissism also casts light on another of Satanism's conundrums: why do individuals adopt principles that are largely unsupported by fact? Fromm's analysis highlights the power of consistent repetition and reaffirmation of the same principles without dissent, the echo chamber effect of Satanic insularity. Another complementary explanation is confirmation bias, a well-documented form of selective thinking whereby one tends to notice and to look for whatever confirms one's beliefs.[29] Any data that supports, or seems to support, one's beliefs is given disproportionate weight. Conversely, whatever undermines or contradicts these beliefs is conveniently discarded. The person who believes in ghosts, for example, will be more likely to attribute a slamming window to supernatural means than the simpler, more plausible explanation of the wind blowing. Superstition, religion, and ideology can play an important role in the subject giving credence to articles of faith over reason. If one's beliefs are little more mere prejudices, the effect is exacerbated; when the beliefs are based on solid evidence, data that confirms existing beliefs is less likely to lead the subject astray.

As confirmation bias is often used to explain why people maintain pseudoscientific beliefs, its relevance to Satanism is clear. The attractiveness of its outsider credos and bogus scientific basis are supported, in Nietzschean fashion, by highly emotional language rather than supporting data. Scientific terminology (particularly the vocabulary of Darwinism) is used in an ostensibly plausible fashion that buttresses the claims of Satanism, but the statements seldom withstand scrutiny. The perceived authority of those making such pronouncements also facilitates their acceptance. As Moriarty noted from his experiences dealing with young Satanists:

> While claiming to be very intellectual, they usually report beliefs predicated on the basis of information that is seriously lacking in logic or substance. In many cases, these Satanists believe that the truth is that which is found in the printed word. Having read a book (of their choice) makes it unequivocally true.[30]

The brazen self-confidence of their primary reading material, *The Satanic Bible*, masks its lack of legitimate authority, and heavy reliance on emotional appeals, flattery, and arguments that do not withstand sustained examination. In addition to the lack of critical thought, organizations such as the Church of Satan are institutionally opposed to any data that may contradict its official doctrines—they simply refuses to engage in any dialogue with parties that do not hold the same beliefs. Nowhere is this intellectual fraudulence more evident than the bigotry of LaVey's later writings:

> I have made a rule that I will not meet with or entertain anyone who petitions me without their having advanced some praise for me or my work. If asked, "Does someone have to agree with you to be your friend?" my answer is a resounding "YES!"...Anyone who doesn't like the way I do things can go fuck themselves. They are not entitled to their own opinion.[31]

This piece, fittingly titled "In Praise of Sycophants," appeared in LaVey's last book, *Satan Speaks!*, separated by a mere six pages from his oft-repeated dictum "the most important word to a Satanist is 'Why?'"[32]

AESTHETIC AND IDEOLOGICAL SATANISM

Satanism has, until now, been discussed as a uniform subculture. Though this assumption is certainly possible when regarding its general characteristics, it is also necessary to acknowledge its internal diversity. There are notable divergences in the positions of different factions, and even between individual Satanists. A moderate group like the League of Independent Satanists would take issue with many of the doctrines espoused by a group such as Satanic Skinheads. As noted in the discussion of Satanism's lengthy flirtation with fascism and neo-Nazism, there are members of the wider Satanic community who require, and readily accept, reassurances that Satanism is *not* a fascist ideology, Satanists who are quite explicitly opposed to racism and extremism.

While there is clearly a faction within Satanism that takes the ideology very seriously, there are also many whose adoption of the creed is based on a less strident interpretation of its doctrines. Any explanation of Satanism, therefore, has to be able to explain how some Satanists see the cause as an entirely benign alternative subculture, whereas others find it entirely compatible with National Socialism, racism, xenophobia, nationalism, and anti-Semitism.

There are obviously moderate and strong interpretations of modern Satanism and, moreover, a range of positions between the two. The more moderate interpretation adopts the idea of a principled rebellion against mainstream values but does not venture too deeply into the political and philosophical issues underlying the creed. This form of Satanism can be referred to as *aesthetic*, as opposed to the harder-edged, more *ideological* interpretation. A clear indication of the basis of aesthetic Satanism is found at the very beginning of *The Satanic Bible*, in the Nine Satanic Statements:

1. Satan represents indulgence, instead of abstinence!
2. Satan represents vital existence, instead of spiritual pipe dreams!
3. Satan represents undefiled wisdom, instead of hypocritical self-deceit!
4. Satan represents kindness to those who deserve it, instead of love wasted on ingrates!
5. Satan represents vengeance, instead of turning the other cheek!
6. Satan represents responsibility to the responsible, instead of concern for psychic vampires!
7. Satan represents man as just another animal, sometimes better, more often worse than those that walk on all-fours, who, because of his "divine spiritual and intellectual development", has become the most vicious animal of all!
8. Satan represents all of the so-called sins, as they all lead to physical, mental, or emotional gratification!
9. Satan has been the best friend the church has ever had, as he has kept it in business all these years![33]

The general principles of the Nine Satanic Statements present the core beliefs of most Satanists: the focus on man as an animal, anitauthoritarian antagonism to established religious authorities, inversion of dominant values, substitution of materialism for spiritualism, justification of hedonism, and individualist zeal. This immediately accessible message and validation of otherness establishes the framework for the principled rebellion of the "discriminating iconoclast." At the same time, the statements are limited by their brevity and superficiality. As catch phrases, they flatter the reader, bolster self-esteem, and promote a romantic conception of Satanism without expressing the concepts they entail in any depth. For example, the statement "man as just another animal…the most vicious animal of all!" can be either a simple representation of primal vitality or, if used to determine social policy à la *Might Is Right*, an entirely fascist concept. LaVey's Statements are broad enough to support both interpretations.

The greater understanding of what the creed represents comes with the counterpoint to aesthetic Satanism: ideological Satanism. The ideologically inclined Satanist has investigated its doctrines enough, and ventured far enough beyond the primary text, to recognize the obvious parallels to the principles it advocates. As soon as an individual begins to regard The Infernal Diatribe (the *Might Is Right* passages in *The Satanic Bible*) as anything more than dramatic hyperbole, he or she has taken the first step towards political extremism. Even within LaVey's works there is a steady progress toward stronger, less ambiguous formulations of many of the concepts introduced in his original work. Ultimately, the grim social vision of *The Satanic Bible*'s broad principles can be situated within a general synthesis of the works of Machiavelli, the Marquis de Sade, Malthus, Redbeard, Nietzsche, Oswald Spengler, and, frequently, Hitler.

This contrast between *aesthetic* and *ideological* Satanism is, admittedly, not a distinction made by adherents, who simply consider themselves Satanists (and all of whom are interested in aesthetics). It merely serves as a framework to capture and make sense of the diversity within the subculture. It explains how contradictory positions can be held by persons who nonetheless consider themselves Satanists and base this identification on the same text. It is more beneficial to think in terms of a spectrum of beliefs, with aesthetic Satanists on one side and the ideological adherents on the other. The far edge of aesthetic Satanism is largely indistinguishable from everyday goths (with the addition of the occasional pentagram or Baphomet). Toward the other end, Satanists are indistinguishable from neo-Nazis (or, frequently, *are* neo-Nazis). The Church of Satan and Temple of Set obviously tend toward the ideological end of the spectrum, and as such generally harbor the more extreme, ideologically driven members.

Thinking of Satanism in this way can help explain why an aesthetic Satanist can be perplexed or even offended by the more extreme, neo-Nazi courting figures within the scene. It can account for the deep involvement with the extreme right by long-term members of the Church of Satan, while simultaneously explaining why Moriarty's study of adolescent Satanists reported that the majority struggled to justify their adherence to the religion beyond recitation of catch phrases. It also accounts for the fact that 22% of the apparently independent Satanists polled by Lewis identified their political affiliation as Democrat or Green, associations seemingly at odds with many of the creed's underlying principles.[34]

Given the considerable distance between moderate and strong interpretations of the creed, it is necessary to ask: which reading, if either, is mistaken?

Obviously, there is a large overlap between those referred to here as aesthetic Satanists and those traditionally referred to as dabblers. By focusing on the confrontational image, rebelliousness, and alternative lifestyle elements of Satanism, those interested in the countercultural trappings of Satanism alone are largely oblivious to the deeper implications of the doctrines that they are embracing. As aesthetic Satanism requires less investment—both financially and intellectually—than membership to a particular organization, it may well be that this geographically disparate, completely decentralized grouping constitutes the majority of Satanists. The Church of Satan's $200 membership fee and Temple of Set's extensive vetting system and study demands obviously discourage more casual applicants. Unfortunately, these Satanists have an understanding of LaVey's work that is itself frequently superficial, championing Satanism as a philosophy of individualism but missing the underlying philosophical parallels with extremist ideologies. (The fault is largely LaVey's, as he clearly obscured his extremist tendencies within the drama and hyperbole of this bible.) The more extreme ideologues within the Church of Satan, Temple of Set, and other stronger organizations display a far stronger grasp of the central message of Satanism and its wider political and social implications.

SOCIOLOGISTS AND SATANISM

One commentator on Satanism who dissents from this line of interpretation is the previously mentioned James Lewis. To Lewis, Satanism is a largely positive movement, a means of self-affirmation that can promote "buoyant self-confidence" in its adherents. He argues that the conventional interpretation of Satanism—as predominantly a reaction against Christianity and a need to rebel—is incorrect, instead claiming "Satanists are reflective individuals who...have come to appropriate Satanism as a mature religious option."[35] The faith is fundamentally no different from any other religion. "One becomes a Satanist for much the same reasons one joins any religion—to achieve a sense of meaning, a supportive community, personal empowerment, and so forth."[36] Lewis, however, pays little attention to the ideological presuppositions that buttress this empowerment, seeing the religion as rational and based in naturalism: "Anton LaVey's primary legitimation strategy was to appeal to the authority of science, specifically to the secularist world view derived from natural science and to an animalistic image of the human being derived from the Darwinian theory of evolution."[37]

As one of the few academics who have devoted sustained attention to Satanism in the past decade, Lewis's shortcomings are unsettling. He dismisses Moriarty's analysis of adolescent Satanism as weak, without engaging any of the substantive claims the latter makes. He gives no indication that LaVey's appeal to the authority of science is a crude and unscientific application of Darwinian concepts, nor is there any indication that Lewis recognizes this crucial fact. Lewis also appears unaware of the extremist undercurrents in Satanism. In three papers devoted to the topic—one of which is subtitled "A Demographic and Ideological Profile"—he does not refer once to social Darwinism or any of the more intemperate pronouncements of LaVey, despite citing Redbeard's *Might Is Right* in the bibliography of each.[38] He further accepts, citing Moynihan's *Lords of Chaos*, the dubious proposition that neo-Nazi affinities are merely an aberration present in a small subset of "northern European Satanists" and that "[m]ost other Satanists, particularly outside of continental Europe, regard these individuals negatively."[39]

Other commentators have acknowledged that Satanism is not entirely negative, although without slipping into full apologetics. Lewis cites the mid-1970s work of sociologist Edward Moody approvingly, particularly Moody's observation that the practice of Satanism or black magic may enhance the practitioner's self-confidence and ability to interact with others.[40] Similarly, Randall Alfred's late-1960s infiltration of the Church of Satan portrayed LaVey as a showman who "recognizes the theatrical nature of enthusiastic religion,"[41] which was undoubtedly true of the early church. Alfred saw Satanism as fulfilling a certain religious function, and largely validated it as an alternative movement. "Satanism, specifically, and the other witchcraft traditions generally recognize some basic factors of human existence, and one way or another they will have their place."[42] An influential series of early-1970s articles by Marcello Truzzi, which laid the groundwork for most sociological analysis of the topic, also presented a largely favorable view. Truzzi typified Satanism as an "elitist, materialist, basically atheistic philosophy…the Church of Satan takes a position of extreme Machiavellianism and cynical realism towards the nature of man…This Satanist, then, is the *ultimate pragmatist*."[43]

As one overview of the academic treatment of Satanism acknowledges, sociological commentaries are mostly sympathetic analyses that emphasize "Satanism's ostensibly harmless character."[44] Those that examine the ideology and content of Satanism itself in any depth, such as Moriarty's work on adolescent psychology and Kristiansen's analysis of Internet Satanism, are generally far more critical of the movement. Furthermore, a number of sociologists have been accused of bias in their approaches.[45] The influential early-1970s work of Truzzi, Moody, and Alfred in particular can be criticized for a lack of critical distance. All three were enthusiastic participants in Church of Satan activities beyond research purposes. Moody and Truzzi were admirers and friends of LaVey's, and their names were even included in the original short-lived dedication page to *The Satanic Bible*. Alfred presented his interest in Satanism as an entirely academic matter, despite continuing his association with the church for many years after, eventually rising to the senior rank of magister. Arthur Lyons, author of *Satan Wants You,* similarly concealed his Church of Satan membership and posed as an impartial observer when discussing the topic publicly. Aquino later labeled the four men a "parade of parasites" for denying or obscuring the depth of their association "when in a position to stand up publically for Satanism and the Church of Satan."[46] From a non-Satanist perspective, the considerable insights of the most frequently cited commentators are unfortunately compromised.

A MATURE RELIGIOUS OPTION?

Ultimately, a number of different factors working in tandem can help explain the attraction of modern Satanism. The parallel to the Nietzsche legend is helpful in understanding its continuing appeal. A critical part of the psychology and attractiveness of Satanism is the desire to be special, to not be one of the crowd. Satanists define themselves by what they claim they are not—herdish, stupid, ordinary, conformist, and so on. The doctrines they embrace substitute the dominant norms of society with those diametrically opposed. Yet these doctrines are frequently stupefyingly superficial. They rest on claims that are advanced by the voice of authority, serving to flatter the follower into the belief that he is intrinsically better than the vast majority, while offering little substance to support these claims. To take one example, the claim that one is born a Satanist is obviously fallacious. There is nothing intrinsically—genetically or otherwise—different between a Satanist and non-Satanist. The factors that motivate one toward the creed are mostly contingent: feelings of alienation and resentment, low self-esteem, rebelliousness, and lack of critical analysis. The claim that Satanists are born, not made is, however, instructive in terms of how Satanism attracts followers. It operates predominantly at the level of rhetoric—promulgated, accepted, and repeated as a self-evident truism.

The lack of depth means that many who identify with Satanism are merely interested in the creed in a superficial way, as a means to bolster self-confidence and justify an alternative lifestyle. Undoubtedly, Satanism does promote confidence in its adherents. For the more casual followers, this confidence may indeed be largely harmless, constituting an outsider stance that expresses itself primarily in catch phrases and aesthetic choices calculated to offend mainstream society. But it is a confidence born of a skewed view of the world, bolstered by rhetoric and bluster rather than fact, and it is clearly a first step toward extremist ideologies. Given its consistent predation on narcissistic tendencies, it is difficult to see how Satanism can be considered a "mature religious option." Though it is possible to identify why it is attractive to those who adopt it, that alone does not validate the faith. Its doctrines consistently lead to a dogmatic insistence on the superiority of one's views, a profound absence of empathy, and complete disinterest in the interests or rights of others. Satanists are largely unable to see any issue from outside the prism of their own limited interests, and subsequently express opinions that tend toward the sociopathic. At its worst, it results in the disassociated moral vacuum of a figure such as Boyd Rice. From a 2003 interview:

> I think AIDS is probably the best thing that's happened to Africa. I mean, just imagine; this is a place with so much population that the land can't support it, and they can't feed themselves, and they're starving to death—to me it seems that something like AIDS would be a godsend...I think it would be great if that place were just turned into a big animal preserve—what about the animals? Fuck the human beings! Let them all slaughter each other with machetes, let them die of AIDS, let that entire continent turn back into a wild kingdom again.[47]

Though it would be preferable to regard Rice as a worst-case scenario, comments of this nature are all too common in Satanic publications, Web sites, bulletin boards, and online social networks.

The consistent inversion of mainstream values makes the outsider status of Satanism self-perpetuating. Even within secular societies, only a small minority will ever adopt Satan as a positive symbol. By adopting a figurehead that is anathema to large segments of society, the Satanist becomes permanently marginalized. No matter what definition LaVey choose to give the term, for the vast majority of people "Satanism" is synonymous with evil and the absolute negation of any moral order. By publicly labeling oneself a Satanist, the individual can only exacerbate any feelings of alienation from general society. This situation may appear self-defeating, but it has the benefit of providing a perpetual justification to the elitism of Satanism. As only a small minority will ever accept the designation, they can maintain the illusion that they are indeed a privileged minority that has accessed knowledge unknown to the masses. In the strained logic of Satanists, the fact that most people regard them with distaste if not contempt only reinforces their belief in their uniqueness and superiority.

Apocalypse Cheerleaders: Satanism in Popular and Not-So-Popular Culture

Satan is now a firm fixture in our cultural consciousness, due in no small part to the contributions of Milton, Blake, and others. Popular culture is permeated with references to Satan and satanic themes. From presidential warnings of an "Axis of Evil" and counter indictments of "The Great Satan," it is hard to escape the archfiend. References to him imbue our daily language: "I've had a hell of a day," "speak of the devil," "go to hell," "idle hands are the devil's workshop," "the devil's luck," "a devil's advocate," and many others. With representations in everything from movies and comics to hot sauce, the devil is very nearly omnipresent. Regardless of whether or not one literally believes in him, he remains Western culture's primary symbol for evil, with the possible exception of whatever dictator is splashed all over the current media.

Prior to 1966, the main satanic presence in popular culture—other than the rumors swirling around Crowley—were the Crowley-inspired novels of British spy/historical writer Dennis Wheatley. Occasionally, Wheatley took leave of espionage and drew upon the works of the Great Beast and Catholic occult scholar Montague Summers to write black magic novels. The first, and most well known, was *The Devil Rides Out* (1934), later made into an equally classic film starring Christopher Lee (1968).[1] Both the book and the film center around the activities of a devil-worshipping cult. The lead Satanist, Mocata, was based almost transparently on Crowley, and the occult terminology was drawn freely from his *Magick in Theory and Practice*. The mix of middle-class secret societies, ritual sacrifice, and a vivid depiction of a witches' Sabbat—attended by Satan himself—painted a convincing and unsettling picture of the power of black magic, and reaffirmed the popular culture power of the demon in red.

With its debt to Crowley's theories and personality, *The Devil Rides Out* is at least tangentially related to modern Satanism. It is difficult to say the same of other satanic works. Later blockbusters such as *Rosemary's Baby* and *The Omen* have little in common with the specific principles of modern Satanism, and the same can be said of most other satanically themed popular fictions. The vast plethora of hell, demonic possession, poltergeist, or Satan-themed horror films and thrillers that followed are often focused on pure shock value, accented with cursory occult references. Numerous, less obvious cinematic works can be said to better embody or explore various themes of modern Satanism. For example, the extended engagement with Nietzschean philosophy in Hitchcock's *Rope*, the vigilante ethic of the *Dirty Harry* or the *Death Wish* movies, the killer-takes-all code of De Palma's *Scarface*, the group-specific morality of Scorsese's gangster epics, Orson Welles's scornful assessment of the fruits of democracy in *The Third Man*,[2] and even the cartoonish homage to Spartan values in the 2006 blockbuster *300*. The latter, a vapid strength-and-honor–exhorting adaptation of Frank Miller's graphic novel, was particularly popular with Satanists. Following its release, even Magus Gilmore began to pepper his public appearances with references to the ethical and social practices of classical Greece—the film's abandonment of unfit infants to the elements is, philosophically speaking, one the most Satanic themes in recent cinema. Away from the mainstream, the avant-garde and Crowley-derived occult surrealism of Alejandro Jodorowsky and Kenneth Anger are also notable.

THE DEVIL AND HEAVY METAL

The most visible and confrontational contemporary adoption of Satan—and most frequent intersection with modern Satanism—is undoubtedly the world of popular music. Hard rock and heavy metal music have since their inception been repeatedly accused of being satanic/Satanic (traditional or modern conceptions), for reasons that are hardly obscure. Rock and roll in general, and heavy metal in particular, is driven by the need to adopt an antagonistic pose. Both are by definition antiauthoritarian, championing decadence, dissolution, and the transgression of conventional values. When looking for an antisocial standard nothing can be more provocative than the adoption of your society's leading personification of evil. Adopting a Satanic pose is a particularly effective means of validating one's rebellion, as Lord Byron, the hedonistic template for the modern rock star, realized more than two centuries ago. Rock music has seen a parade of rock stars follow the wayward poet in adopting the androgynous, effete sensuosity of the Romantic Luciferian figure, as exemplified by Jim Morrison, Mick Jagger, and Robert Plant, and so forth.

Heavy metal singers have gravitated toward the harsher, more demonic side of the devil, as can be seen in the exaggerated personae of Alice Cooper, Ozzy Osbourne, Glenn Danzig, and Marilyn Manson. All have tapped into the immense power of Satan/Lucifer to embody primal instincts and taboo-smashing. Pure escapism is another factor, as is a desire to shock the church congregation or, more to the point, mom and dad. What is difficult, however, is establishing when heavy metal Satanism is real and when it is show.

Satan entered mainstream rock music in the era of *The Devil Rides Out*, *Rosemary's Baby*, and the establishment of the Church of Satan. The Rolling Stones engaged in a late-1960s flirtation with Satanic imagery and themes, beginning with the psychedelic *Sgt. Pepper*–inspired misfire *Their Satanic Majesties Request* in 1967, which saw Mick Jagger appear on the cover in a sorcerer's hat. Their 1969 single "Sympathy for the Devil" confirmed for many that the band was of the devil born, an impression reinforced by their licentious lifestyles. Jagger and most of the band also had central roles in Anger's short film *Invocation of my Demon Brother*, which included a cameo from LaVey. The violence and deaths that marred the Altamont Speedway Free Festival of the same year—delegating security duties to the Hell's Angels in exchange (reportedly) for free beer proved an injudicious decision—quickly ended The Stones' run with the devil, and they quickly abandoned the theme. After being immortalized in the documentary *Gimme Shelter*, The Rolling Stones' appearance at Altamont became, along with the Tate/LaBianca murders, a powerful symbol of the collapse of counterculture values and the end of the 60s.

The same era saw the emergence of a more menacing form of rock, heavy metal, and the beginning of a trend toward darker subject matter and imagery. Black Sabbath were in the vanguard, detuning their instruments and employing the devil's tone (the tritone) to perform doom-laden epics. In the 1970s the three primary metal bands—Black Sabbath, Deep Purple, and Led Zeppelin—were seen as the embodiment of evil, an unholy trinity of noise and distortion. There was little substance to the rumors, apart from a few devil-related songs from Black Sabbath and Jimmy Page's friendship with Anger and significant interest in Crowley (Page is a major collector of Crowley memorabilia and at one point owned Crowley's Boleskine House in Scotland). It has long been tempting, for some commentators, to see the connections between these figures as evidence of an underlying conspiracy, despite mostly sketchy evidence. While it is true that members of Led Zeppelin and The Rolling Stones had various connections with Kenneth Anger, the Church of Satan, the Process Church (Marianne Faithful, Jagger's then girlfriend and costar in *Invocation*, was a member), and therefore the Manson Family, these facts do not indicate an organized proliferation of evil.

With rock music the established mode of defiance, there was no shortage of bands ready to play devil's advocate. Alice Cooper was a poster boy for diabolism throughout the 1970s, although he regarded his shock-rock antics as entirely benign—even mocking his own predicament on *Goes to Hell* (1976). He nonetheless established the use of the aesthetics of evil in rock, and numerous bands followed his lead in adopting similar trappings. Kiss were a vaudeville act from the beginning, and while Van Halen's "Runnin' with the Devil" may sound dangerous at first, it was a largely meaningless celebration of freedom and hedonism. Equally superficial would have to be the dance with the devil of Los Angeles umlaut enthusiasts Mötley Crüe. The band is a prime example of heavy metal's exploitation-for-infamy approach to satanism. Desperate to shock, their 1983 album *Shout at the Devil* saw the quartet adorned in penta-grams surrounded by hellfire. Yet by their 1985 follow-up *Theatre of Pain*, the diabolism had been largely dispensed with in favor of an ultra-glam aesthetic based primarily on pink feather boas and eyeliner. Across the Atlantic, British metal stalwarts Iron Maiden were accused of being satanists after the title track of their 1982 album *Number of the Beast* described a band member's nightmare in frenzied detail. More than willing to put their collective tongue in cheek, the band included a nonsensical backwards message about a three-headed monster in the track "Still Life" on their following release *Piece of Mind* (1983).

Backwards messages, called "backmasking," did not remain benign for long. The strong association of heavy metal with satanism eventually drew more determined opposition. Heavy metal was in the center of the storm during the SRA scare, with a number of prominent bands accused of utilizing back-masking and subliminal messages to influence their listeners. Two Arizona teenagers attempted suicide with a shotgun in 1985 after drinking, smoking marijuana, and listening to the Judas Priest album *Stained Glass*. One was suc-cessful, the other lost half his face and later successfully committed suicide with painkillers. Judas Priest were sued for causing the original suicide with a backwards message supposedly saying "I took my life!" on the track "Beyond The Realms of Death." The band was acquitted after they identified a num-ber of ludicrous backwards messages in their songs. Judas Priest members later observed that if they were to put subliminal messages in their music, telling their fans to kill themselves wouldn't make much sense—"buy more albums" was a far more bankable suggestion.

Ex–Black Sabbath frontman Ozzy Osbourne was similarly sued over his provocatively titled track "Suicide Solution." The song, which dealt with the alcohol-related death of original AC/DC singer Bon Scott, was connected to the 1984 suicide of a teenager suffering from depression. Osbourne was accused of using an advanced mind-control technique dubbed "hemi-synch" on the track along with the subliminal lyrics "Get the gun and try it! Shoot, Shoot, Shoot!" Cleared of the charges, the perpetually baffled Osbourne later commented, "Does this guy [the opposing attorney] think I'm a fucking sci-entist or a rock star? The only sink I've ever heard of is the one you wash your fucking face in every morning."[3] As the self-proclaimed "Prince of Darkness," Osbourne is a leading example of how far from reality a cloven-hooved public persona can be, as his hapless turn as a reality TV dad clearly establishes.[4]

Despite—or more likely because of—the rising controversy, heavy metal continued to get uglier and more provocative. As the old guard were fighting off lawsuits, a new breed of faster, more aggressive bands were championing satanism in a far more direct fashion. British black metal pioneers Venom made no attempt to hide their backmasking, inserting reversed *Paradise Lost* excerpts along with threats to "burn your soul" and "crush your bones" at the start of "In League with Satan."[5] With Venom, however, the subliminal satanic messages were largely irrelevant, as they were generally less disturbing that the lyrics recorded in the correct direction, as testified by the tracks "Sons of Satan," "Live Like an Angel (Die Like a Devil)," and others. As the most genuinely frightening band of the era, they were widely regarded as genuine devil-worshippers, even by many heavy metal fans. Practicing (LaVeyan) Satanists, the band adopted and immortalized the Baphomet and inverted pentagram of the Church of Satan. They placed the combined images on the cover of their 1981 debut *Welcome to Hell*, helping to popularize the myth that both were legitimate and traditional satanic symbols. Venom was joined in the move toward greater extremes by Sweden's Bathory and Denmark's Mercyful Fate, influential underground bands that both had a heavy focus on the devil. King Diamond, lead singer of Mercyful Fate, was friends with LaVey and a long-term member of the Church of Satan, further cementing the ties between the music and the creed.

In the wake of Venom's base sexual obsessions and at times laughably camp satanism a legion of bands followed. One of the first and most prominent were American thrash metal pioneers Slayer, who quickly established themselves as Hell's de facto house band. With their greater technical ability and blistering song tempos providing a more terrifying vehicle for the devil's music than early black metal's primitive and often crude performances, Slayer became one of the world's top-selling extreme metal acts, and a perennial lightning rod for critical excoriation. For many opponents of heavy metal, Slayer were irrefutable proof that the entire genre was hell-bound. The band's extraordinarily bad reputation—built on the sulfurous albums *Hell Awaits*, *Reign in Blood*, *South of Heaven*, and *God Hates Us All*—was eventually revealed to be grossly overstated, and it has slowly become apparent that half of the band are practicing Christians. Nonetheless, in the realm of extreme and satanic metal, their influence is enormous.

Propelled as it is by a rejection of the mainstream, heavy metal has consistently been confronted with the paradox of eventually becoming mainstream itself, and has each time responded by becoming more extreme. The late 1980s and early 1990s rise of death metal and the second wave of black metal saw heavy metal became home to countless artists claiming to be genuine devil-worshippers, on their albums and in the music magazines at least. With the commercial success of bands like Slayer and death metal act Morbid Angel, both of who could sell half a million copies of an album, the number of bands adopting a satanic stance exploded. By the end of the millennium there were numerous prominent bands professing a satanic allegiance of some form. Discerning between those that merely adopt this stance for provocative purposes and those that are more dedicated to the topic is difficult, if not impossible, for the outsider. Even the fans find it difficult. There has been so much satanic metal produced that it is now seen as largely passé by many long-term followers of the genre. Many contemporary metal bands have moved away from the topic, as it has simply been exhausted. As the 1970s' high priest of shock, Alice Cooper (now a born-again Christian), commented in relation to black metal: "The satanism that you see is not satanism, it's some kind of caricature satanism…if you're looking for satanism in the first place you don't look to rock and roll, a bunch of kids playing loud guitars [and making the sign of the devil], that's Halloween."[6]

At the same time, many bands go beyond simply adopting the imagery of satanism and endorse values that invariably owe a great deal to LaVey's influence. The intersection of heavy metal and satanic imagery is extremely powerful, and undoubtedly the most visible Satanic influence in popular culture. Heavy metal's natural tendency toward greater extremes invites the adoption of extremist thought. Misanthropy, nihilism, violence, and other antisocial themes are standard. Included here are The Electric Hellfire Club, Morbid Angel, Danzig, Deicide, Satyricon, and countless black metal and death metal acts. The doctrines and rhetoric of modern Satanism provide a convenient quasi-intellectual crutch to antisocial rebellion and a ready-made vocabulary/ mythology of opposition. Yet degrees of allegiance vary from band to band. Whereas Slayer's lengthy satanic excursion was nothing more than a theatrical exercise in provocation that they abandoned in the early 1990s for near pathological anti-Christian vitriol (the primary songwriter is not Christian), Morbid Angel was—and remains—deeply interested in the ideology of modern Satanism, particularly in the lyrics of vocalist David Vincent.

HEAVY METAL SATANISM IN THE HEADLINES: MARILYN AND VARG

An especially high-profile meeting of popular music and Satanism is the case of shock rocker Marilyn Manson. Drawing his name from twin icons of the 1960s, Marilyn Monroe and Charles Manson, the gothic/fascist androgyne achieved fame with his 1996 release *Antichrist Superstar*. Part rock album, part manifesto, *Antichrist Superstar* effectively stated that Manson could become extraordinarily successful by being extraordinarily provocative. It was hardly an original concept, but with the endorsement of LaVey and unwitting complicity of American religious conservatives, it worked perfectly. A reverend of the Church of Satan, Manson quickly became the highest profile Satanist ever. His blasphemous nonconformity, strong anti-Christian views, social Darwinist leanings, and extensive exploitation of quasi-fascist imagery were well suited to the creed, although Manson's ongoing and well-publicized drug abuse was directly contrary to church policy. Though Manson's contact with the church was minimal, the mutually beneficial association was mentioned in almost every article regarding the singer at the height of his late-1990s fame. Being a priest of the Church of Satan boosted Manson's most valuable commodity—notoriety—and provided the church with what it most desired—publicity and exposure to a new generation of angry, alienated youth with a predisposition to gothic theatrics.

The importance of Manson's flirtation with the Church of Satan is easily overstated, by critics and fans alike. LaVey apologist Gavin Baddeley's *Introducing Marilyn Manson* (2000) is notable only for its absurd tendency to refer every aspect of Manson's life and career back to the Black Pope and Satanism. Yet Manson's position in the church was largely honorary, the outcome of a single visit to LaVey in the early 1990s. The musician expressed admiration for LaVey as a philosopher, and eventually wrote the foreword to *Satan Speaks!*, honoring LaVey as "the most righteous man I've ever known."[7] In recent years, however, the singer has consistently downplayed the extent of the association, particularly following the extensive criticism he faced in the wake of the 1999 Columbine High School massacre.

Manson's Satanic connection may have dominated American attention, but in Europe the focus was on the early-1990s Norwegian black metal scene. The then small subculture attracted international attention for its involvement in an explosive catalogue of murder, arson, and apparent devil-worship. This dramatic series of events provides the subject matter of Church of Satan and Abraxas member Michael Moynihan's engrossing *Lords of Chaos: The Bloody Rise of the Satanic Metal Underground* (co-written with Didrik Søderlind). The work details how second wave black metal bands Mayhem, Burzum, and Emperor instigated a series of church burnings in Norway, a radical means of protesting the cultural dominance of Christianity and its supplanting of pagan Nordic values. The book also analyzes a number of supposedly satanic heavy metal–related murders, including Emperor drummer Bård Eithun (aka Bård Faust) and his stabbing to death of a homosexual suitor. Eschewing melodramatic impulses (except in its title), the work's sober analysis makes a convincing case that the various murders were generally opportunistic or random acts of violence, with the satanic aspect significantly overstated in mainstream media coverage.

The central figure of *Lords of Chaos* is Varg Vikernes, Burzum founder and member of Mayhem. In August 1993, Vikernes stabbed Mayhem bandmate Øystein Aarseth (aka Euronymous) to death over a dispute born, it would seem, of jealousy and financial matters. The book charts the progression of Vikernes from an antisocial misfit and shock-Satanist to explicitly racist violent insurgent who considers Christianity a "Jewish implant" and identifies strongly with Norse paganism and fascism. In detailing Vikernes's development, the work provides considerable space for Vikernes and other extremist figures to detail their ideological beliefs, ostensibly serving the purpose of investigating the black metal scene. The narrative's openness to the ideas presented raises questions about its objectivity, particularly given author Moynihan's lengthy association with the extreme right and reputation as an esoteric neo-Nazi propagandist. Moynihan was criticized by investigative journalist Kevin Coogan for advancing a barely concealed subcurrent of radical right politics and allowing numerous racist claims in the book to pass unopposed, with criticisms limited to token "some people might disagree"-style statements.[8] Vikernes's ideals of racial purity are, for example, characterized by their base simplicity, a crude "blue eyes are like the sea, brown eyes are like shit"-type. The book nonetheless credits him with possessing a "fertile mind" and being an insightful visionary.

The criticisms of *Lords of Chaos* are well-founded, as the work's extended exploration of racists and esoteric themes goes far beyond the purported interest within the scene. Jung's doctrine of archetypes and identification of Nazism with Wotan is discussed at length, with a chapter devoted to "Resurgent Atavism"—the concept of timeless racial/cultural archetypes making their presence felt again. The topic is addressed with notable credulity, and the text is often at pains to make the theories appear plausible; for instance drawing tenuous links between Vikernes's actions and the etymology of his adopted name "varg" (wolf). Vikernes is presented as a mythic outlaw or modern day heretic, analyzed as a representation of a both wolflike and "Odinic paradigm."[9] Ultimately, the Vikernes of *Lord of Chaos* emerges as a dark antihero, rather than the more realistic assessment as a simple killer and extremist ideologue with a passion for publicity.

Lords of Chaos culminates with a distinctly religious-poetic discussion of the myths of Ragnarök and Prometheus, extolling them as archetypes that represent explicitly Eurocentric ideals. Prometheus is utilized to eulogize the creative fire of "the spirit of artistry," the Nietzschean "will-to-create" that smolders beneath the surface of asinine contemporary culture. "Prometheus represents an important archetype for the Satanist: he is the adversary, the willful iconoclast who spurs change with his actions."[10] In effect, the book concludes with a strong stamp of approval for the very theories and mythologies that underpin the racialist groups and ideologies it documents. Though the text provides an engrossing glimpse into an extremist subculture, it clearly serves a twofold purpose: its manifest function as an investigation of supposedly Satanic crime, and its covert role as a primer on extremist politics and neo-pagan metaphysics.

THE NEW COUNTERCULTURE

With Vikernes, Norwegian black metal, and *Lords of Chaos*, the analysis of Satanism's cultural presence shifts toward the margins again. Far away from the world of multimillion-selling heavy metal stars is an underground scene of countercultural nihilism that frequently intersects with the doctrines and cultural preoccupations—not merely the aesthetics—of Satanism. A major nexus is the alternative electronic music scene, an amorphous cluster of genres that is variously described as noise, industrial, martial, experimental or neofolk (with the latter frequently functioning as a blanket term). Though difficult to define, the scene is characterized by its extensive use of heathen themes and pagan runes, and its strong focus on expressing an exclusively European cultural consciousness. Often present is a strong apocalyptic edge, a belief that Western civilization has entered a phase of decline that can only be countered by a retrenchment in traditional cultural roots. As it flirts extensively with the rhetoric and imagery of the far right, the scene has courted controversy and faced frequent accusations of promoting political extremism, racism, and xenophobia.

Boyd Rice's one-man noise/industrial outfit NON has been an innovator and key player in the alternative underground music scene for over 30 years. Influential and provocative, admirers consider him an iconoclast and outlaw intellectual, "a fountain of ideas and inspiration for culture mavens."[11] Rice has consistently used NON to advocate social Darwinism, its albums permeated with references to "nature's eternal fascism" and the like. An entire album, *Might* (1995), is an exploration of Redbeard's *Might Is Right*. The NON track "Total War" (1992), which is essentially Rice bellowing neo-pagan slogans about Thor repeatedly over a techno-militaristic drum loop, is a classic of the genre. Rice has maintained his personal allegiance to the fascist formulations of natural law (the strong crush the weak) for over a quarter of a century, and does not hide his extremism. "I feel that I'm a fascist, but 'Nazi' is a real specific term...I'm a fascist in the sense of the modern bastardised meaning of the word. I'm completely against democratic values and liberalism. I think that they have very little to do with life on Earth. I think they're an ideological abstraction."[12]

When challenged on racism and NON's extensive connections with the radical right, Rice is more circumspect: "I think people have a misunderstanding with my whole slant on that. They think I'm some sort of racial idealist and I feel I'm just a cynic and a realist."[13] He has trodden carefully about the issue since 1989, when he appeared on a magazine cover with Bob Heick, founder of the white supremacist skinhead gang American Front, each wearing American Front uniforms and holding a knife. Rice claims it was a spur of the moment prank with a friend, though it is also claimed he was a member of Heick's organization.[14] Prior to the criticism this episode instigated, Rice was more forthcoming with his views. In the mid-1980s he was interviewed on White Aryan Resistance (W.A.R.) TV's "Race and Reason" show, hosted by owner and former Ku Klux Klan grand master Tom Metzger. In the interview, Rice accepts the designation "a cult figure in the racial underground musical world" and the description of his own work as "white racialist music." In response to the comment that "Electronic music is very white, just by its very nature…it just seems intrinsically white," Rice replies, "Yeah, that's what I feel too…This music that I do, the press dubbed it 'industrial music' after this one band [Throbbing Gristle]…and it had been said that this was the first white music to come out in hundreds and hundreds of years, because a lot of the popular music has been influenced with black influences, Little Richard and so on." Asked to mention "racialist-type music" in Europe he names David Tibet of Current 93, "who is moving more and more towards racialist stuff," and Death in June, who are "very racialist oriented."[15]

The racist and neofascist undercurrents of the industrial/neofolk scene have been present since its inception. Throbbing Gristle was an early industrial band that pioneered the provocative use of Nazi symbolism, defended as an attempt to challenge preconceptions. Rice/NON became a frequent collaborator with Death in June, another band infamous for its paramilitary stylings and extensive use of fascist symbolism and rhetoric, which has extended to appearing on stage in Nazi uniforms. Like many neofolk acts, Death in June deny that the symbolism indicates a neo-Nazi affiliation, yet maintain a popular following within the far right. David Tibet's Current 93 is a British experimental act with a strong occult/apocalyptic edge. Similarly oriented acts include Sol Invictus, Above the Ruins, Allerseelen (aka Kadmon, who contributed an article on neo-paganism to *Lords of Chaos*), and Moynihan's Blood Axis. More subtle than out-and-out neo-Nazi hardcore or white power bands, these artists rely on fostering an air of ambiguity around their political stance. In doing so, they generally avoid the persecution and censorship faced by skinhead bands and the like, particularly in Europe with its stricter censorship rules, although Death in June have faced numerous show cancellations due to their reputation and far right following.

A recent development in the industrial/neofolk world has been the rise of so-called white power electronics, a subgenre which makes extensive use of affordable computing technologies and is closely connected with the Satanic community. Frequently little more than feedback loops with jarring, dissonant samples piled on top, this do-it-yourself music eschews traditional musical elements and is regarded as intrinsically white, a specifically European culture product. Most contributors are one or two-person acts and have few pretensions of being actual musicians. Barriers to entry are extremely low and virtually no musical ability is presupposed. Modern editing software allows tracks to be composed on any personal computer or basic mixing equipment. Artistic aims are generally simple: to promote discomfort in one's audience. As one Church of Satan member describes his "Ritual HateNoise project," "Dauðarorð is my outlet for negativity, hate, annoyance. My goal is to trigger your fears, offend your senses. To rape your mental asshole, so to speak. However, for the able of mind, this should provide a rather pleasurable listening experience. Those who are not able minded, I hope your ears bleed."[16]

Promotion for these acts frequently takes place on online social networking sites. MySpace, which is perfectly geared toward promoting independent music at minimal or no cost, is the primary hub of activity. Although extremist, racist, and hate profiles face constant deletion, MySpace is nonetheless home to an enormous online ghetto of hate propaganda. Deletions may be an annoyance but are easily overcome. When ejected, acts simply create a new profile, re-add all their former contacts, and await re-deletion. Frequent deletions are often worn as a badge of countercultural honor. In this environment, numerous Satanist-related power-electronic acts exist: Genocide Lolita, Necrofascist, Eugenics Council, Sewer Goddess, Rosemary Malign, Grey Wolves, Genetik Terrorists, Torturecide, and numerous others. Most are characterized by virulent misanthropy, extreme nationalism, xenophobia, anti-immigration hostility, fascist imagery and violent rhetoric, and explicit or implicit/coded racism. Many are released by small independent record labels, such as France's militant Zero Tolerance and the anti-Semitic American label Third Position Recordings. Many of these acts are clearly associated with, or at very least supportive of, the Church of Satan. The aesthetics of choice are standard: a vast medley of sig runes, Totenkopfs, Black Suns, Wolfsangles, Baphomets, paramilitary or neo-fascist uniforms, and a universal obsession with gas masks. Church of Satan Magister James Sass is also active within the scene, his Necrofascist industrial noise project promoted by Zero Tolerance alongside the viciously anti-Semitic hate-project Genocide Lolita and other explicitly racist Satanic/neo-Nazi ensembles.

APOCALYPSE CULTURE AND
THE OTHER MANSON

The alternative industrial/noise/power electronics scene is frequently far closer associated with the ideals of modern Satanism than mainstream heavy metal. While metal bands often do little more than adopt the imagery and mythology of traditional satanism, the alternative scene shares key elements of the ideological basis of its contemporary counterpart. In contrast to the metal scene, many of the key figures in the industrial/neo-folk world are as deeply involved in publishing, writing, and other forms of mass media as they are with making music. Moynihan, Rice, Kadmon, Nikolas Schreck and others are also writers and display a degree of resourcefulness beyond that of the average rock star. Their publications are generally occult-related and/or a form of cultural analysis, usually with a heavy focus on the presumed corruption of contemporary civilization and predictions of its imminent demise. The theme of radical cultural pessimism was partly established by Feral House's Adam Parfrey and *Apocalypse Culture* (1987), continued in *Apocalypse Culture II* (2000). A recent contribution is made by Parfrey's long-time collaborator George Petros in his 2007 collection *Art That Kills: A Panoramic Portrait of Aesthetic Terrorism 1984–2001*. Featuring contributions from familiar figures—LaVey, Gilmore, Rice, Moynihan, Parfrey, James Mason, and Marilyn Manson, among others—the work bills itself as "where art meets crime." As the work's publisher blurb states:

> The book…chronicles the evolution of a new aesthetic movement, a terrifying fringe of Underground Art where enlightenment and depravity combined. Murder, rape, torture, pedophilia, cannibalism, drugs, sedition, racism and blasphemy mixed with literature, history, politics, news, movies, TV, punk rock, philosophy and science.[17]

The continued involvement in works of this nature predictably draws criticism, for which a series of well-established defenses are offered: The works are merely giving a voice to dangerous ideas, pushing the boundaries of discourse, and their publication does not mean endorsement as people can make up their own minds. At the same time, any commentator will look long, hard, and in vain to find any critique or condemnation of extremist content.

Despite these frequently heard disclaimers, these ideological and cultural preoccupations are clearly taken seriously. The 1988 San Francisco "8/8/88" rally and white power electronics clearly do not treat them as mere hypotheses.[18] Another clear example is the 1991 "Manson Maniacs" episode of evangelist Bob Larson's *Talkback* radio show, where (then) close friends Moynihan and Rice were interviewed along with neo-Nazi James Mason, author of *Siege* and founder of the militant collective Universal Order, of which Moynihan was a member. In the course of a belligerent and confrontational interview, the three presented their apocalyptic vision of society. The stated premise of the three is a profound belief that Western society is in a state of advanced decay, and a return to a pre-Christian order and the values of natural law is somehow imminent, to be brought about by a cataclysmic collapse of the existing social order. Much of the show is dominated by discussion of the merits of Charles Manson and the Family's 1969 murders, with Moynihan, Rice, and especially Mason praising the incarcerated killer as a visionary who has seen through the corruption of modern society. The mother of Sharon Tate, also involved, is berated and repeatedly told that her daughter deserved to die because of her association with so-called Jewish Hollywood.

Besides it's extremist content, one telling aspect of the interview is the contrast between the styles of the three protagonists. Mason, a lifelong neo-Nazi, is completely forthcoming with his racism and fanatical anti-Semitism, becoming increasingly irate and paranoid as the interview progresses, pegging the various ills of the world, both real and (mostly) imagined, on a massive Jewish conspiracy theory. Central to his thought is an apocalyptic fantasy of hiding out while the world is consumed by civic chaos. In his work *Siege*, he predicts massive social upheaval, with the whites sitting on the sidelines watching the cities tear themselves apart. "The riots of the Sixties barely scratched the surface in the amount of direct coordinated VIOLENCE and TERROR that's going to be required to intimidate and melt the System."[19] Mason's racialist fantasies are eerily reminiscent of Manson's purported plan to hide out in Death Valley while the race wars instigated by the Family's murders raged. Moynihan and Rice, for their part, support an identical assessment of cultural decay and coming apocalypse, with one simple difference: in place of Mason's undisguised racial paranoia, Moynihan and Rice substitute self-satisfied evasiveness. Despite advancing the same analysis as Mason and consistently supporting and echoing his calamitous vision, both avoid making a single explicitly racist comment.

The reverence for Charles Manson is one of the stranger and more widespread aspects of the countercultural ethos, evident throughout Satanism and neofolk circles. Yet it is easy to determine how the Manson reverence ties in with the general themes of both. Manson is viewed as a seer who has recognized and revealed the hypocrisy of modern society. He, like LaVey, has come to represent a direct repudiation of the values of the 1960s, contained within a form of prophetic and charismatic rebellion. This interpretation is only reinforced by the stark unrepentance of Manson and his codefendants during their trial, as they jeered the press and court, laughed at their verdicts, and turned the proceedings into a public spectacle. Similarly, Manson later made an infamous appearance at a parole hearing with a swastika tattooed onto his forehead. To defenders, Manson remains a hero whose brilliance is incomprehensible to the average mind. He is a martyr for the truth who is unafraid to express his racist theories and fascist belief in violence as a legitimate form of political action. His rejection of mainstream society is seen as a first strike against the corrupt values of Western egalitarianism, and he is applauded for the apparently racially motivated murders he engineered. (Manson did not personally kill anyone, he was convicted on conspiracy charges and his role in tying up the LaBiancas prior to their murder.) This idealized interpretation is maintained despite being difficult to reconcile with the rambling, paranoid figure present in his extensive interview footage and writings. Besides his obvious charisma and impish sense of humor, there is little reason to regard Manson's disjointed and repetitive conspiratorial chatter seriously.

Manson's supposed innocence is a frequent point of contention. Prominent Manson advocates—Nikolas Schreck, Moynihan, and Rice—all present the same defense of Manson. He killed no one and therefore should not be in prison; he is a political prisoner rather than convicted criminal. That he was organizer and accessory for a succession of particularly brutal murders is either never discussed or flatly denied. (James Mason is the exception on this point—he admits that Manson is a killer, and praises him for it. He is particularly insistent that Sharon Tate's eight-month-old fetus deserved to die as "it was, after all, a Jew."[20]) Nonetheless, supporters argue that the victims of the Tate/LaBianca murders deserved to die, and their deaths represent Manson's philosophy in action. There is a glaring contradiction here: Manson is regarded as an entirely innocent man, but his victims died as a direct result of his revolutionary leadership and philosophy; he didn't kill anyone, but he is nonetheless praised for deaths he (apparently) didn't cause.

ESOTERIC APOCALYPTIC CULTURE THEORISTS

The reverence for Charles Manson is merely one facet of a wider phenomenon, a complex intersection of apocalyptic countercultural pessimism, neofascism, Nazi occultism, and Satanism. Intellectually, this fringe movement is a promiscuous cluster of ideas drawn from the speculative margins of cultural theorizing. One of its earliest influences is Thomas Malthus and his bleak predictions of unsustainable population growth, which find contemporary voice in dire prophesies of global overpopulation. These scenarios are in turn used as rhetorical justification of elitist and repressive social engineering programs (or, with LaVey, a fantasy of firing the herd into space in rockets).[21] Another complementary line of thought is Oswald Spengler's pessimistic assessment of the achievements and permanence of Western culture, which had a substantial influence on Nazi thought. Spengler's 1918 work *The Decline of the West* posited an organic, cyclical interpretation of Western culture and history. According to Spengler, periods of cultural decay are an inevitable fact of history and an unavoidable phenomenon in the future. Capitalism and democracy will be challenged and defeated by exceptional individuals of great mental strength and vision who will gain and wield political power ruthlessly.

In the postwar era, an international potpourri of radical intellectuals have contributed to this fatalistic, racist, conspiratorial admixture. Spengler's most visible postwar successor was Francis Yockey, an American fascist writer who released his Hitler-dedicated *Imperium* in 1948. Intended as a continuation of *The Decline of the West*, the work drew heavily from Spengler's diagnosis of profound and inescapable cultural decay but recast his theories in the context of profound anti-Semitism and fears of a global Jewish conspiracy. Also popular amongst Satanists are French racialist psychologist Gustave Le Bon, Japanese Nationalist and traditionalist Yukio Mishima, Italian occult neofascist Julius Evola, Indian neo-Nazi mystic Savitri Devi, Chilean esoteric neo-Nazi Miguel Serrano, and the numerous publications of the prominent Holocaust-denying Institute for Historical Review. There are many overlapping themes with these writers. Most are staunchly opposed to democracy and its values, and instead posit a return to some form of traditionalist values of strength and elitism. Strict ideals of racial purity are prevalent, finding voice in Eurocentrism or, particularly in America, staunch nationalism and adherence to racial identity. Devi and Serrano both lauded Hitler as an archetype through whom the collective unconscious of his race flowed. Strongly esoteric in nature, these figures are further interconnected by a spider's web of occult influences, including Theosophy (Madame Blavatsky's teachings), *völkisch* racist theories, neo-paganism, Jungian archetypes, and Black Sun esotericism (a collection of myths and theories based around Nazi occultism and Wewelsburg castle).

Venomous anti-Semitism is a prevalent theme, both within these theorists and their modern countercultural proponents. White power electronics in particular is heavily focused on racial ideals and is frequently obsessed with the purported Zionist master plan. Within this scene, which overlaps frequently with the extremes of Satanism, an all-powerful and all-controlling international Jewish shadow government is the key enemy. All perceived social and political ills are systematically subsumed into one overarching conspiracy theory: egalitarian ethics, democratic governance, racial-integration, interracial breeding, multiculturalism, and globalization are simply part of a Zionist plot to dilute the purity of the white race and ferment the establishment of a new world order. A powerfully obsessive insistence on Holocaust denial is standard, as so-called Holocaust guilt is regarded as a cynical tool of manipulation. The phenomena is self-perpetuating and all-consuming, its logic circular and immune to criticism. If any issue has the slightest hint of a Jewish connection, it is inevitably analyzed entirely in reference to anti-Semitic paranoia. Every transgression—real or perceived—of either the State of Israel, American foreign policy, individual Jews, or the supposedly Jewish media is seen as further proof of an underlying conspiracy. If the infeasibility of the scenario is pointed out, this criticism is dismissed as the result of Jewish influence and manipulation. Criticism, in fact, is taken as further proof of the all-powerful conspiracy, for only a deluded or manipulated individual would deny what is (to believers) self-evidently true.

APOCALYPSE FALLACIES

None of the assorted themes discussed here are essential aspects of Satanism or industrial/neofolk music—they are all adopted at the (in)discretion of the individual. Many Satanists do not adhere to anti-Semitic conspiracy theories and are not occult fascists. Neofolk artists are not necessarily racist or nationalistic; many clearly aren't. Unfortunately, this fluidity provides cover for more extremist figures, by giving disavowals more credence. There is, nonetheless, an identifiable body of beliefs adopted by the extremes of the counterculture, one that is readily compatible with the wider concerns of Satanism and often closely aligned. Satanism is in no way the cause of this extremist underground; its broad principles simply fuse with and reinforce independently existing ideas. Neither is there any overarching conspiratorial or organizational architecture, merely individuals who have similar agendas. As with neo-Nazism and neofascism, Satanism can nonetheless be viewed as a soft entry point to these issues, its general principles opening up the path to extremist doctrines.

Apocalyptic diagnoses of decline and collapse sit well with the conservative social pessimism of Satanism. They combine easily with its outsider stance, discriminatory doctrines, and antihumanist belief in the superfluity of the majority of humankind. The standard Satanic hostility to Judeo-Christian morality, with its basis in quasi-conspiratorial Nietzschean genealogy, is easily transformed into an explicitly anti-Semitic narrative. These theories also work in tandem with the underlying Satanic drive for elite, privileged status. The culture of self-imposed and self-perpetuating alienation within Satanism only amplifies their plausibility. As Nicholas Goodrick-Clarke observes in his benchmark work on neo-Nazi esotericism, *Black Sun*: "Conspiracy theories always flourish when people feel excluded from the political process."[22] With esoteric theorists, Western culture's primary symbols of evil—Manson, Hitler, and so forth—are first exhorted as heroic ideals, then championed as the modern embodiment of ancient archetypes.

The key counterculture figures are adept at maintaining a mist of ambiguity around their true beliefs. The leading Satanist proponents of apocalyptic theorizing will never simply state their position on controversial issues. Accused of being fascist, they will quibble over the definition of fascism. Asked if they support the racist or neofascist contents of books they publish and contribute to, they will instead discuss the importance or value of publishing dangerous works, or draw attention to irrelevant details. (As a way of defending his publication and championing of Julias Evola's neofascist tract *Men among the Ruins*, Moynihan points out that Evola also wrote books on yoga and mountain climbing. Similarly, Peggy Nadramia addresses the issue of Boyd Rice's longstanding Hitler fetishism by calling attention to his Barbie collection.) If Death in June or Boyd Rice are challenged over their use of Nazi symbols, they reply that it is merely a matter of aesthetics, or claim that they are merely challenging people's perceptions. Other common strategies include ambiguous, partial denials or retreats behind freedom of speech.

This pattern is visible throughout Satanism, from the adoption of pagan symbols, the defense of fascist doctrines as mere representations of reality, to the championing of racist texts (*Might Is Right*, *Mein Kampf*, *Siege*, etc.). Satanists such as Boyd Rice attempt to flirt with extremism while remaining legitimate—hence the constant disavowals of Nazism and racism. Yet they constantly align themselves with hate figures such as Tom Metzger and James Mason, passing off their associations as open-mindedness and cynically defending fascist propaganda under the banner of free speech. The strategy finds its paradigm case with Rice and Moynihan's appearance on Bob Larson's radio show, snidely complicit with the hate speech of James Mason, yet carefully moderating their own comments. The major Satanic organizations, meanwhile, maintain enough distance to plausibly deny any racist, neo-Nazi, or neofascist elements, while consistently pandering to extremist themes.

The most telling aspect of the counterculture's end-times enthusiasm is its lack of reputable support. Since its inception, Satanism has consistently maintained and popularized a superficial diagnosis of nature's eternal fascism. Satanic fascists advance, through their constant trumpeting of natural law, an anthropology that states humans and human societies are by nature aggressive, destructive, and combative—and that it should be so. At the same time modern political and anthropological sciences have been moving toward exactly the opposite conclusions. Contemporary research maintains that primitive hunter-gatherer societies were by necessity egalitarian, in order to defray the risks of uneven hunting success and support the necessary division of tasks. Earlier modern humans, of around 100,000 years ago, were considerably more aggressive and violent than modern humans. In order to develop the complex, large scale societies we have today, humans had to develop the capacity to treat nonkin as kin. Trust, an essential component of trade and economic activity, was essential. No nonhuman species has developed the ability to allow nonkin to perform crucial tasks. For example, the ability to enter an operating room, be anaesthetized, and let nonrelated individuals perform surgical procedures presupposes an extraordinarily complex network of social relations, and an extraordinary amount of trust in human codes of conduct and moral/behavioral norms. Fascist anthropologies simply cannot account for these phenomena, as everything is subordinated to mere power politics. Entering the operating room of a Dr. Ragnar Redbeard would not be recommended, particularly if you had paid in advance. Dr. Redbeard would not remove your life-threatening stomach ulcer—he would remove your kidneys, heart, and other vital organs and sell them on the black market.

In addition to its flawed anthropology, the extremist/pagan fringe's adoption of Jungian archetypes is equally unsupported. While the theory was mildly influential in the mid-twentieth century, it has since been almost universally discarded. Ideas of racially delimitated collective unconscious and genetic memory are simply not substantiated by modern science. While it is fairly certain that we have psychological *intuitions* and *behavioral norms* that are carried by our genes, that is very different from saying we have *memories* (collective or individual) that are carried by our genes. Individuals die with the same genetic code that they were born with; nothing that happens in their life affects it in any way. There is no way a person's memories will become part of their genetic code, any more than their hairstyle or tattoos will. Though Freud and Jung both supported the idea of the transmission of memories to subsequent generations, both were mistaken. The countercultural/neo-pagan enthusiasm for Jungian archetypes is born of convenience and opportunism. It functions as an important prop for the claims of a unique European racial/cultural identity, strengthening ideals of racial solidarity in a way that science does not, and creating the illusion that ethnic and national identities are truly ingrained in one's bloodline.

Alternative culture Satanism has developed into a strangely credulous environment, a subculture where crazed conspiracy theories are given extra credence merely because the majority rejects them. The gleeful diagnosis of cultural decay and apocalyptic end-times mirrors mainstream religious fundamentalism with neofascist fundamentalism. Each joyfully prophesizes the end of the world, the purifying triumph of its ideology and salvation of the true believer. The underlying psychology of each remains the same: the world is seen in terms of absolute ideals, the victim of profound moral decline, its inhabitants divided into rigid categories of us and them. It is surely no coincidence that with all apocalyptic scenarios it is always the individual prophesying doom who is destined to prevail. In terms of worldview and critical rigor, these end-times theorists have more in common with the authors of the Rapture-awaiting *Left Behind* series than any other cultural commentators. All await judgment day, convinced that they alone have grasped the truth, dogmatically convinced that their reactionary values will triumph. Spengler and his ilk may be curious footnotes in the history of intellectual thought, but to self-identified outsiders, apocalypse cheerleaders and other cultural hypochondriacs, their theories are just too convenient to pass up.

Conclusion

Worst Case Scenario: Satanism, Egalitarianism, Darwinism, Atheism, and Nihilism

All human beings are born free and equal in dignity and rights. They are endowed with reason and conscience and should act towards one another in a spirit of brotherhood.

—United Nations Universal Declaration of
Human Rights, Article 1, December 10, 1948

The essential unity of the human race and consequently the fundamental equality of all human beings and all peoples, recognized in the loftiest expressions of philosophy, morality and religion, reflect an ideal towards which ethics and science are converging today.

—UNESCO Declaration on Race and
Racial Prejudice, November 27, 1978

Stratification—The point on which all others ultimately rest. There can be no myth of equality for all—it only translates to mediocrity and supports the weak at the expense of the strong.

—Anton LaVey, *The Devil's Notebook*, p. 93

In studying the phenomenon of modern Satanism, one point comes repeatedly to the fore—the deeply entrenched opposition to so-called egalitarian values. It is the rallying cry of all Satanists, the call to arms against a corrupt and unnatural Judeo-Christian social order. The term is taken to mean a complete leveling of all differences between human beings. In LaVey's view, "Egalitarianism is a condition whereby society is governed by the whim of its inferior members, whose strength lies solely in numbers."[1] It is a synonym for "equality," in the sense than all members of society are presumed to have equal abilities and no one differs from anyone else. Instead of each being able to perform to the best of our abilities, egalitarian values descend and compress all into bland uniformity where no one is allowed to be different, and no one is allowed to excel. This conformist homogeneity is anathema to the Satanist, who sees it as a contradiction of the natural order. As LaVey further explains, "Water must be allowed to seek its own level without interference from apologists for incompetence."[2]

GETTING EGALITARIANISM RIGHT

This assessment is misleading. Egalitarianism is simply the claim that all people should be treated as equal, that all people are fundamentally *equal in moral worth and status*.[3] In relation to Satanism, the most important aspect of egalitarianism is the concept of human rights, the principle that all people have (or should have) a core set of immutable rights that should not be infringed upon. The vocabulary of human rights is pervasive today, and for good reason. Human rights are norms that are designed to protect all individuals from abuse, be it social, political, or legal. As such, they are *minimal*, not maximal, standards; their primary goal is preventing the worst, not enabling the best. Human rights are not a crude leveling tool, and they have no bearing on ability. They exist to protect the vital interests of every individual, not to artificially succor so-called incompetents or homogenize society. Any individual who has the ability to win a marathon is free to do so, and any individual who doesn't never will. The same is true for anyone who pursues goals in the arts, science, or any other field of endeavor. Human rights are designed to see that none are subjected to repression or persecution in pursuit of their respective goals, not determine what individuals can achieve with their natural abilities, or level out the differences between those abilities. Again, egalitarian values represent the claim that all humans are of *equal moral worth*, not *equal ability*.

To label support for egalitarian values, properly understood, as merely Judeo-Christian values is to miss the point (and to be more than a little misled by Nietzsche's dubious genealogical scholarship). They are the values that any person who supports a stable, civil society would support, religious or not; values that form a basis from which individual liberty is able to grow, and offer protection from arbitrary injustice, persecution, and violence. Certainly, core Judeo-Christian values of mutual respect and shared humanity are, broadly speaking, pervasive within Western society, again for good reason—they are commendable ideals. This fact is evident from their being upheld by religious and secular figures. We find egalitarian virtues with theological overtones enshrined in the United States Declaration of Independence, in its claim that "all men are created equal." But they are also at the heart of secular declarations such as the United Nations Universal Declaration of Human Rights, quoted at the head of this chapter, and are firmly enshrined in numerous international laws, treaties, and domestic constitutions and bills of rights. To dismiss them as the product of a single religious tradition is to overlook their secular origins. Many modern egalitarian principles were born of the Enlightenment and adopted in spite of religious opposition. In addition, their historical origin is of far less importance than their effectiveness and the benefits that they provide to all.

It is certainly not coincidental that the drive toward universal human rights was given crucial impetus in the wake of World War II a conflict that took more than 60 million lives worldwide and left entire nations in ruins. They are, in an important historical sense, a direct response to the fruits of rabid social Darwinism, fantasies of genetic purity, pitiless elitist philosophies, and the politics of arbitrary discrimination, dehumanization, and systematic eradication of empathy. They arose to prevent the recurrence of the question posed by Auschwitz: How does it happen that people become things? The horrors of this era provided the urgency in providing a base level of protection for all human beings, to recognize every person as a person, as enshrined in the United Nations' 1948 declaration. Egalitarian values are necessary, as every developed and successful nation acknowledges, to ensure a civil society in which its citizens can pursue fulfilling lives. With their fundamental liberties protected, individuals are free to pursue whatever life they find rewarding, as long as others' rights are respected. Otherwise, millions are left defenseless in the face of policies that lead directly to the gulag, gas chamber, and killing field.

Support for principles such as egalitarianism and human rights need not presuppose, as a Satanist would say, that one put on a "Goodguy Badge."[4] In complex, high–population density modern societies an individual's self-interest is inextricably intertwined with the self-interest of others. No one wants to be subjected to arbitrary discrimination, no one wants to be incarcerated without due legal process or protection, and no one wants to be the victim of random violence. Therefore, in order to protect ourselves and those we care about, we support the principles that provide a stable environment and grant everyone certain inviolable rights. The basis of these principles can, therefore, be regarded as rising from mutual self-interest. *Reciprocity* is the central issue: I respect the rights of others because I need other people to respect my rights. Such reciprocal arrangements can, as game theory proves, result in a stable, mutually beneficial social environment, and provide sufficient basis for altruistic behavior. It is in everyone's self-interest to cooperate with others; it is in everyone's self-interest to behave altruistically at times; it is in everyone's interest to support the principles of an egalitarian society.

THE ETHICS OF ARBITRARINESS

Unfortunately, the rhetoric of modern Satanism is too blunt to capture any of the preceding points. Satanic ethics, to the extent that they ever rise out of the quagmire of jingoistic nihilism, are characterized by their near-sightedness. Consider *The Satanic Bible*'s discussion of "Love and Hate":

> Satanism represents kindness to those who deserve it instead of love wasted on ingrates!
>
> You cannot love everyone; it is ridiculous to think you can. If you love everyone and everything you lose your natural powers of selection and wind up being a pretty poor judge of character and quality. If anything is used too freely it loses its true meaning.[5]

As is his custom, LaVey advances his cause by attacking a position only a very small number of people hold. Only the most idealistic individual would claim to truly love everybody equally. The admonition to love thy neighbor is generally interpreted as advocating the extension of a basic level of respect and regard for others, not its most literal interpretation. Few people, even the most devout, have pretenses of Messiah-hood or Buddha-hood. As a far more astute philosopher noted: "If men had been overwhelmingly benevolent, if each had aimed only at the happiness of all, if everyone had loved his neighbour as himself, there would be no need for the rules that constitute justice."[6] It is not necessary to love everyone equally, only to afford every individual a basic level of respect and dignity.

Obviously, ethical concerns must be prioritized. Immediate family and close friends do come first in our consideration, with the sphere of concern expanding gradually to encompass acquaintances, colleagues, one's community, nation, and so forth. However, prioritizing who we pay the most regard to does not mean we can't reserve a level of respect for every individual—the fundamental principle underpinning egalitarianism and the concept of human rights. The ethics of Satanism, by contrast, provide no reason to treat with any dignity any person who is not a blood relative, personal friend, or fellow Satanist. Rather, the creed and its representatives engage in continual, systematic belittling of all non–group members. By Satanism's discriminatory and arbitrary reasoning, anyone who is not a Satanist is fundamentally of lesser moral worth or of none at all. As Magus Gilmore stresses, "Human life, in and of itself, is *not* considered valuable; it is the worth of *particular* humans that matters to the Satanist."[7] Here, we can see exactly how people become things—worth as a human being is only extended to others on an ad hoc basis. Satanic ethics provide no basis for showing consideration toward anyone outside their limited circle of acquaintances. As such, Satanic ethics can provide no arguments against slavery, torture, genocide, rape, racism, sexism, or murder—so long as these don't affect anyone in their small sphere of concern. Any of these can be said to occur naturally and, as Satanic ethics are determined by the law of nature, any can be—and frequently are—accepted as legitimate actions.

Ethically, the ideology if Satanism is crippled by its short-sightedness and failure to realize or accept that Satanists exist within a larger society and that their interests intersect with the interests of others. On occasion, even Satanists display awareness of this problem. In a 2007 interview on Canadian television, Church of Satan Reverend Jack Malebranche was asked if the world would be a better place if everyone were a Satanist. "No," he replied, "I don't think so. Satanists would be at each other's throat in a heartbeat."[8] What was apparently black humor to Malebranche is in truth extraordinarily revealing. When a group's principles are only feasible while they remain a small minority within the larger whole, the ideology is clearly a classic example of the free-rider problem. This problem arises whenever a social good or service is not excludable—when it can't effectively be denied to those who don't contribute to it, making any such people free-riders. In this case, the social good is egalitarianism and its accompanying benefits, for example, the *right* to free speech or the *right* to freedom of religion—rights that Satanists are quick to appeal to. Satanists benefit from the stability provided by key democratic principles, yet their entrenched hostility to egalitarianism places them in diametric opposition to these rights. They readily receive the benefits of a free society but are not prepared to support them or contribute to it, thus rendering their creed fundamentally parasitic and hypocritical.

The product of Satanism's self-serving account of human societies and ethics is an ideology that is all too frequently little more than a fancy-dress facsimile for fascism. Boyd Rice, speaking in the Church of Satan's mid-1990s documentary *Speak of the Devil*, makes the logical conclusions of Satanic philosophy all too clear:

> A Satanic world is a world reborn in purity, a world where the instinct and the intellect will be complementary to one another rather than being at odds with one another. It will be a world in which we follow laws of nature instead of just the rules that man has made up to regulate his conduct. It will be a world in which masters will be masters and slaves will be slaves, and never the twain shall meet.[9]

He is echoed in the same work by another church magister, Rex Church (aka Rex Diabolus):

> The Church of Satan has declared total war on ignorance. This has often been misconstrued by mainstream media, this is not a war of race, it a war of the

intelligent versus the stupid, of predator and prey, master and slave, domination and servitude. Satan represents the powers of force in nature and we feel that a cleansing of the idiot ideology of the pallid, incompetent Christ is in order. And so, this is something that the Church of Satan is conducting on many different avenues. We are doing this through the use of what we are calling "aesthetic terrorism." This involves the creative use of art, music, writing; effectively, what we call propaganda, the dissemination of information to influence what we call "iron youth."[10]

The principles being advanced here are odious, whether or not they involve racism, but even that denial rings hollow. The numerous instances of Satanists becoming involved in openly racist organizations, the presence of worthlessly outdated race theory works on the Temple of Set reading list, the numerous relationships between prominent Satanists (including Rice and LaVey) and explicitly racist figures, the championing of *Might Is Right* as a work of merit, and the often ambiguous disavowals converge to raise very serious questions about Satanic denials of racism. The boundaries between Satanism doctrines and racism are obviously extremely porous, if it can be said that there are any boundaries at all. Once one adopts the bogus scientism of genetic and evolutionary superiority, expressing this superiority in racialist terms is seldom far behind. Racism is, after all, simply discrimination based on skin color or ethnicity, and Satanism is fundamentally discriminatory. If one prepared to exercise prejudice on the flimsy basis of having read and agreed with a particular book, other forms are scarcely ruled out. It hardly seems coincidental that Satanists—specifically senior members of the Church of Satan—have been deeply involved with some of late twentieth-century America's most notorious racists and white supremacists, including James Madole, James Mason, Tom Metzger, and David Lane. As the latter noted in his influential "88 Precepts," in rhetoric only marginally removed from that of Satanism: "In accord with Nature's Laws, nothing is more right than the preservation of one's own race."[11]

DARWINISM, ATHEISM, AND THE SPECTER OF THE ABSURD

At a point in history when evolution and atheism/nonbelief have become such hotly debated issues, discussion of Satanism seems particularly timely, given the frequency with which it intersects with both these topics, and the creed's prominent identification as an atheistic religion. It is timely, however, for the extent to which Satanism diverges from the positions of both evolutionary science and secular atheism. While biologists and other scientists are fighting a constant battle to address public misconceptions and misrepresentations of their disciplines, Satanists are content to endorse an unscientific and long-since debunked form of pseudo-Darwinism. While the vast majority of nonbelievers are just as concerned with being morally engaged in the world as the average theist, Satanists are content to indulge in ethical egoism and embrace simplistic nihilism. In advancing an extremist ideology as the logical position for anyone who rejects traditional religion, Satanism in many ways presents a worst-case scenario for evolutionary biology and atheism, by interpreting the former as supporting fascism and the latter as leading to nihilism. By actively promoting the most egregious distortions of each, Satanism provides material for the enemies of legitimate science and secular values.

The tenets of social Darwinism are, to restate, utterly incorrect. Social Darwinism begins with false assumptions about the natural world and evolutionary theory and proceeds to false conclusions regarding social policies. "Survival of the fittest" does not necessarily mean that the strong crush the weak. Evolutionary fitness means possessing characteristics that enhance survival and reproduction, which is by no means limited to brute strength or aggressiveness. Furthermore, it is now known that cooperation and mutually beneficial actions are an integral part of the dynamics of nature. This point is particularly true of human societies, where our advanced cognitive and linguistic abilities greatly improve our ability to cooperate. And even if none of these were correct, and nature were simply a Hobbesian "war of all against all," there would be no reason to conclude that the harshness of nature provided ethical carte blanche to structure our societies along similar lines. As Darwin's bulldog, T. H. Huxley, noted presciently—in a decidedly nonbulldogish moment—"Whatever difference of opinion may exist among the experts, there is a general consensus that the ape and tiger methods of the struggle for existence are not reconcilable with sound ethical principles."[12] We can now, of course, do even better than general consensus, having established that it is not possible to derive an *ought* from an *is* so greedily: the bare facts of nature do not determine ethical norms in this way. Ultimately, the only thing Darwinian biology and social Darwinism have in common is the brand name, which is adopted by the latter in order to leech off the scientific legitimacy of the former.

Rational atheism or nonbelief, for its part, does not entail the collapse of all moral order. The overwhelming majority of nonbelievers acknowledge that society needs moral rules and principles if humans are to live together and overcome their limited concerns for each other. History books overflow with secular writers who have striven to advance moral values that promote tolerance, equality (of moral worth and opportunity), individual rights, intellectual freedom, and conditions whereby people can benefit from mutual society and pursue rewarding lives. The fact that nonbelievers don't see morality as inscribed on stone tablets, or issuing from the pages of a given text, doesn't mean that they simply reject moral values and embrace nihilism. One prominent atheist labels this tired and oft-heard accusation "The Myth of Secular Moral Chaos."[13] Rather, morality is a product of social interactions between humans, evolving over time into basic norms of behavior that reflect the interdependency of social action and are sufficiently persistent to enable civil societies. These standards may not be absolute, in the traditional religious sense, but that does not make them arbitrary. They are those values that have, over the course of time, by trial and error, proven to best enable a just, equitable society in which people can lead mutually beneficial lives and reconcile conflicting interests. Furthermore, they are shaped by the application of human reason. Rationality is prescriptive—it can tell us how to behave, it can guide us in developing fair and equitable moral principles, it can help adjudicate as to what is fair and just. A prime example is the 1948 establishment of universal human rights, which are both moral and legal norms established by rational deliberation. A lack of belief in either God or moral absolutes, then, poses no impediment to our explaining why murder, torture, theft, and so forth are morally wrong. There is simply no reason to accept the sophomoric moral nihilism so present in the work of LaVey, Aquino, Gilmore, Rice, and company.

Despite the preceding comments, the close association, in many people's minds, between atheism and moral nihilism cannot be denied. But if morality is, as argued, a product of our societies and thus unreliant on divine fiat, why is nihilism a recurrent issue in modern Western intellectual culture? Why does it appear the logical conclusion to individuals such as Satanists? What is *its* cause? Though religious thinkers frequently identify the influence of Darwinism, scientific materialism, secularism, and atheistic philosophy as the obvious culprits, its ultimate source may be quite different. In truth, a lack of understanding of the gradual development of moral principles, combined with deeply entrenched cultural and religious presumptions regarding the nature of our world, may well be largely responsible: specifically, the metaphysical, eschatological, and existential expectations advocated for centuries by the Christian worldview.

In his comprehensive examination of modern nihilism, *The Specter of the Absurd: Sources and Criticisms of Modern Nihilism*, philosopher Donald Crosby draws attention to the conflict between Western scientific materialism and the traditional Christian account of nature. Crosby identifies a number of points of the classical Christian vision that have been challenged by scientific advances: Christianity's strong anthropocentrism (and the subservience of nature to humanity), belief in a objective moral order rooted in the will of God, belief in the existence and immortality of the soul, belief in an afterlife of greater importance than the current world, belief in the meaningfulness of history, and the externalization of existential value (life is meaningful because God makes it so). These principles undoubtedly provide enormous ready-made existential comfort in the form of meaning, purpose, order, and certainty. As such, they help explain the continuing attraction of the faith. Yet merely being comforting or attractive does not make them true, and each of these presuppositions has faced serious, often devastating, challenges from the enormous and ever-increasing explanatory power of the naturalistic, scientific worldview. The result is a discernible reduction in the persuasiveness of the Christian vision, a "gaping hole that can be torn in the fabric of social and individual existence when that vision ceases to convince or compel, and nothing else seems to take its place."[14] Christianity has historically

> provided what in many ways must be recognized as a richly satisfying and comforting vision of human existence, one that has exerted a profound, long-lasting influence on the Western world. Its decline is bound to force the question of whether anything comparable can be found to put in its place. To the extent that one concludes that the answer is "No," one tends in the direction of nihilism, in the sense of having no alternative pattern of commitment and belief from whose perspective the meaningfulness of human life can be confidently affirmed. In this sense the fading of Christian conviction in the West must be seen as a major historical root of modern nihilism.[15]

By so effectively and extensively promoting base assumptions about the world that do not accurately reflect reality, Christianity only exacerbates the sense of loss that is felt as its vision is disproved. The problem is not that science is nihilistic or immoral, but that against the unrealistic expectations of Christianity it appears so, by failing to offer the same level of comfort or certainty. It is significant that the nihilistic malaise does not affect Eastern cultures to the same extent it affects the West. Most Asian countries have conceptions of morality and purpose that are rooted far more deeply in social practice than supernatural justification. Importantly, the rigid anthropocentrism and otherworldly focus at the heart of Christianity is often absent. The Japanese, for example, have no problem accepting the fact of human evolution, as they have traditionally regarded themselves as a part of the natural world. Japanese morality is similarly unaffected, as it is directed more toward social harmony than external standards of good and evil. Scientific naturalism does not conflict with any of their cultural/religious presuppositions, as it merely explains natural processes, and as it therefore poses no threat it provokes not hostility. In the West, however, the steady, systematic assault and dismantling of the core presuppositions of Christianity, combined with how deeply these presuppositions are embedded into all segments of our society, has often resulted in a profound sense of loss.[16]

It should be clear how Satanism fits into this debate. The common ground of the Satanist and other secular non-believers is the assertion that this world and this life are the only important considerations. For both groups, the individual must create or find meaning and purpose for himself. But beyond these broad assumptions, the two quickly part company. In contrast to Satanists, secular atheists avoid the pitfalls of crude nihilistic posturing. It can also be noted that the high level of interest in the occult makes Satanism a *very* strange form of atheism. Atheists, generally, eschew any supernatural beliefs and support a naturalistic account of the world. The close association with skepticism and naturalism provides little room for occult beliefs and practices.

The Satanist's response to this specter of nihilism is particularly illuminating. To so openly embrace the worst interpretation of a naturalistic worldview betrays a mindset that has failed to escape the traditional Christian intellectual framework. The psychology of Satanism is, despite its claims of basis in rationality, in many ways of a profoundly religious nature. Many Satanic beliefs are identical to those of other conservative religious figures: the same (mis)understanding of the implications of Darwinism (that it simply reduces us to the status of animals), the same nihilistic assessment of the entailments of rational atheism (the fallacy popularized by Dostoyevsky that if there is no God there can be no basis for ethics), the same claims of privileged access to fundamental truths of the world (and similarly based on a revelatory scripture), a willingness to believe in nonnatural phenomena, and similar claims to special group privileges (a chosen people who deserve preferential rights). All of these factors betray the extent to which Satanists remain ensnared in the underlying cultural and intellectual presuppositions of the classical Christian worldview. The adoption of the prime Christian bogeyman as a standard of rebellion is simply further proof.

THE TWILIGHT OF THE IDOLS

Of the ideology of modern Satanism itself, little remains to be said. Its key doctrines are not just odious and repugnant, they are demonstrably false. It is an immature, intolerant, and hateful ideology that is only a philosophy of life to those who adhere to it. Like the very worst of political doctrines it transforms people into abstractions, systematically stripping them of dignity, humanity, and rights. Founded on bluster and insecurity, Satanism appeals to inchoate minds that feel Crowley's "Do what thou wilt" provides significant guidelines for social interaction, and that reading and agreeing with a single book qualifies one as the elite of society. Fears of extremist tendencies or affinities within Satanism are not overstated or unjustified. By packaging extremist rhetoric in such a theatrical, superficially persuasive form, modern Satanism is often little more than a soft entry point for the doctrines of neo-Nazism and neofascism.

Shorn of its dramatic and deliberately provocative title, modern Satanism is little more than a grab-bag of nineteenth-century philosophical misadventures. It purports to be a rational philosophy yet demonstrates all the trademarks of bad thinking: its proponents display an undue deference to authority, a strong tendency to see every issue in terms of simplistic dichotomies, misuse of scientific terminology, dogmatism, profound ignorance of developments in areas of direct relevance (evolutionary biology, sociobiology, moral philosophy), hostility toward anyone who supports contrary ideas, and unwillingness to engage non-group members in open debate. In this regard, we can heed a warning made by Bertrand Russell: "I suggest that philosophy, if it is bad philosophy, may be dangerous, and therefore deserves that degree of negative respect which we accord to lightning and tigers."[17]

Modern Satanism is, undoubtedly, bad philosophy. Nonetheless, this fact doesn't negate the value of studying it. Satanism brings into sharp focus a number of key issues regarding the type of society we want to live in, the values we hold as important, and why it is important to defend them. It is a cautionary tale as to the dangers of seeking easy answers to complex issues, the lure of rhetoric in place of content, and the pitfalls of a cult of personality. Fortunately, modern Satanism appears fated to remain a fringe philosophy, taken up by a small minority, and misunderstood, shunned, or vilified by the vast majority—quarantined by its own reputation. Satanists, no doubt, are only too happy with this fate.

The existence of a subculture like modern Satanism can be seen as one of the costs of living in a democratic society. Their ability to maintain a diabolical stance and promote discriminatory bigotry in complete opposition to reality, decency, and common sense is part and parcel with living in a free society. States such as Stalinist Russian, Communist China, modern day North Korea or Iran would not tolerate their pretensions for a minute, and countermeasures would be swift and brutal. There are no free-riders in totalitarian (nonegalitarian) states. The fact that Western democracies allow groups such as Satanists to freely disseminate their hateful folly is an important part of what makes Western democracies better societies. Satanists' rights to say and believe whatever they want must be affirmed, as they are rights *egalitarian* societies afford all their citizens, regardless of whether said citizens reciprocate or not. But by the same standards, we must also affirm the right of critics to subject Anton Szandor LaVey's crypto-fascist ideology and its various permutations to a rigorous critique, and ultimately declare it intellectually, scientifically, and morally bankrupt.

Notes

INTRODUCTION

1. Goethe, *Faust*, bilingual ed., trans. and ed. by J.F.L. Raschen (Ithaca, NY: The Thrift Press, 1949), p. 202.
2. Quoted in Gavin Baddeley, *Lucifer Rising: A Book of Sin, Devil Worship, and Rock 'n' Roll* (London: Plexus Publishing Limited, 2006), p. 66.
3. Anton Szandor LaVey, "The Church of Satan, Cosmic Joy Buzzer," in *The Devil's Notebook*, pp. 28–32 (p. 28).
4. John Lennon, quoted in *The Evening Standard*, London, March 4, 1966.
5. Uncredited neighbor of LaVey, *Satanis: The Devil's Mass*, dir. Ray Laurent (Sherpix, 1970), rerelease DVD, Something Weird Video (2003).
6. LaVey, *The Satanic Bible* (New York: Avon Books, 1969), p. 50.
7. Ayn Rand, *The Virtue of Selfishness* (New York: Signet, 1957), p. vii.
8. Anton Szandor LaVey, "Pentagonal Revisionism: A Five-Point Program," in *The Devil's Notebook* (Los Angeles: Feral House, 1992), pp. 93–96 (p. 93).
9. LaVey, *The Satanic Bible*, p. 65.
10. "Evil, anyone?," *Newsweek*, August 6, 1971, quoted in Arthur Lyons, *Satan Wants You: The Cult of Devil Worship in America* (New York: Mysterious Press, 1988), p. 118. The full *Newsweek* quote is included at the head of Chapter 8 of this book.
11. Quoted in Blanche Barton, *The Secret Life of a Satanist* (Los Angeles: Feral House 1990), p. 205.
12. Pastor David Todeschini, *The Truth about the Devil* (n.p.: Barry Campbell, 2005), p. 3.
13. Mark Twain, *Letters from the Earth: Uncensored Writings*, ed. Bernard DeVoto (New York: Harper & Row, 1962), pp. 7–8.

CHAPTER 1

1. All biblical quotations are from the New International Edition.
2. Job 1:7–8.
3. Job 1:9–11.
4. Zechariah 3:1.
5. Zechariah 3:2.
6. Matthew 4:3–10.
7. Just as Satan is merely Yahweh's chief prosecutor, the Islamic the figure of Iblis (or Shaitan) is similarly merely a part of God's creation. The enemy of humanity and not God, Iblis is a formless creature that attempts to lead humans to evil by suggestion.
8. Luke 11.
9. 2 Corinthians.
10. Isaiah 14:12.
11. Henry Kelly, quoted in "Professor Protests Satan's Modern Image," http://www.dailybruin.ucla.edu/news/2006/nov/15/professor-protests-satans-mode/ (accessed January 23, 2007). See also Peter Stanford, *The Devil: A Biography* (London: Mandarin Paperbacks, 1996); Henry Kelly, *Satan: A Biography* (Cambridge: Cambridge University Press, 2006). The problem of writing biographies of the devil or Satan is highlighted in a review of Kelly's *Satan:* "[Kelly] can hardly write a biography because Satan, as he demonstrates, does not have a life. He was never a person, and is absent from the Old Testament" (Peter Conrad, "Better the Devil You Know," http://www.guardian.co.uk/theobserver/2006/aug/27/society (accessed January 22, 2007)).
12. Luke 10:17.
13. 1 Peter 5:8.
14. Isaiah 27:1.
15. Revelation 12:9.
16. Genesis 6:4.
17. St. Augustine, *Confessions*, VII, ch. 3.
18. St. Augustine, *City of God*, XIX, ch. 8.
19. St. Augustine, *City of God*, XIX, ch. 8.
20. H. J. Schroeder, *Disciplinary Decrees of the General Councils: Text, Translation and Commentary* (St. Louis: B. Herder, 1937), p. 236.
21. Malcolm Lambert, *Mediaeval Heresy: Popular Movements from the Gregorian Reform to the Reformation* (New York: Holmes & Meier, 1977), p. 7.
22. John 12:31.
23. *The Malleus Maleficarum*, Part I, Question III, http://www.malleusmaleficarum.org/ (accessed January 25, 2007).
24. William Manchester, *A World Lit Only by Fire: The Medieval Mind and the Renaissance* (London: Macmillan London Limited, 1993), p. 62.
25. Aleister Crowley, *Gilles de Rais: The Banned Lecture* (Logan, OH: Black Moon Publishing, 2008), p. 11. The title "Banned" or "Forbidden" Lecture is somewhat

misleading. It was not the lecture but rather Crowley himself that was prevented from appearing at Oxford University in 1930—due entirely to his thoroughly rotten reputation.

26. Voltaire, Letter from Voltaire to Frederick, January 5, 1767. *Letters of Voltaire and Frederick the Great*, trans. Richard Aldington (New York: Brentano's, 1927), no. 156.

27. *Applebee's Original Weekly Journal*, May 6, 1971. Reprinted in Rictor Norton, "The Hell Fire Club," *Early Eighteenth-Century Newspaper Reports: A Sourcebook*, http://www.infopt.demon.co.uk/grub/hellfire.htm (accessed January 25, 2007).

28. J. K. Huysman, *La Bas*, quoted in Nikolas Schreck, ed., *Flowers from Hell: A Satanic Reader* (New York: Creation Books, 2001), p. 159.

29. Galatians 5:16–21.

30. Richard Cavendish, *The Black Arts* (New York: Perigee, 1967), p. 303.

CHAPTER 2

1. Numbers 16:30.

2. Leviticus 16:21.

3. Dante Alighieri, *The Divine Comedy*, Book I Canto 34:29–36.

4. William Shakespeare, *Macbeth*, Act IV, Scene III, 55–57.

5. John Milton, *Paradise Lost*, I.26.

6. Milton, *Paradise Lost*, I.56–58.

7. Milton, *Paradise Lost*, I.258–263.

8. Milton, *Paradise Lost*, I.600–4.

9. Milton, *Paradise Lost*, II.305–6.

10. Michel de Montaigne, "Of Repenting," in *Essays*, trans. John Florio (London: V. Sims, 1603), book 3, ch. 2. Of course, Montaigne gets one important detail wrong—it wasn't just *men* being burnt alive by the Inquisition, it was in fact mostly women.

11. Percy Shelley, "In Praise of Poetry," in *Shelley's Prose*, ed. David Lee Clark (New York: New Amsterdam, 1988), p. 290.

12. William Blake, "The Marriage of Heaven and Hell," in *The Complete Prose and Poetry of William Blake*, ed. David V. Erdman, revised edition (Berkeley: University of California Press, 1982), p. 35.

13. Benita Eisler, *Byron: Child of Passion, Fool of Fame* (New York: Vintage Books, 2000) p. 340.

14. Eisler, *Byron: Child of Passion, Fool of Fame*, p. 716

15. Goethe, *Goethe, Selected Poems*, trans. Michael Hamburger, ed. Christopher Middleton (Princeton, NJ: Princeton University Press, 1983), p. 27.

16. Baudelaire, "Litany to Satan," in *Flowers of Evil*, eds. Marthiel and Jackson Mathews (New York: New Directions, 1962), p. 170.

17. Niccolò Machiavelli, *The Prince*, trans. George Bull, intro. Anthony Grafton (London: Penguin, 1961), p. 54.

18. Thomas Hobbes, *De Cive*, I, 12, in *Man and Citizen* (*De Homine* and *De Cive*), ed. and intro. Bernard Gert [*De Cive* trans. attributed to Thomas Hobbes] (Indianapolis, IN: Hackett Publishing Group, 1991).

19. Of course, the simplest argument against Malthus is the most obvious one: the population continued to grow and the great famine he predicted never happened. Not only did the population continue to grow through the nineteenth century, it positively exploded in the twentieth. From the estimated 1 billion people in the time of Malthus, the world now hosts near to 7 billion individuals.

20. Thomas Malthus, *An Essay on the Principle of Population*, ed. Geoffrey Gilbert, (New York: Oxford University Press, 1999), p. 26.

21. Herbert Spencer, "Progress: Its Law and Causes," *The Westminster Review* 67, no. 132 (1857): pp. 445–85 (p. 445).

22. Social Darwinism was for a long time attributed squarely to Spencer, largely due to the American capitalists and social theorists who championed the theory in his name, in conjunction with the influence of G. E. Moore's *Principia Ethica* (1903) and Richard Hofstadter's *Social Darwinism in American Thought* (1955), works that both explicitly laid responsibility on Spencer. Subsequent interpreters have, until recently, largely followed their lead. It is now generally regarded as only a minor theme in his work.

23. William Graham Sumner, *The Challenge of Facts and Other Essays*, ed. A. G. Keller (New Haven, CT: Yale University Press, 1914), p. 25.

24. Max Stirner, *The Ego and Its Own*, trans. Steven T. Byington, ed. James J. Martin (New York: Dover Publications, 2005), p. 169.

25. Stirner, *The Ego and Its Own*, p. 318. Italics in original.

26. There are claims that similarities between Stirner and Nietzsche are more than mere echoes; in 1891 Nietzsche's contemporary, German philosopher Eduard Von Hartmann, accused Nietzsche of plagiarizing Stirner. There are no references to Stirner in Nietzsche's works or letters, but Nietzsche had his student borrow Stirner's books from Basel Library in 1874, and spoke favorably of them to the student and acquaintances afterwards. See Rüdiger Safranski, *Nietzsche: A Philosophical Biography*, trans. Shelley Frisch (London: Granta Publications, 2002), pp. 126–27.

27. Friedrich Nietzsche, "The Antichrist," in *The Portable Nietzsche*, ed. and trans. Walter Kaufmann (New York: Penguin Books, 1976), §62, pp. 655–56. Italics in original.

28. Friedrich Nietzsche, "The Gay Science," in *The Portable Nietzsche*, §125, pp. 95–96. Italics in original.

29. Friedrich Nietzsche, *Twilight of the Idols / The Anti-Christ*, trans. R. J. Hollingdale (Middlesex: Penguin Books, 1968), p. 187.

30. Friedrich Nietzsche, "Thus Spake Zarathustra," in *The Portable Nietzsche*, "Zarathustra's Prologue," §3, p. 124.

31. Nietzsche, *The Antichrist*, in *The Portable Nietzsche*, §2, p. 570.

32. The Marquis de Sade, while completely disinterested in any religious idea of Satan, was nevertheless not above having a character evoke him for the purposes of blasphemy and to further intensify perversion:

> Behold, my love, behold all that I simultaneously do: scandal, seduction, bad example, incest, adultery, sodomy! Oh, Satan! one and unique God of my soul, inspire thou in me something yet more, present further perversions to my smoking heart, and then shalt thou see how I shall plunge myself into them all! (Marquis de Sade, "Dialogue the Fifth," in *Philosophy in the Bedroom*, trans. Richard Seaver and Austryn Wainhouse. [London: Arrow, 1991], p. 272)

33. Jack London, *The Sea Wolf*, (New York: Award Books, 1970), p. 192.

34. London, *The Sea Wolf*, p. 67.

35. London, *The Sea Wolf*, pp. 57–58.

36. London, *The Sea Wolf*, pp. 197–98. It is important to note that Jack London would be unimpressed by his work's later adoption by Satanism. London, a staunch socialist, intended *The Sea Wolf* as an attack on the radical Nietzschean individualism exemplified by Wolf Larsen and later adopted by LaVey. LaVey's appraisal of London as a Satanic writer was based on a misinterpretation of the latter's work. In *The Sea Wolf*, Wolf Larsen's brutal individualism ultimately sees him abandoned by his crew and shipwrecked, and he dies a broken—though defiant—cripple.

37. Ayn Rand, *Atlas Shrugged* (New York: Signet, 1957), p. 936.

38. Rand, p. 948.

39. Ayn Rand, *The Virtue of Selfishness* (New York: Signet, 1964), p. vii. Italics in original.

40. Although Rand's expansive philosophical system encompasses epistemology, metaphysics, ethics, politics, and art, her philosophy of rational self-interest has not been influential with academic philosophers, who generally hold that her work lacks philosophical rigor, makes numerous basic errors, and that many of the main themes of her work are presented far better and with greater clarity by other, less famous theorists. The most prominent example is undoubtedly Robert Nozick, *Anarchy, State, and Utopia* (New York: Basic Books, 1974).

41. Martin Booth, *A Magick Life: A Biography of Aleister Crowley* (London: Coronet Books, 2000), p. 394.

42. Aleister Crowley, *The Book of the Law / Liber Al Vel Vegis* (York Beach, ME: Weiser Books, 2004), Book I, §40,

43. Crowley, *The Book of the Law / Liber Al Vel Vegis*, Book III, §44.

44. Aleister Crowley, *Magick in Theory and Practice* in *Magick: Liber Aba: Book 4 (Magick Bk. 4)* (York Beach, ME: Weiser Books, 1998), "Introduction," p. 126.

45. Crowley, *The Book of the Law / Liber Al Vel Vegis*, Book I, §57.

46. Aleister Crowley, "Letter to Gerald Kelly," October 1905; quoted in Lawrence Sutin, *Do What Thou Wilt* (New York: St Martin's Press, 2000), p. 160.

47. Crowley, *The Book of the Law / Liber Al Vel Vegis*, Book III, §18.

48. Aleister Crowley, *The Law Is for All*, ed. Israel Regardie (Phoenix: Falcon Press, 1986), p. 177.

CHAPTER 3

1. Anton Szandor LaVey, *The Satanic Bible* (New York: Avon Books, 1969) "Introduction," by Burton H. Wolfe (1976–2005). This is Wolfe's second introduction to *The Satanic Bible*. His first was from 1969–1972; replaced by Michael Aquino's from 1972–1976. The current introduction is written by Peter H. Gilmore (2005–).

2. Lawrence Wright, "It's Not Easy Being Evil in a World That's Gone to Hell," *Rolling Stone* 612, September 5, 1991, pp. 63–68 (p. 67).

3. LaVey, *The Satanic Bible*, "Introduction" (Burton H. Wolfe, 1976–2005).

4. Blanche Barton, *The Secret Life of a Satanist: The Authorized Biography of Anton LaVey* (Los Angeles: Feral House 1990) p. 42.

5. Barton, *The Secret Life of a Satanist*, p. 50.

6. Burton H. Wolfe, "Introduction," *The Satanic Bible*, p. 11. Wolfe's account was later expanded into the first biography of LaVey, *The Devil's Avenger*, which appeared in 1974.

7. Arthur Lyons, *Satan Wants You: The Cult of Devil Worship in America* (New York: Mysterious Press, 1988) pp. 104–5.

8. Barton, *The Secret Life of a Satanist*, p. 55. Of course, the very idea of a return to San Francisco presupposes LaVey ever left. However, the fact that Michael Levey owned 6114 California Street from the early 1930s and was at one point a legitimate liquor salesman (presumably before Prohibition) makes the claim that the Black House once served as a speakeasy somewhat plausible, if casting it in a different light.

9. Wright, "It's Not Easy Being Evil in a World That's Gone to Hell," p. 106.

10. Barton, *The Secret Life of a Satanist*, p. 60.

11. According to Blanche Barton, Togare died at San Francisco Zoo in 1981, on Walpurgisnacht, no less (see Barton, p. 124).

12. For details of these—and many other—biographical embellishments, see Zeena Schreck and Nikolas Schreck, "Anton LaVey: Legend and Reality," 1998, http://www.churchofsatan.org/aslv.html (accessed February 21, 2007).

13. Burton Wolfe, Michael Aquino, and current Magus Peter Gilmore all made their contributions. As an indication of how actively the Church of Satan promotes LaVey's mythography, Gilmore's 2005 introduction repeats the main claims of the biography—Marilyn, the Mayan Theatre, the police career, the 1956 purchase of the Black House—14 years after Wright's article and in face of solid proof such as the transfer of the deed to 6114 California Street on July 9, 1971.

14. Anton Szandor LaVey, "The Liars Club," in *Satan Speaks!* (Los Angeles: Feral House, 1998), pp. 101–2 (p. 101).

15. Arthur Lyons, *The Second Coming: Satanism in America* (1970) quoted in Aquino, *Church of Satan*, 5th ed. (Self-published, 2002), p. 80. Lyons's account should be treated with caution as he was, at the time of writing this passage, a member of the Church of Satan. Nonetheless, Lyons's assessments of this period are by far the most reliable, objective, and insightful of any of the early members of LaVey's circle.

16. Barton, *The Secret Life of a Satanist*, p. 90. The invocation is printed in full in Anton Szandor LaVey, *The Satanic Rituals* (New York: Avon Books, 1972) pp. 214–18.

17. Barton, *The Secret Life of a Satanist*, p. 91.

18. Anton Szandor LaVey, 1967, http://www.churchofsatan.com/ (accessed January 25, 2007).

19. Barton, *The Secret Life of a Satanist*, p. 98.

20. Anton Szandor LaVey, "To: All Doomsayers (etc.)," in *Satan Speaks!*, pp. 4–7 (p. 5).

21. LaVey, *The Satanic Bible*, p. 61.

22. LaVey, *The Satanic Bible*, pp. 21–22.

23. LaVey, *The Satanic Bible*, pp. 23–24.

24. LaVey, *The Satanic Bible*, p. 66.

25. LaVey, *The Satanic Bible*, p. 44. LaVey's description of God as a cosmological projection of humanity is very similar to the theories put forward by nineteenth-century theorists such as Ludwig Feuerbach, Karl Marx, David Strauss, and Friedrich Nietzsche—a philosophical epoch that LaVey was obviously familiar with.

26. LaVey, *The Satanic Bible*, p. 89.

27. LaVey, *The Satanic Bible*, p. 162.

28. LaVey, *The Satanic Bible*, p. 168.

29. Regardie's comments come from his introduction to Aleister Crowley's *The Vision and the Voice* (San Francisco: Red Wheel Weiser, 1972): "a California group sensationally engaged in the practice of Satanism…appropriated and published the Enochian rituals or Calls in a so-called Satanic Bible…The author of this debased volume had made enough changes in the various Calls to rule out any likelihood of confusion with those presented here in their original form. Wherever the word God is used, the author had substituted the name of Satan or one of the equivalent terms in its stead. The same holds true for several other pieces of similar stupidity."

30. Quoted in Shane Bugbee, "The Doctor is in…" *MF Magazine 3*, http://www.churchofsatan.com/Pages/MFInterview.html (accessed January 17, 2007).

31. Quoted in *Satanis: The Devil's Mass*, directed by Ray Laurent (Sherpix, 1970, re-released DVD, Something Weird Video, 2003).

32. Randall H. Alfred, "The Church of Satan," *The New Religious Consciousness*, ed. Charles Y. Clock and Robert N. Bellah (Berkeley: University of California Press, 1976), pp. 180–202 (p. 193). Alfred noted a large number of people dropping in and out of the church, making it difficult to ascertain exact numbers. In a 16-month

period, he recorded 140 "different members observed in more or less regular attendance at the rituals" (p. 194).

33. Aquino, p. 868. Aquino is generally much more realistic—and open—with membership numbers of both the Church of Satan and the Temple of Set, and his figure is probably the most reliable. It is also supported by statements by both Diane and Zeena LaVey that the Church of Satan membership never exceeded 300 members between 1966 and 1990 (see Zeena Schreck and Nikolas Schreck, "Anton LaVey: Legend and Reality").

34. Lyons, *Satan Wants You*, p. 115.

35. Anton Szandor LaVey, *The Satanic Witch*, intro. Zeena LaVey (Los Angeles: Feral House, 1989), p. 106. By all accounts, LaVey was completely serious about his salad dressing theory.

CHAPTER 4

1. Anton Szandor LaVey, *The Satanic Bible* (New York: Avon Books, 1969), p. 45. Capitals in original.

2. Peter H. Gilmore, "Rebels without Cause," in *The Satanic Scriptures* (Baltimore: Scapegoat Publishing, 2007), pp. 186–94 (p. 193). References to LaVey as 'Dr' or 'Doctor' are a widespread custom among Satanists, but are entirely honorary. There is no evidence that LaVey completed *any* formal education after dropping out of high school.

3. A number of the more extreme Satanists were put off by LaVey's view that even a housewife could be a Satanist. As the black metal musician Ihsahn notes, a backlash against LaVey began because "his form of Satanism is very humane. No one wanted a humane Satanism; you should almost be Satan himself" (Michael Moynihan and Didrik Søderlind, *Lords of Chaos: The Bloody Rise of the Satanic Metal Underground*, rev. and exp. ed. (Los Angeles: Feral House, 2003), p. 220.

4. LaVey, *The Satanic Bible*, p. 33. This passage is taken verbatim from Ragnar Redbeard's *Might Is Right*, with LaVey's only alteration being the substitution of "SMASH him on the other" for the original "smash him down" (Ragnar Redbeard, *Might Is Right* (n.p.: Evilnow, 2006), p. 32).

5. Quoted in Baddeley, *Lucifer Rising: A Book of Sin, Devil Worship, and Rock 'n' Roll* (London: Plexus Publishing Limited, 2006), p. 75.

6. LaVey, *The Satanic Mass* (Mephisto Media, 1968) rerelease CD, Reptilian Records, 2001.

7. The edition of *Might Is Right* used here is published independently by Church of Satan member Shane Bugbee. It includes a "forward" [*sic*] by LaVey and an afterword by Peter Gilmore.

8. Ragnar Redbeard, *Might Is Right*, p. 3.

9. Redbeard, *Might Is Right*, p. 31. For an analysis of (far more subtle) elements of anti-Semitic conspiracy elements in Nietzsche, see Robert Nola, "Nietzsche as

Anti-Semitic Jewish Conspiracy Theorist," *Croatian Journal of Philosophy* 3, no. 7 (2003): pp. 35–62.

10. Ibid., p. 123. Redbeard's views of women are strikingly similar to those expressed by Arthur Schopenhauer in his infamous essay "On Women," and are in all likelihood lifted wholesale from the German Idealist: "Women are also remarkably good liars. Deception is an essential and necessary part of their mental equipment. They are inherently deceitful...When women *think*, they think falsely" (p. 178). Redbeard continues later with a faux scientific justification of misogyny, again echoing Schopenhauer: "A woman is primarily a reproductive cell-organism, a womb structurally embastioned by a protective, defensive, osseous network; and surrounded with the antennae, and blood vessels, necessary for supplying nutriment to the growing ovum or embryo" (p. 177). See also Arthur Schopenhauer, "On Women," in *Essays and Aphorisms*, trans. R. J. Hollingdale (London: Penguin Books, 1970), pp. 80–88.

11. Redbeard, *Might Is Right*, p. 123.

12. Redbeard, *Might Is Right*, p. 77.

13. Redbeard, *Might Is Right*, p. 186. *Panmixia* is a late nineteenth-century term used to describe the random mating of individuals within a population with no regard to choosing partners with particular traits.

14. LaVey, *The Satanic Bible*, p. 34. (Redbeard, pp. 45–46.)

15. Redbeard, *Might Is Right*, p. 46.

16. One of the few points of divergence between *Might Is Right* and *The Satanic Bible* is on the issue of sexuality. In regard to sexual mores, Redbeard is extraordinarily conservative and—irony notwithstanding—strikes a resolutely *moralistic* tone.

17. LaVey, "Pentagonal Revisionism," in *The Devil's Notebook* (Los Angeles: Feral House, 1992), pp. 93–96. The essay's conflation of ideology and pure fantasy is disturbing. In a proposal that sounds suspiciously like fascist theorizing, LaVey makes open references to Buck Rogers and Flash Gordon.

18. LaVey, "The Goodguy Badge," in *The Devil's Notebook*, pp. 20–27 (pp. 20–22).

19. Ayn Rand, *The Virtue of Selfishness* (New York: Signet, 1957), pp. x–xi.

20. Charles Darwin, *The Descent of Man, and Selection in Relation to Sex*, Volume 1 (London: John Murray, 1871), p. 105. Darwin continues to state: "The moral sense perhaps affords the best and highest distinction between man and the lower animals" (p. 106).

21. See George Williams, "Huxley's Evolution and Ethics in a Sociobiological Perspective," *Zygon* 23:4 (1988), pp. 383–407.

22. In a discussion of the concept of universal rights in human societies, biologist E. O. Wilson makes the following intriguing observation: "A rational ant—let us imagine for a moment that ants and other social insects had succeeded in evolving high intelligence—would find such an arrangement biologically unsound and the very concept of individual human freedom intrinsically evil" (E. O. Wilson, *On Human Nature* (Cambridge, MA: Harvard University Press, 1978), pp. 198–99).

23. Peter H. Gilmore, "Satanism: The Feared Religion," in *The Satanic Scriptures*, pp. 25–39 (p. 35).

24. The Fallacy of Mediocrity is the claim that any member of a set is limited to the attributes it shares with the other members of the set. For example: My calculator is made of plastic, metal, and glass; plastic, metal, and glass can't perform mathematical calculations; therefore, my calculator can't perform mathematical calculations. Satanism argues that because humans share a large biological basis with other animals, we are therefore merely animals.

25. LaVey, *The Satanic Bible*, p. 44.

26. Friedrich Nietzsche, *Beyond Good and Evil*, §75, in Hollingdale, *A Nietzsche Reader*, trans. and ed. R. J. Hollingdale (London: Penguin Books, 1977), p. 160.

27. Interestingly, LaVey's ideas on sexuality belie how traditionally structured his thinking often was. The close connection between sex and evil is a central theme in Christianity, whose scriptures closely associated the spirit with God and the flesh with the devil. LaVey exploits this association to fallaciously conclude that religious faith is incompatible with a healthy sexual life, therefore making the liberating sexuality of Satanism the only option. Yet by focusing so heavily on sexuality, LaVey again betrays both the profound influence that Christianity had on his thinking and his inability to think independently of Christian sexual mores. While the comments LaVey makes about promiscuity and masturbation are reasonably sensible, the extremely limited definition of man as a carnal animal can be read as an overreaction to perceived Christian puritanism. In the context of *The Satanic Witch*, LaVey's stereotypical account of human nature and interactions between the sexes becomes insulting to both sexes: the prime resource of women is their ability to use their sexual allure to entrap feeble, sexually compelled males.

28. Quoted in Blanche Barton, *The Secret Life of a Satanist* (Los Angeles: Feral House 1990), p. 218.

29. See Marquis de Sade, *Juliette*, trans. Austryn Wainhouse (New York: Grove Press, 1968), p. 418.

30. Anton Szandor LaVey, "Two Wrongs Make A Right," in *The Devil's Notebook*, p. 117.

31. LaVey, "Diabolica," in *The Devil's Notebook*, pp. 143–47 (p. 144).

32. LaVey, *The Satanic Bible*, p. 52.

33. LaVey, *The Satanic Bible*, pp. 69–70.

34. LaVey, *The Satanic Bible*, p. 33. Once again, this passage is taken directly from *Might Is Right* (Redbeard, p. 31).

35. Friedrich Nietzsche, *On the Genealogy of Morals*, First Essay, §13, trans. Walter Kaufman and R. J. Hollingdale (New York: Vintage Books, 1984), p. 47.

36. Nietzsche, *On the Genealogy of Morals*, First Essay, §11, p. 45.

37. Herodotus, *The Histories*, trans. Robin Waterfield, ed. Carolyn Dewald (Oxford: Oxford University Press, 1998), p. 122 (§68). Herodotus's observations may be interesting, but his skills as a zoologist were hardly beyond reproach: in the same

section he also notes that the crocodile "is the only creature in the world without a tongue," that it "does not move its lower jaw" and that "it is blind in the water." Nonetheless, he can probably be forgiven for not getting close enough to verify these claims.

38. R. L. Trivers, "The Evolution of Reciprocal Altruism," *Quarterly Review of Biology* 46 (1971): pp. 35–57.

39. Plato, *The Republic*, trans. and intro. Desmond Lee (London: Penguin Books, 2003), p. 18.

40. Plato, *The Republic*, p. 25.

41. Plato, *The Republic*, p. 32.

42. Robert Axelrod, *The Evolution of Cooperation* (New York: Basic Books, 1984), p. 20. In the interests of space, only a short overview of the Prisoner's Dilemma is provided here. For a far more detailed assessment, Axelrod's book is recommended. The best short, general overview is probably chapter 12 of Richard Dawkin's *The Selfish Gene*, an extremely concise and clear assessment of the main points (Oxford: Oxford University Press, 1976).

43. LaVey, *The Satanic Bible*, p. 51.

44. Stephen Jay Gould, "The Most Unkindest Cut of All," in *Dinosaur in a Haystack* (London: Penguin Books, 1996), pp. 309–19 (p. 315).

45. Gilmore, "A Match Made in Hell: Afterword," in Ragnar Redbeard, *Might Is Right*, pp. 202–5 (p. 205).

46. Gilmore, "Opening the Adamantine Gates," introduction to *The Satanic Bible*, pp. 9–18.

47. Gilmore, "Satanism, The Feared Religion," p. 35.

CHAPTER 5

1. Arthur Lyons claims that the cause of West's expulsion was "inflicting the group's rituals with his personal preferences for bondage and homosexuality" (*Satan Wants You* (Los Angeles: Feral House, 1998), p. 116), whereas Aquino claims it was due to disagreement over reduction in size of *The Cloven Hoof* and removal of content regarding magical practice (Michael A. Aquino, *Church of Satan*, 5th ed. (Self-published, 2002), pp. 140–43).

2. Letter, Anton LaVey to Michael Aquino, June 24, 1974. Quoted in Aquino, *Church of Satan*, p. 366. See also Lyons, *Satan Wants You*, pp. 117–19.

3. Aquino, *Church of Satan*, p. 99.

4. Letter, Michael Aquino to Anton and Dianne LaVey, June 10, 1975. Quoted in Aquino, pp. 831–34 (p. 834).

5. Peter H. Gilmore, "Pretenders to the Throne," http://www.churchofsatan.com/ (accessed January 1, 2007).

6. Aquino, *Church of Satan*, p. 411.

7. Michael A. Aquino, "The Book of Coming Forth by Night," in *Temple of Set*, draft 6 (Self-published, 2006), pp. 90–95 (p. 91).

8. *The Occult Experience*, Dir. Frank Heiman, VHS, Premiere Entertainment International, 1985.

9. Roald E. Kristiansen, "Satan in Cyberspace: A Study of Satanism on the Internet in the 1990s," prepared for the Lomonosov Conference in Archangelsk, Russia, November 1995, http://www.love.is/roald/satanism.html (accessed March 3, 2007). The abbreviations CoS (Church of Satan) and ToS (Temple of Set) in Kristiansen's text have been replaced throughout. As an analysis of the beliefs and practices of both organizations, Kristiansen's article is highly recommended.

10. Quoted in *The Occult Experience*.

11. Temple of Set membership figures for 1975 and 2002 come from Aquino, *Temple of Set*, p. 390. The mid-1980s figure is quoted in *The Occult Experience*. Aquino's claim of establishing the Temple of Set with 50 ex–Church of Satan members in 1975 is hardly a wild contradiction of Gilmore's claim that only 30 left, and certainly not grounds for the assertion "the exact numbers are heavily disputed" made by Gavin Baddeley in *Lucifer Rising: A Book of Sin, Devil Worship, and Rock 'n' Roll* (London: Plexus Publishing Limited, 2006), p. 102.

12. Aquino, "Order of the Trapezoid—Statement," *The Crystal Tablet of Set* (self-published, 1990).

13. Aquino, *Temple of Set*, p. 334.

14. Aquino, *Temple of Set*, p. 335. The same work under discussion, *Hitler's Secret Conversations 1941–1944* (New York: Farrar, Straus & Young, 1953), has also been released under the title *Hitler's Table Talk 1941–1944*.

15. Aquino, *Temple of Set*, p. 336.

16. Aquino clearly regards the fall from grace of Madison Grant's *The Passing of the Great Race* (New York: Charles Scribner's Sons, 1918) as the result of postwar intellectual trends rather than the exposure of its lack of proper scientific basis: "In this book he argues a forceful case for a European race history that would have done credit to Hitler or Rosenberg. The most interesting aspect of this book is that only a few years ago it was accepted as a responsible contender in the academic/scientific community. After World War II it was, in Orwell's terms, guilty of Crimethink and thus condemned to be an Unperson. There is a lesson to be learned here concerning the durability and invulnerability of 'established scientific fact' when it becomes politically or socially inconvenient. I hereby suggest that you make up your mind as to whether the book is convincing. After all, I wouldn't want to get in trouble for even appearing to endorse it" (*Temple of Set*, p. 336). A more balanced appraisal is simply to note that science is a self-correcting, fallible process that routinely revises or even abandons inadequate hypotheses in favor of better ones. *The Passing of the Great Race* has not been disregarded because it is "politically or socially inconvenient"; it has been disregarded because it is nonsense.

17. Aquino, *Temple of Set*, p. 369.

18. Paul Valentine, speaking in *Scream Greats, Vol. 2: Satanism and Witchcraft*, directed by Damon Santostefano, VHS, Paramount Home Video, 1986.

19. Mike Pencow, "An Essay on War," May 14, 2006, http://www.black-goat.tk/ (accessed August 11, 2007).

20. For a detailed history of Myatt, see Nicholas Goodrick-Clarke, *Black Sun: Aryan Cults, Esoteric Nazism and the Politics of Identity* (New York: New York University Press, 2002), pp. 215–24.

21. Anton Long, *Diablerie*, p. 10. Quoted in Nicholas Goodrick-Clarke, *Black Sun: Aryan Cults, Esoteric Nazism and the Politics of Identity*, p. 217.

22. Kerry Bolton, quoted in Michael Moynihan and Didrik Søderlind, *Lords of Chaos: The Bloody Rise of the Satanic Metal Underground*, rev. and exp. ed., (Los Angeles: Feral House, 2003), p. 360.

23. Darrick Dishaw, http://cocthulhu.proboards105.com/index.cgi?board=satanism &action=display&thread=1157504034 (accessed December 10, 2006).

24. E-mail, Darrick Dishaw to Peggy Nadramia, in "I Choose to Reign in Hell," http:// www.cultofcthulhu.net/satanism.htm, May 2005, (accessed August 9, 2007).

25. Venger Satanis, "Prologue," *Cult of Cthulhu* (n.p.: Lulu, 2007), p. 10.

26. Church of Satan Reverend Lestat Ventrue's comments about Valentine's purported lying, stalking, character assassination, and incestuous alter egos are made in "The Internet Satanic Bunco Sheet," http://members.chello.at/herbert.paulis/isbs.html (accessed August 8, 2007). Valentine's replies can be viewed on his YouTube videoblog http://www.youtube.com/profile?user=PDValentine (accessed August 8, 2007).

27. "Satanism: Description, Philosophies and Justification of Satanism," http://www. dpjs.co.uk/index.html (accessed August 18, 2007).

28. "Theistic Satanism," http://www.theisticsatanism.com/index.html (accessed August 18, 2007).

29. Church of Satan, http://www.churchofsatan.com/ (accessed August 18, 2007).

30. Rev. Michael S. Margolin, Sinagogue of Satan, http://www.sosatan.org/ (accessed October 10, 2007).

31. Teens_for_Satan Yahoo Group, http://groups.yahoo.com/group/Teens_for_Sa tan/ (accessed October 10, 2007).

32. Bob Ferguson, "Adversarial Evolution," www.leagueofsatanists.com (accessed August 12, 2007).

33. Hegarty/LaVey Property Agreement, April 25/26, 1985. Quoted in Aquino, *Church of Satan*, pp. 899–906.

34. *The Hour*, CBC, July 6, 2006 (television interview).

35. *Magic Mind*, ENG Productions, August 22, 2006 (radio interview).

36. *Hell: The Devil's Domain*, History Channel, produced by Noah Morowitz, A&E Television Networks, 2004.

37. Gilmore's *The Satanic Scriptures* has received rave reviews from Church of Satan members. Magister Svengali (aka James Sass) produced a particularly unrestrained

torrent of sycophancy: "Now all can see what those in the know have appreciated for some time; the steely intellect, lethally razor-like wit, cogently charged writing style, and deeply diabolical erudition of Peter H. Gilmore. Having followed his writing since the 1980's, I had some idea what to expect, but in all earnestness, and all partisan interests aside, in 300+ pages, *The Satanic Scriptures* exceeds all expectations in depth and breadth of thought and subject matter covered." Retrieved from http://www.scapegoatpublishing.com/blog/the-satanic-scriptures-by-peter-h-gilmore/ (accessed October 11, 2007).

38. The interview is an interesting display of just how far Satanism is from standard interpretations of atheism. While Gilmore argues, "We are atheists, we are sceptics, we embrace science as a method for understanding the universe," the host points out that any atheist who supports secular humanism would be directly opposed to a number of ideas that Gilmore advances. The host, a secular humanist and atheist, also challenged Gilmore on his claim that lack of belief in God leads to pure moral subjectivism. In the online forum discussion that followed, a number of atheists were concerned about the negative impact of being associated in any way with the ethical position represented by Gilmore. When atheists, one of America's least popular minorities, want to distance themselves from Satanism, it is clear that any Satanic public-relations campaign will be an uphill battle (D. J. Grothe, Peter Gilmore, *Peter H. Gilmore—Science and Satanism*, Point of Inquiry podcast, August 10, 2007, http://www.pointofinquiry.org/?p=122 (accessed August 11, 2007)).

39. Anton Szandor LaVey, *Satan Speaks!* (Los Angeles: Feral House, 1998), p. 169.

40. Peter H. Gilmore, "Rebels without Cause," in *The Satanic Scriptures* (Baltimore: Scapegoat Publishing, 2007), p. 186–94 (p. 193).

CHAPTER 6

1. Richard Cavendish, *The Black Arts* (New York: Perigee, 1967), p. 1. More than four decades after its publication, Cavendish's work remains the authoritative study on the topic (even appearing in the bibliography for LaVey's *The Satanic Witch*). This chapter's debt to *The Black Arts*, as well as David S. Katz's *The Occult Tradition: From the Renaissance to the Present Day* (London: Pimlico, 2005) is freely acknowledged.

2. Pico della Mirandola, quoted in David S. Katz, *The Occult Tradition: From the Renaissance to the Present Day* (London: Pimlico, 2005), p. 43.

3. Cornelius Agrippa, *Three Books of Occult Philosophy* (London: Gregory Moule, 1651), p. 66.

4. LaVey, *The Satanic Bible* (New York: Avon Books, 1969), p. 155–56.

5. LaVey, *The Satanic Bible*, p. 136.

6. Éliphas Lévi, *Doctrine and Ritual of High Magic, Part II: The Ritual of Transcendental Magic*, trans. A. E. Waite (England: Rider & Company, 1896), p. 82.

7. Aleister Crowley, *Magick in Theory and Practice* in *Magick: Liber Aba: Book 4 (Magick Bk. 4)* (York Beach, ME: Weiser Books, 1998), "Introduction," p. 129.

8. LaVey, *The Satanic Bible*, p. 52.

9. LaVey, *The Satanic Bible*, p. 51.

10. LaVey, *The Satanic Bible*, p. 110.

11. Michael A. Aquino, "Lesser Black Magic/Ethics," in *Temple of Set*, draft 6 (Self-published, 2006), pp. 215–26 (p. 215).

12. Peter H. Gilmore, speaking in *Hell: The Devil's Domain*, DVD, produced by Noah Morowitz (A&E Television Networks, 2004).

13. Crowley, *The Book of the Law / Liber Al Vel Vegis* (York Beach, ME: Weiser Books, 2004), Book II §22.

14. LaVey, *The Satanic Bible*, p. 89.

15. Larry Wessel, *Speak of the Devil*, directed by Nick Bougas, VHS (Wavelength Video, Dist. Feral House Video, 1993).

16. LaVey, *The Satanic Bible*, p. 90.

17. LaVey, *The Satanic Rituals*, p. 34.

18. CBS2 News, "Satanic Celebration," television broadcast, July 6, 2006.

19. Anton LaVey, "The Nine Satanic Sins," 1987, http://www.churchofsatan.com/Pages/Sins.html (accessed October 10, 2007).

20. See Gavin Baddeley, *Lucifer Rising: A Book of Sin, Devil Worship, and Rock 'n' Roll* (London: Plexus Publishing Limited, 2006), p. 33–42.

21. Zeena LaVey's 1998 fusillade against her unfather is particularly damning on the topic of his German holiday. "Young Howard [Anton] spent the entirety of 1945 in suburban northern California, and never visited Germany at any time in his life. The uncle who he claimed brought him to Germany was incarcerated at McNeill Island Penitentiary for involvement with Al Capone-related criminal activity during 1945, and was never in the armed forces. Allied martial law forbade U.S. citizens from visiting postwar Germany. The 'German' rituals in *The Satanic Rituals* are written in extremely poor, Anglicized German. They are clearly uncredited adaptations of the short story *The Hounds of Tindalos* by Frank Belknap Long and H. G. Wells' famous novel *The Island of Dr. Moreau*." Zeena Schreck and Nikolas Schreck, "Anton LaVey: Legend and Reality." 1998, http://www.churchofsatan.org/aslv.html (accessed February 21, 2007). For LaVey's version of the story, see Blanche Barton, *The Secret Life of a Satanist* (Los Angeles: Feral House 1990), p. 23.

22. For a detailed account of the *völkisch* movement and critique of the wilder Nazi occultism myths, see Nicholas Goodrick-Clarke, *The Occult Roots of Nazism: The Ariosophists of Austria and Germany, 1890–1935* (Wellingborough, UK: Aquarian Press), 1985.

23. Nicholas Goodrick-Clarke, *Black Sun: Aryan Cults, Esoteric Nazism and the Politics of Identity* (New York: New York University Press, 2002), p. 257.

24. David Lane, "Mystery Religions and the Seven Seals," in *Deceived, Damned and Defiant: The Revolutionary Writings of David Lane* (St. Maries, ID: 14 Words Press, 1999), p. 81. Quoted in Goodrick-Clarke, *Black Sun*, p. 274.

25. C. G. Jung, "The Concept of the Collective Unconscious," in *The Archetypes and the Collective Unconscious*, trans. R.F.C. Hull (Princeton, NJ: Princeton University Press, 1959), pp. 42–53 (p. 43).

26. Jung, "The Concept of the Collective Unconscious," p. 42.

27. C. G. Jung, "Wotan," in *Civilization in Transition*, trans. R.F.C. Hull (Princeton, NJ: Princeton University Press, 1964), pp. 179–93 (p. 180).

28. Peter H. Gilmore, "Rite of Ragnarök," in *The Satanic Scriptures* (Baltimore: Scapegoat Publishing, 2007), pp. 275–91 (p. 276).

29. Gilmore, "Rite of Ragnarök," p. 291. For the relevance of the phrase "strength through joy," see chapter 8.

30. Gilmore, "Rite of Ragnarök," p. 287. The phrase "total war" is similarly a reference to a neo-pagan anthem of the same name by Boyd Rice/NON.

31. Gilmore, "Apocalypse Now," in *The Satanic Scriptures*, pp. 58–59 (pp. 58–59).

32. Gilmore, "Apocalypse Now," p. 59.

33. Kenneth Grant, *The Magical Revival* (New York: Samuel Weiser, 1972), pp. 114–15.

34. For a discussion of how Lord Cthulhu's unfathomable tentacles have reached into the fragile souls of the occult world, see Erik Davis, "Calling Cthulhu: H. P. Lovecraft's Magick Realism," *Gnosis* 37 (1995): pp. 56–63.

35. Friedrich Nietzsche, *Thus Spake Zarathustra*, in *The Portable Nietzsche*, trans. and ed. Walter Kaufmann (New York: Penguin Books, 1976), "The Shadow," fourth part, p. 386. (Also in *On the Genealogy of Morals*, trans. Walter Kaufman and R. J. Hollingdale (New York: Vintage Books, 1984), third essay, §24.)

36. Ray Sherwin, "Chaos Magick," http://www.chaosmatrix.org/library/chaos/texts/sher2.html (accessed October 26, 2007).

37. To compare LaVey's reworking of the Al-Jilwah with the original, see LaVey, *The Satanic Rituals*, pp. 161–72, and Isya Joseph, *Devil Worship: The Sacred Books and Traditions of the Yezidiz* (Boston: Richard G. Badger, 1919), pp. 35–72. The rite in *The Satanic Rituals* is actually two works combined, the Al-Jilwah and "The Poem in Praise of Seth-Adi." For LaVey's comments on the Yedizis in *The Satanic Bible*, see "*Wanted!*: God—Dead or Alive," pp. 40–43 (p. 43).

38. Crowley, "Introduction," *Magick in Theory and Practice*, p. 126.

39. Blanche Barton, *The Secret Life of a Satanist: The Authorized Biography of Anton LaVey* (Los Angeles: Feral House 1990), pp. 97–98. Discussed in chapter 3 of the current work.

40. Barton, pp. 195–98.

41. Reverend Harris, "Satanism 101," *Satanism Today* (podcast), October 23, 2007, http://www.satanismtoday.net/.

42. Cavendish, *The Black Arts*, p. 338.

CHAPTER 7

1. Michelle Smith and Lawrence Pazder, *Michelle Remembers* (New York: Congden & Lattes, 1980).

2. Jerry Johnston, *The Edge of Evil: The Rise of Satanism in North America* (Dallas: Word Publishing, 1989), p. 4.

3. Lauren Stratford, *Satan's Underground: The Extraordinary Story of One Woman's Escape* (Eugene, OR: Harvest House, 1988).

4. "Devil Worship: Exposing Satan's Underground," *Geraldo* (syndicated TV show), October 25, 1988.

5. James T. Richardson, "Satanism in the Courts: From Murder to Heavy Metal," in *The Satanism Scare*, eds. James T. Richardson, Joel Best, and David G. Bromley (New York: Aldine de Gruyter, 1991), pp. 205–217 (p. 209).

6. Bob Larson, *Satanism: The Seduction of America's Youth* (Nashville, TN: Thomas Nelson Inc, 1989), pp. 124–25.

7. Ted Gunderson, speaking in *Scream Greats, Vol. 2: Satanism and Witchcraft*, directed by Damon Santostefano, VHS (Paramount Home Video, 1986).

8. Kenneth V. Lanning, "Satanic, Occult, Ritualistic Crime: A Law Enforcement Perspective," in *Police Chief* 56 (1989): pp. 62–83 (p.63).

9. Lanning, "Satanic, Occult, Ritualistic Crime," p. 71

10. Lanning, "Satanic, Occult, Ritualistic Crime," p. 81.

11. Kenneth V. Lanning, *Investigator's Guide to Allegations of "Ritual" Child Abuse* (Quantico, VA: FBI National Center for the Analysis of Violent Crime, 1992), §1.

12. Robert D. Hicks, "The Police Model of Satanic Crime," in *The Satanism Scare*, (pp. 175–89) p. 175. See also Hicks's book-length study, *In Pursuit of Satan: The Police and the Occult* (New York: Prometheus Books, 1991).

13. Lawrence Wright, *Remembering Satan: A Case of Recovered Memory and the Shattering of an American Family* (New York: Knopf, 1994).

14. Jean La Fontaine, *The Extent and Nature of Organised and Ritual Abuse* (London: HMSO, 1994).

15. Jean La Fontaine, *Speak of the Devil: Tales of Satanic Abuse in Contemporary England* (Cambridge: Cambridge University Press, 1998).

16. G. S. Goodman, et. al., *Characteristics and Sources of Allegations of Ritual Child Abuse: Final Report to the National Center on Child Abuse and Neglect* (Washington, D.C.: National Center on Child Abuse and Neglect, 1994).

17. Catherine Bennett, "All Aboard with Satan's Sailor," http://www.guardian.co.uk/world/2004/oct/28/religion.military (accessed October 25, 2007).

18. "Harry Potter Books Spark Rise in Satanism among Children," *The Onion*, June 2000, http://www.theonion.com/onion3625/harry_potter.html (accessed April 23, 2007).

19. Anthony Breznican, "Supernatural Themes in Harry Potter Continue to Anger Certain Conservative Christian Critics," *Associated Press*, November 9, 2001.

20. William H. Kennedy, *Satanic Crime: A Threat in the New Millennium* (Mystic Valley Media, 2006).

21. Blanche Barton, *The Secret Life of a Satanist* (Los Angeles: Feral House 1990), p. 216.

22. Barton, *The Secret Life of a Satanist*, p. 218.

23. See Barton, *The Secret Life of a Satanist*, p. 198 (also discussed in chapter 6 of the current work).

24. Aquino's full reaction to this claim of LaVey's is: "Are we to admire someone who would slay a restaurant full of people simply because he was sulking over a court-order to keep him from threatening his wife?" (Michael A. Aquino, *Church of Satan*, 5th ed. (Self-published, 2002), p. 422).

25. Barton, *The Secret Life of a Satanist*, p. 218.

26. The meaninglessness of this key Satanic phrase can be displayed by considering the comparable logical constructions *library membership to those who belong to libraries* or *intelligence to the intelligent*.

27. Anton Szandor LaVey, "Pentagonal Revisionism," in *The Devil's Notebook* (Los Angeles: Feral House, 1992), pp. 93–96 (p. 94).

28. *Speak of the Devil*, directed by Nick Bougas, VHS (Wavelength Video, Dist. Feral House Video, 1993).

29. Barton, *The Secret Life of a Satanist*, p. 219.

30. LaVey, "Pentagonal Revisionism," pp. 93–94.

31. LaVey, *The Satanic Bible*, p. 25.

32. LaVey, *The Satanic Bible*, p. 33. Also quoted in chapter 4 of the current work.

33. LaVey, "Destructive Organisms," in *The Devil's Notebook*, p. 97.

34. See Peter H. Gilmore, "Satanism, The Feared Religion," in *The Satanic Scriptures* (Baltimore: Scapegoat Publishing, 2007), pp. 25–39 (p. 35); Robert A. Lang, "Gladiatorial Combat Anyone?" http://members.chello.at/herbert.paulis/gca. html (accessed April 27, 2007). Judging by the tone of Lang's disturbingly fascist vision of justice the piece appears to be half—but only half—tongue-in-cheek.

35. See Nicholas Agar, *Liberal Eugenics: In Defence of Human Enhancement* (Malden, MA: Blackwell Publishing, 2004), pp. 3–6.

36. Robert Proctor, *Racial Hygiene: Medicine under the Nazis* (Cambridge, MA: Harvard University Press; 1988), p. 108.

37. Gilmore, "Eugenics," in *The Satanic Scriptures*, pp. 92–94 (pp. 93–94).

38. Barton, *The Secret Life of a Satanist*, p. 212–13.

39. LaVey, "The Third Side: The Uncomfortable Alternative," in *Satan Speaks!* (Los Angeles: Feral House, 1998), pp. 29–32 (p. 30). Bizarrely, LaVey was strongly opposed to abortion—"Satanically speaking"—and saw mandatory birth control and forced sterilization as a way to bypass the issue.

40. Gilmore, "Eugenics," p. 93.

41. Barton, *The Secret Life of a Satanist*, p. 212.

42. Michael A. Aquino, "Lesser Black Magic/Ethics," in *Temple of Set*, draft 6 (Self-published, 2006), pp. 215–26 (p. 226).

43. Aquino's ethical discussion makes numerous simple errors. In discussing Plato's *Republic*, Aquino falsely identifies Glaucon as the egoist, when he is in fact the equivalent of a modern social contract theorist—it is Thrasymachus who is the egoist (see Plato, *The Republic*, trans. and intro. Desmond Lee (London: Penguin Books, 2003), pp. 15–40). Aquino also states "Socrates is unable to directly refute Glaucon's egoist charge that justice is merely a rationalization for the prevailing

interest of the stronger" (Aquino, "Lesser Black Magic/Ethics," p. 220). As shown in chapter 4, Socrates does exactly that, and it is his argument that has ultimately been validated. The main point of Aquino's discussion of ethics appears to be the sophomoric observation that as there are a number of different accounts of ethics, therefore it's too difficult to reach a conclusion.

44. Aquino, "Lesser Black Magic/Ethics," p. 218.
45. LaVey, "Diabolica," in *The Devil's Notebook*, pp. 143–47 (p. 144).

CHAPTER 8

1. "The Cult of the Occult," *Newsweek*, April 13, 1970. Quoted in Michael A. Aquino, *Church of Satan*, 5th ed. (Self-published, 2002), p. 72.

2. Isaac Bonewits, *Real Magic* (York Beach, ME: Red Wheel / Weiser, 1989), p. 101.

3. Isaac Bonewits, "My Satanic Adventure or I Was a Teenaged Satanist," Version 2.3, 1975/2005, http://www.neopagan.net/SatanicAdventure.html (accessed May 25, 2007).

4. Willy Werby, letter to *S.F. Weekly*, July 1–7, 1988. Quoted in Aquino, *Church of Satan*, p. 432.

5. Donald Nugent, "Satan Is a Fascist," *The Month*, April 1972. Quoted in Aquino, *Church of Satan*, p. 218.

6. Peter H. Gilmore, "A Map for the Misdirected," http://www.churchofsatan.com/home.html (accessed February 22, 2007).

7. Reverend Jack Malebranche, "Where Does Satanism Stand on Politics?," *Letters to the Devil*, Church of Satan online discussion forum, http://www.satannet.com/forum/ubbthreads.php?ubb=showthreaded&Number=83839&page=26 (accessed February 24, 2007).

8. Anton Szandor LaVey, "The Lawyer Is Your Friend," in *Satan Speaks!* (Los Angeles: Feral House, 1998), pp. 126–27 (p. 126).

9. Robert O. Paxton, *The Anatomy of Fascism* (New York: Vintage Books, 2004), p. 218.

10. *Charles Manson: Superstar*, directed by Nikolas Schreck, VHS (Video Werewolf 2002).

11. James Mason, *Siege*, "Introduction," http://www.solargeneral.com/library/siege/0001.htm (accessed February 28, 2007). The dedication is, at the time of writing, viewable at this URL (a white supremacist site run by Stormfront). Relationships between Satanism and white supremacists are complex, especially given that the latter are frequently Christian (the Ku Klux Klan, for example, is a Christian organization). In a 2003 interview, Mason observed, apropos of LaVey, "Satan will never approach you as Satan. Never. He will always approach as 'an angel of light'. So to call one's self a 'Satanist', I believe, is no more than a cry for attention." (AAC, "Universal Order: An Interview with James Mason," http://www.solargeneral.com/library/siege/interview.htm (accessed February 28, 2007).

12. Boyd Rice, "FAQ," http://www.boydrice.com/home.html (accessed February 12, 2007).

13. Adolf Hitler, *Mein Kampf*, trans. Ralpf Manheim. intro. D. Cameron Watt (London: Pimlico, 1969), p. 121–22.

14. Boyd Rice, "FAQ."

15. Boyd Rice, "Opening Speech," (August 8, 1988 recording), http://www.boydrice.com (accessed September 14, 2007).

16. "Do You Want a Total War?," *The Fifth Path*, http://www.boydrice.com/interviews/fifthpath.html (accessed September 28, 2007).

17. LaVey, "A Plan," in *Satan Speaks!*, pp. 20–22 (p. 20).

18. Peggy Nadramia, "Re: Boyd Rice, A Nazi?," posted at alt.satanism, May 6, 1995.

19. Peggy Nadramia, "Re: Boyd Rice, A Nazi?"

20. Michael Moynihan, *Lords of Chaos: The Bloody Rise of the Satanic Metal Underground*, rev. and exp. ed. (Los Angeles: Feral House, 2003), p. 261.

21. Walter Benjamin, "The Work of Art in the Age of Its Technological Reproducibility," in *Selected Writings, Volume 3 1935–1938*, ed. Howard Eiland and Michael W. Jennings (Cambridge, MA: Belknap Harvard, 2002), pp. 101–22 (p. 121). See also Paxton, p. 17.

22. George L. Mosse, "Fascist Aesthetics and Society: Some Considerations," *Journal of Contemporary History* 31, no. 2, special issue: "The Aesthetics of Fascism" (April 1996): pp. 254–52 (p. 251).

23. LaVey, *The Satanic Bible* (New York: Avon Books, 1969), p. 82. Italics in original.

24. See Tim Mason, "The Containment of the Working Class," in *Nazism, Fascism, and the Working Class: Essays by Tim Mason*, ed. Jane Caplan (Cambridge: Cambridge University Press, 1995), p. 238. The four means of control of German workers that Mason lists are: terror, division, occasional concessions, and integration devices such as the party rallies, youth groups, and leisure-time associations.

25. Letter, M. A. Aquino to Thomas and Colleen Huddleston, Arthur Zabrecky, and Stephen Hollander, July 1, 1974. Quoted in Aquino, *Church of Satan*, p. 367.

26. Letter, Anton LaVey to M. A. Aquino, July 1, 1974. Quoted in Aquino, *Church of Satan*, p. 368.

27. Robert Bannister, *Social Darwinism: Science and Myth in Anglo-American Social Thought* (Philadelphia: Temple University Press, 1979), p. 204.

28. LaVey, "Foreword," in Ragnar Redbeard, *Might Is Right* (n.p.: Evilnow, 2006), pp. 4–9 (p. 7).

29. David Lane also authored the racist 88-Precepts of "Natural Law." The number 88 is, once again, a reference to "Heil Hitler."

30. Peter H. Gilmore, "A Match Made in Hell: Afterword," in Ragnar Redbeard, *Might Is Right*, pp. 202–5 (p. 205).

31. Mason, *Siege*.

32. LaVey, "A Plan," in *Satan Speaks!*, pp. 20–22 (p. 21).

33. LaVey's logic in the "Jewish/Satanic connection" was a formal fallacy, Aristotle's law of the undistributed middle. That the two groups can be described with a middle term—in this case, "outsider"—does not make them equivalent. Consider the following use of "black and white": All pandas are black and white / some police cars are black and white / therefore, some police cars are pandas. LaVey's argument is structured identically: All Satanists bear the devil's name / Jews bear the devil's name / therefore, Jews and Satanists are confederates of some sort.

34. LaVey, "A Plan," p. 22. LaVey's most likely meaning with this quote is simply another attempt to make his philosophy as appealing as possible to as wide a number of people as possible. Nonetheless, it is an inscrutable statement that presents a minefield of obvious contradictions: "Imperialist" with "Socialism"; "Bolshevik" and "Socialism" with "Fascism" and "Nazi"; "Zionist" with both "Nazi" and "Bolshevik."

35. LaVey, "The Jewish Question? Or Things My Mother Never Taught Me," in *Satan Speaks!*, pp. 69–72 (p. 71). The quality of LaVey's thought in these *Satan Speaks!* extracts are indicative of the quality of the work as a whole.

36. *The Secret Life of a Satanist* contains claims that LaVey worked in the early 1950s as a "Zionist operative" but provides no supporting evidence. Given that the comment was made at a time that Satanism was facing stiff criticism for it's lurch to the far right, there is no reason to believe this story is anything but another creation of LaVey's overactive imagination. (See Blanche Barton, *The Secret Life of a Satanist* (Los Angeles: Feral House 1990), p. 56–57)

37. Barton, *The Secret Life of a Satanist*, p. 212.

38. Gilmore, "A Match Made in Hell: Afterword," in Ragnar Redbeard, *Might Is Right*, pp. 202–5 (pp. 202–3).

39. Gilmore, "A Match Made in Hell: Afterword," p. 205.

40. James D. Sass, "Am I a Racist? Do I Care?," November 16, 2006, http://magister svengali.blogspot.com/2006/11/am-i-racist-do-i-care.html (accessed April 24, 2007).

41. Motto on the MySpace profile of James D. Sass, http://www.myspace.com/trapezoid (accessed January 18, 2008).

42. *The Devil's Disciples*, DVD, (Mondo Macabro, 2006). It is assumed that Baddeley means "neo-fascism" rather than "proto-fascism." At the time of LaVey's birth in 1930, Benito Mussolini had already been in power for eight years.

43. Gavin Baddeley, *Lucifer Rising: A Book of Sin, Devil Worship, and Rock 'n' Roll* (London: Plexus Publishing Limited, 2006), p. 138.

44. Roald E. Kristiansen, "Satan in Cyberspace: A Study of Satanism on the Internet in the 1990s," prepared for the Lomonosov Conference in Archangelsk, Russia, November 1995, http://www.love.is/roald/satanism.html (accessed March 13, 2007).

45. Gilmore, "The Fascism Question," in *The Satanic Scriptures*, pp. 82–91 (p. 88).

46. Don Webb, Concerning the Task of Becoming Evil and Ruling the World, http://www.xeper.org/hyperborea/setnakt_eng.pdf (accessed October 12, 2008). [Also

known as "Uncle Seknakt Sex—Become Evil and Rule the World:2"]. Webb continues to attempt to differentiate the two creeds: "Both Satanism and Nazism push at the individual; however, Satanism has replaced the destructive hatred of Nazism with the pure black light of challenge." There is, however, absolutely no evidence for the existence of hate-free Satanism, and plenty to the contrary.

47. Bannister, *Social Darwinism*, p. 204. Bannister concludes that the author of *Might Is Right* was most likely a Chicago journalist with satirical and financial motivations.

48. Jonathan Glover, *Morality: A Moral History of the Twentieth Century* (London: Pimlico, 2001), p. 343. At the beginning of the book, Glover devotes an entire chapter to Nietzsche's amoral response to the crisis of values instigated by the loss of faith in God and to the German philosopher's extraordinary influence in the twentieth century (pp. 11–17).

49. Glover, *Morality*, p. 17.

50. Gilmore, "Satanism: The Feared Religion," in *The Satanic Scriptures*, pp. 25–39 (p. 34).

51. Brian L. Silver, *The Ascent of Science* (New York: Oxford University Press, 1998), p. 291.

CHAPTER 9

1. Australian Bureau of Statistics, 2006 Census Tables, http://www.abs.gov.au/web sitedbs/d3310114.nsf/Home/census (accessed September 4, 2007).

2. Statistics New Zealand, 2006 Census, http://www.stats.govt.nz/census/default. htm (accessed September 4, 2007).

3. General Register Office for Scotland, Scotland's Census 2001, http://www. gro-scotland.gov.uk/census/censushm/index.html (accessed September 4, 2007).

4. National Statistics (UK), The Census in England and Wales (2001), http://www. statistics.gov.uk/census/ (accessed September 4, 2007).

5. Northern Ireland Statistics and Research Agency, 2001 Census, http://www.nis ranew.nisra.gov.uk/census/start.html (accessed September 4, 2007).

6. Statistics Canada, 2001 Census of Canada, http://www12.statcan.ca/english/cen sus01/home/Index.cfm (accessed September 4, 2007).

7. Estimated number of Satanists in Russia in 2003: "several thousand, with 500 members each in Moscow and Petersburg" (Russian Interior Ministry on February 4, 2003, as reported by Associated Foreign Press [Moscow] on the same day.).

8. Estimated by extrapolating from the admittedly limited data available—the combined population of the United Kingdom, Canada, and Australasia are 112,000,000 in comparison to 498,400,000 for the European Union/Norway (excluding Turkey) and 303,000,000 for the United States—and assuming that the European Union and United States both sit within the band of 3–10 Satanists per 100,000 population (a figure between the United Kingdom/Canada figures and those of

Australia, with the New Zealand figure of 29 Satanists per 100,000 treated as an anomaly.) The figure also assumes that the number of Satanists in Asia, Africa, and South America is negligible.

9. James R. Lewis, "Who Serves Satan? A Demographic and Ideological Profile." *Marburg Journal of Religious Studies* 6, no. 2 (June 2001), http://web.uni-marburg. de/religionswissenschaft/journal/mjr/lewis2.html (accessed September 10, 2007). The difficulty with Lewis's survey of 140 Satanists is that it is a highly biased, self-selecting sample. Respondents were selected by "e-mail addresses posted on Satanist websites" and by assistance from "organizations [that] agreed to post the questionnaire on their respective websites." The sample is largely self-selecting and there is no indication that either of the larger Satanic churches were involved in any way, meaning the survey is only of select groups of independent Satanists, and even then only those who had an interest in responding.

10. Randall Alfred and Arthur Lyons both present demographic information generally in line with Lewis's. A meta-survey of studies on Satanism notes "Church of Satan members are predominantly ages 25 to 30, white, and middle-class, with a number of professionals included." See Dianne E. Taub and Lawrence D. Nelson, "Satanism in Contemporary America: Establishment or Underground?" *The Sociological Quarterly* 34, no. 3 (August 1993), pp. 522–41 (p. 530).

11. R. J. Hollingdale, "The Hero as Outsider," in Bernd Magnus and Kathleen Higgins, *The Cambridge Companion to Nietzsche* (Cambridge: Cambridge University Press, 1996), pp. 71–89 (pp. 87–88).

12. Nietzsche, *A Nietzsche Reader,* p. 205 (from *Daybreak,* §575).

13. Nietzsche, *A Nietzsche Reader,* p. 205 (from *The Gay Science,* §124).

14. Anton Szandor LaVey, "Nonconformity: Satanism's Greatest Weapon," in *The Devil's Notebook* (Los Angeles: Feral House, 1992), pp. 63–65 (p. 63).

15. Peter H. Gilmore, "Rebels without Cause," in *The Satanic Scriptures* (Baltimore: Scapegoat Publishing, 2007), pp. 186–94 (p. 193).

16. A.S.P. "MySpace profile," http://www.myspace.com/a_s_p_84 (accessed September 14, 2007).

17. Arthur Lyons, *Satan Wants You: The Cult of Devil Worship in America* (New York: Mysterious Press, 1988), p. 134.

18. Lyons, *Satan Wants You,* p. 118.

19. Anthony Moriarty, *The Psychology of Adolescent Satanism* (Westport, CT: Praeger Publishers, 1992), p. 38.

20. Moriarty, *The Psychology of Adolescent Satanism,* p. 12.

21. LaVey, *The Satanic Bible,* p. 30.

22. Jack Malebranche, *Androphilia: A Manifesto Rejecting the Gay Identity, Reclaiming Masculinity* (Baltimore Scapegoat Press, 2007).

23. Gini Scott Graham, *The Magicians* (Oakland, CA: Creative Communications, 1984), p. 182, quoted in Lyons, *Satan Wants You,* p. 130.

24. Michael A. Aquino, *The Church of Satan,* 5th ed. (Self-published, 2002), p. 30.

25. Randall H. Alfred, "The Church of Satan," in *The New Religious Consciousness*, pp. 180–202 (pp. 192–93).

26. The criteria for narcissism are drawn from the *Diagnostic and Statistical Manual of Mental Disorders*, 4th edition (Arlington, VA: American Psychiatric Publishing, 1994).

27. Erich Fromm, *The Anatomy of Human Destructiveness* (London: Pimlico, 1973), pp. 272–73.

28. Fromm, *The Anatomy of Human Destructiveness*, p. 277.

29. See R. S. Nickerson, "Confirmation Bias: A Ubiquitous Phenomenon in Many Guises," *Review of General Psychology* 2 (1998): pp. 175–220. The account given here also draws from the description given by Robert Todd Carroll at *The Skeptic's Dictionary*, http://skepdic.com/confirmbias.html.

30. Moriarty, *The Psychology of Adolescent Satanism*, p. 18.

31. LaVey, "In Praise of Sycophants," in *Satan Speaks!* (Los Angeles: Feral House, 1998), pp. 37–38 (p. 38).

32. LaVey, "The Third Side: The Uncomfortable Alternative," in *Satan Speaks!*, pp. 29–32 (p. 32).

33. LaVey, *The Satanic Bible*, p. 25.

34. Lewis, "Who Serves Satan? A Demographic and Ideological Profile."

35. Lewis, "Who Serves Satan? A Demographic and Ideological Profile."

36. Lewis, "Who Serves Satan? A Demographic and Ideological Profile."

37. Lewis, "Diabolical Authority: Anton LaVey, The Satanic Bible and the Satanist Tradition." *Marburg Journal of Religious Studies* 7, no. 1 (September 2002), http://web.uni-marburg.de/religionswissenschaft/journal/mjr/lewis3.html (accessed September 15, 2007). Lewis's favorable assessment is echoed by Jesper Aagaard Petersen, who declares "Satanism is legitimate because it is rational," it is "a reasonable religion built on a sound understanding of human nature and the empirical world." ("Modern Satanism: Dark Doctrines and Black Flames," in *Controversial New Religions*, eds. James R. Lewis and Jesper Aagaard Petersen (New York: Oxford University Press, 2004), pp. 423–57 p. 434).

38. Lewis, "Who Serves Satan? A Demographic and Ideological Profile," "Diabolical Authority: Anton LaVey, *The Satanic Bible* and the Satanist Tradition," and "The Satanic Bible: Quasi-Scripture / Counter-Scripture." The 2002 CESNUR International Conference, Salt Lake City and Provo (Utah), June 20–23, 2002, http://www.cesnur.org/2002/slc/lewis.htm (accessed September 15, 2007).

39. Lewis, "Who Serves Satan? A Demographic and Ideological Profile."

40. See Edward J. Moody, "Magical Therapy: An Anthropological Investigation of Contemporary Satanism," in *Religious Movements in Contemporary America*, ed. Irving I. Zaretsky and Mark P. Leone (Princeton, NJ: Princeton University Press, 1974), pp. 355–382. Despite acknowledging possible positive effects of ritual magic, Moody also notes that many initiates perceive themselves as evil and are inclined towards sadism and masochism, identifying with Satanism as it validates or even encourages their behavior.

41. Randall H. Alfred, "The Church of Satan," in *The New Religious Consciousness*, ed. Charles Y. Glock and Robert N. Belleah (Berkeley: University of California Press, 1976), pp. 180–202 (p. 197).

42. Alfred, "The Church of Satan," p. 210.

43. Marcello Truzzi, "Satanism and Witchcraft," *On the Margin of the Visible: Sociology, the Esoteric, and the Occult*, ed. Edward A. Tiryakian (New York: Wiley Interscience/John Wiley and Sons, 1974), pp. 215–22 (p. 220). Italics in original.

44. Dianne E. Taub and Lawrence D. Nelson, "Satanism in Contemporary America: Establishment or Underground?" *The Sociological Quarterly*, pp. 522–41.

45. See Thomas Robbins, "The Transformative Impact of the Study of New Religions on the Sociology of Religion," *Journal for the Scientific Study of Religion* 27 (1988): pp. 12–31.

46. Aquino, *Church of Satan*, p. 421.

47. Brian M. Clark, "The Black Pimp Speaks," interview with Boyd Rice for *Rated Rookie* 6 (2004), http://www.boydrice.com/interviews/blackpimp.html (accessed September 22, 2007). As explained in the interview, "Black Pimp" is a nickname that Charles Manson bestowed on Rice.

CHAPTER 10

1. Dennis Wheatley, *The Devil Rides Out* (London: Hutchinson, 1934); movie: *The Devil Rides Out*, directed by Terence Fisher, DVD (Anchor Bay Entertainment, 1968) (also known in the United States as *The Devil's Bride*).

2. Welles's improvised dialogue shows that Satanic philosophizing can be done just as easily off-the-cuff: "Victims? Don't be melodramatic. Tell me. Would you really feel any pity if one of those dots stopped moving forever? If I offered you twenty thousand pounds for every dot that stopped, would you really, old man, tell me to keep my money, or would you calculate how many dots you could afford to spare?... Like the fella says, in Italy for 30 years under the Borgias they had warfare, terror, murder, and bloodshed, but they produced Michelangelo, Leonardo da Vinci, and the Renaissance. In Switzerland they had brotherly love, they had 500 years of democracy and peace, and what did that produce? The cuckoo clock." Orson Welles, *The Third Man*, directed by Carol Reed, DVD (The Criterion Collection, 1949).

3. Ozzy Osbourne, *Don't Blame Me*, directed by Jeb Brien, DVD (Epic Music Video, Dist. Sony Music Entertainment, 1991).

4. See *The Osbournes*, MTV, 2002–2005.

5. Venom, "In League with Satan," *Welcome to Hell*, Neat Records, 1981.

6. Alice Cooper, interviewed in *Metal—A Headbanger's Journey*, directed by Sam Dunn, DVD (Warner Home Video, 2005).

7. Marilyn Manson, "Foreword," in Anton Szandor LaVey, *Satan Speaks!* (Los Angeles: Feral House, 1998), pp. viii–ix (p. viii).

8. See Kevin Coogan, "How Black Is Black Metal?," *Hitlist* 1, no. 1 (February/ March 1999).

9. Michael Moynihan, *Lords of Chaos: The Bloody Rise of the Satanic Metal Underground*, Revised and Expanded edition, (Los Angeles: Feral House, 2003), pp. 208–13.

10. Moynihan, *Lords of Chaos*, p. 377.

11. Adam Parfrey, "Boyd Rice," (introduction) *Seconds Magazine* 38, 1996, pp. 36–41 (p. 36).

12. Chris A. Masters, "Boyd Rice Interview," *Misanthrope*, 1997, http://www.boydrice. com/interviews/misanthrope.html (accessed September 21, 2007).

13. Parfrey, "Boyd Rice," p. 38.

14. See Nicholas Goodrick-Clarke, *Black Sun: Aryan Cults, Esoteric Nazism and the Politics of Identity* (New York: New York University Press, 2002), p. 207.

15. "Race and Reason," *White Aryan Resistance (W.A.R.) TV,* Hosted by Tom Metzger, 1986.

16. Dauðarorð (MySpace Profile), http://www.myspace.com/daudarord (accessed January 3, 2008).

17. George Petros, *Art That Kills: A Panoramic Portrait of Aesthetic Terrorism 1984–2001* (Washington, DC: Creation Books, 2007).

18. See discussion in chapter 8.

19. James Mason, "Fury Unfelt," in *Siege* 15, no. 1 (January, 1986), http://www.solar general.com/library/siege/0145.htm (accessed November 10, 2007).

20. James Mason, "Hollywood Rogues Gallery," in *Siege*, http://www.solargeneral. com/library/siege/0803.htm (accessed November 10, 2007).

21. Anton Szandor LaVey, "Pentagonal Revisionism," in *The Devil's Notebook* (Los Angeles: Feral House, 1992), pp. 93–96 (pp. 93–96). Also see discussion in chapter 4.

22. Goodrick-Clarke, *Black Sun*, p. 289.

CONCLUSION

1. Anton Szandor LaVey, "Diabolica," in *Satan Speaks!* (Los Angeles: Feral House, 1998), pp. 143–47 (p. 146).

2. LaVey, "Pentagonal Revisionism," (p. 93).

3. Egalitarianism is a complex, multifaceted principle. In modern Western democracies, it is often used to describe a position that supports more equal distribution of wealth throughout society than currently exists. When used in the context of Satanism, the term invariably refers not to economic matters, but rather to ethical concerns and the relative merit of different persons within a society. The discussion here therefore focuses entirely on the question of the moral worth of individuals and the nature of human rights.

4. The "Goodguy Badge" is an influential (among Satanists, obviously) 1975 essay by LaVey that is frequently invoked as a defense against criticism. In it, LaVey

reaffirms his denunciation of altruism and his view that every act is a selfish act. Therefore, anyone who engages the vocabulary of equality, morality, or empathy is merely making a spectacle of their supposed virtue—sporting a "Goodguy Badge" out of nothing but self interest. The entire argument is, however, a form of ad hominem argument (a logical fallacy). By attacking the (presumed) motivation that drives a person's position, it fails utterly to address (and in fact diverts attention away from) the substance of any arguments they make (LaVey, "The Goodguy Badge" in *The Devil's Notebook* (Los Angeles: Feral House, 1992), pp. 20–27).

5. Anton Szandor LaVey, *The Satanic Bible* (New York: Avon Books, 1969), p. 64.

6. John Mackie, *Ethics: Reinventing Right and Wrong* (Harmondsworth, UK: Penguin, 1977), p. 110.

7. Peter H. Gilmore, "A Primer for Fledgling Misanthropologists," in *The Satanic Scriptures* (Baltimore: Scapegoat Publishing, 2007), pp. 45–52 (p. 45). Emphasis in original.

8. *The Standard*, Rogers CHNU Television, November 31, 2007.

9. *Speak of the Devil*, directed by Nick Bougas, VHS, (Wavelength Video, Dist. Feral House Video, 1993).

10. *Speak of the Devil.*

11. David Lane, "88 Precepts." (pamphlet authored and circulated while Lane was incarcerated).

12. T. H. Huxley and J. S. Huxley, *Evolution and Ethics* (London: Pilot Press, 1947), p. 63. Quoted in Michael Ruse, *Taking Darwin Seriously* (Oxford: Basil Blackwell, 1986.), p. 82.

13. See Sam Harris, "The Myth of Secular Moral Chaos," http://www.secularhuman ism.org/index.php?section=library&page=sharris_26_3 (accessed December 31, 2007). It is worth outlining Harris's three main arguments against this myth: (1) "If a book like the Bible were the only reliable blueprint for human decency that we had, it would be impossible (both practically and logically) to criticize it in moral terms. But it is extraordinarily easy to criticize the morality one finds in the Bible, as most of it is simply odious and incompatible with a civil society." (2) "If religion were necessary for morality, there should be some evidence that atheists are less moral than believers." There isn't. (3) "If religion really provided the only conceivable objective basis for morality, it should be impossible to posit a nontheistic objective basis for morality."

14. Donald A. Crosby, *The Specter of the Absurd: Sources and Criticisms of Modern Nihilism* (Albany: State University of New York Press, 1988), p. 123. Crosby's sober and insightful analysis of Christianity and nihilism is found in chapter 5, "Anthropocentrism, Externality of Value, and Religion as Theism," (pp. 122–36).

15. Crosby's argument is presented here in a somewhat less conciliatory fashion than in his work. Crosby, for example, finishes his discussion with the following important provisos: "I do not claim that these assumptions have been operative in exactly

this form in the thinking of every person in the West, or that my characterizations of them do justice in every case to the most sophisticated thinking of Christians themselves, now or in the past...My claim is rather that [these assumptions] have figured prominently in Western thought in general and contributed in crucial ways to the development of nihilism." (Crosby, p. 127.)

16. A Christian apologist, who would presumably be perturbed by both the assumptions and implications of this discussion, would respond that this loss of value in the face of the rejection of classical Christianity is actually reason to believe in the revelation of Christ. The certainty, meaning, moral guidance and spiritual solace offered by Christianity provide powerful reasons for accepting its doctrines. There is a central flaw in this reasoning as it is a false appeal to consequences—the claim that something is true or not depending upon whether the consequences are desirable or not. That the Christian body of belief is attractive and comforting, and ostensibly provides both meaning and certitude, does not make it true. That regarding the world from the perspective of scientific naturalism raises difficult questions regarding existential meaning, the foundation for morality, and offers little consolation in the face of an immense, barely understood cosmos, does not make it false. Truths about the world are truths about the world regardless of our subjective attitudes towards them. The lion about to pounce on an antelope does not become unreal because the antelope does not want to be eaten. Santa does not exist because belief in his existence makes children happy. Desirability does not determine truth.

17. Bertrand Russell, *Philosophy and Politics* (Cambridge: Cambridge University Press, 1947), p. 7.

Selected Bibliography

Aquino, Michael A. *The Church of Satan*. 5th ed. Self-published, 2002.

———. *The Temple of Set*, draft 6. Self-published, 2006.

Baddeley, Gavin. *Dissecting Marilyn Manson*. London: Plexus Publishing Limited, 2000.

———. *Lucifer Rising: A Book of Sin, Devil Worship, and Rock 'n' Roll*. London: Plexus Publishing Limited, 2006.

Bannister, Robert. *Social Darwinism: Science and Myth in Anglo-American Social Thought*. Philadelphia, PA: Temple University Press, 1979.

Barton, Blanche. *The Secret Life of a Satanist: The Authorized Biography of Anton LaVey*. Los Angeles: Feral House 1990.

Biography: The Night Stalker Richard Ramirez. David Healy (Narrator), Richard Ramirez, Philip Carlo, A & E Television Networks, 2004.

Cavendish, Richard. *The Black Arts*. New York: Perigee, 1967.

———. *A History of Magic*. New York: Taplinger Publishing Company, 1979.

Crosby, Donald A. *The Specter of the Absurd: Sources and Criticisms of Modern Nihilism*. Albany: State University of New York Press, 1988.

Crowley, Aleister. *The Book of the Law / Liber Al Vel Vegis*. York Beach, ME: Weiser Books, 2004.

———. *Gilles de Rais: The Banned Lecture*. Logan, OH: Black Moon Publishing, 2008.

———. *The Law Is for All*. Ed. Israel Regardie. Phoenix, AZ: Falcon Press, 1986.

Crowley, Aleister, Mary Desti, and Leila Waddell. *Magick: Liber Aba: Book 4 (Magick Bk. 4)*. Ed. Hymenaeus Beta. York Beach, ME: Weiser, 1998.

Dawkins, Richard. *The Selfish Gene*. 30th ann. ed. Oxford: Oxford University Press, 2006.

Fromm, Erich. *The Anatomy of Human Destructiveness.* London: Pimlico, 1973.

Gilmore, Peter H. *The Satanic Scriptures.* Baltimore: Scapegoat Publishing, 2007.

Glover, Jonathan. *Humanity: A Moral History of the Twentieth Century.* London: Pimlico, 2001.

Goodrick-Clarke, Nicholas. *Black Sun: Aryan Cults, Esoteric Nazism and the Politics of Identity.* New York: New York University Press, 2002.

Hitler, Adolf. *Mein Kampf.* Trans. Ralpf Manheim. Intro. D. Cameron Watt. London: Pimlico, 1969.

Hofstadter, Richard. *Social Darwinism in American Thought.* Rev. ed. Intro. Eric Foner. Boston: Beacon Press, 1955.

Jung, C. G. *The Archetypes and the Collective Unconscious.* Trans. R.F.C. Hull. Princeton, NJ: Princeton University Press, 1959.

———. *Civilization in Transition.* Trans. R.F.C. Hull. Princeton, NJ: Princeton University Press, 1964.

Katz, David S. *The Occult Tradition: From the Renaissance to the Present Day.* London: Pimlico, 2005.

Lanning, Kenneth V. *Investigator's Guide to Allegations of "Ritual" Child Abuse.* Quantico, VA: FBI National Center for the Analysis of Violent Crime, 1992.

———. "Satanic, Occult, Ritualistic Crime A Law Enforcement Perspective." *Police Chief* 56 (October 1989): pp. 62–83.

LaVey, Anton Szandor. *The Devil's Notebook.* Los Angeles: Feral House, 1992.

———. *The Satanic Bible.* Intro. Peter H. Gilmore. New York: Avon Books, 1969.

———. *The Satanic Rituals.* New York: Avon Books, 1972.

———. *The Satanic Witch.* Intro. Zeena LaVey. Los Angeles: Feral House, 1989.

———. *Satan Speaks.* Los Angeles: Feral House, 1998.

Lewis, James R. "Diabolical Authority: Anton LaVey, The Satanic Bible and the Satanist Tradition." *Marburg Journal of Religious Studies* 7, no. 1 (September 2002), http://web.uni-marburg.de/religionswissenschaft/journal/mjr/lewis3.html.

———. "'The Satanic Bible: Quasi-Scripture / Counter-Scripture." The 2002 CESNUR International Conference, Salt Lake City and Provo (Utah), June 20–23, 2002, http://www.cesnur.org/2002/slc/lewis.htm.

———. "Who Serves Satan? A Demographic and Ideological Profile." *Marburg Journal of Religious Studies* 6, no. 2 (June 2001), http://web.uni-marburg.de/religionswissenschaft/journal/mjr/lewis2.html.

London, Jack. *The Sea Wolf and Selected Stories.* New York: Signet Classic, 1964.

Lyons, Arthur. *Satan Wants You.* New York: Mysterious Press, 1988.

———. *The Second Coming: Satanism in America.* New York: Award Books, 1970.

Machiavelli, Niccolò. *The Prince.* Trans. George Bull. Intro. Anthony Grafton. London: Penguin, 1961.

Magnus, Bernd, and Kathleen M. Higgins, Eds. *The Cambridge Companion to Nietzsche.* Cambridge: Cambridge University Press, 1996.

Milton, John. *Paradise Lost.* Ed. and intro. John Leonard. London: Penguin Books, 2000.

Moriarty, Anthony. *The Psychology of Adolescent Satanism: A Guide for Parents, Counselors, Clergy, and Teachers.* Westport, CT: Praeger Publishers, 1992.

Moynihan, Michael and Didrik Søderlind. *Lords of Chaos: The Bloody Rise of the Satanic Metal Underground.* Rev. and exp. ed. Los Angeles: Feral House, 2003.

Nietzsche, Friedrich. *On the Genealogy of Morals* and *Ecce Homo.* Trans. Walter Kaufman and R. J. Hollingdale. New York: Vintage Books, 1984.

———. *A Nietzsche Reader.* Ed. and trans. R. J. Hollingdale. London: Penguin Books, 1977.

———. *The Portable Nietzsche.* Ed. and trans. Walter Kaufmann. New York: Penguin Books, 1976.

Noss, Davis S., and John B. Noss. *A History of the World's Religions.* 9th edition. Upper Saddle River, NJ: Simon and Schuster, 1994.

The Occult Experience. VHS. Directed by Frank Heiman. Premiere Entertainment International, 1985.

Paxton, Robert O. *The Anatomy of Fascism,* New York: Vintage Books, 2004.

Plato. *The Republic.* Trans. and intro. Desmond Lee. London: Penguin Books, 2003.

Rand, Ayn. *Atlas Shrugged.* New York: Signet, 1957.

———. *The Virtue of Selfishness.* New York: Signet, 1964.

Randall, Alfred H. "The Church of Satan." In *The New Religious Consciousness,* ed. Charles Y. Clock and Robert N. Bellah. Berkeley: University of California Press, 1976.

Redbeard, Ragnar. *Might Is Right.* n.p.: Evilnow, 2006.

Richardson, James T., Joel Best, and David G. Bromley. *The Satanism Scare.* New York: Aldine de Gruyter, 1991.

Ruse, Michael. *Taking Darwin Seriously: A Naturalistic Approach to Philosophy.* Oxford: Basil Blackwell, 1986.

Safranski, Rüdiger. *Nietzsche: A Philosophical Biography.* Trans. Shelley Frisch. London: Granta Publications, 2002.

Schreck, Nikolas, Ed. *Flowers from Hell: A Satanic Reader.* Washington, D.C.: Creation Books, 2001.

Singer, Peter. *Writings on an Ethical Life.* London: Fourth Estate, 2002.

Stanford, Peter. *The Devil: A Biography.* London: Mandarin Paperbacks, 1996.

Stirner, Max. *The Ego and Its Own: The Case of the Individual against Authority.* Trans. Steven T. Byington, ed. with intro. James J. Martin. New York: Dover Publications, 2005.

Sutin, Lawrence. *Do What Thou Wilt: A Life of Aleister Crowley.* New York: St Martin's Press, 2000.

Wright, Lawrence. "It's Not Easy Being Evil in a World That's Gone to Hell." *Rolling Stone* September 5, 1991: 63–68, 105–106. (Also reprinted in Wright, Lawrence. *Saints and Sinners.* New York: Vintage, 1995.)

WEB SITES

In addition to the works listed in the notes, the following Internet resources have been
    particularly helpful in researching this work:
The Catholic Encyclopedia: http://www.newadvent.org/cathen/index.html
The Fallacy Files: http://www.fallacyfiles.org/index.html
The Skeptic's Dictionary: http://skepdic.com/
The Stanford Encyclopedia of Philosophy: http://plato.stanford.edu/

Index

About the Author

CHRIS MATHEWS is a writer and university instructor living in Japan. He holds a master's degree in philosophy from the University of Auckland, New Zealand, and has published in magazines and newspapers in New Zealand, Australia, England, and Japan. He currently publishes regularly in a number of English-language magazines in Japan and internationally, writing on philosophy, politics, religion, and culture. He teaches critical thinking and writing composition courses at Meiji Gakuin and Hosei universities in Tokyo.